COUNT YOUR *Blessings*

Our Daily Bread
DEVOTIONAL COLLECTION

Our Daily Bread Publishing.

Count Your Blessings: Our Daily Bread *Devotional Collection*

The devotional readings collected in this book were previously published over a span of years in *Our Daily Bread* devotional booklets that are distributed around the world in more than fifty languages.

Interior design by Michael J. Williams

Printed in China
25 26 27 28 29 30 31 32 / 8 7 6 5 4 3 2 1

Introduction

Gratitude has gone viral.

In the past few years, a host of scientific studies have concluded that feeling and expressing gratitude has emotional, relational, and even physical benefits. Gratitude can improve your mood. It can lower your blood pressure. It can improve your friendships and your marriage. Gratitude is good for you.

As in so many areas of life, modern science is catching up to ancient wisdom that has guided God's people for thousands of years. All throughout the Bible, gratitude is key to a life lived in right relationship with God, others, ourselves, and our world.

In Psalm 8, for instance, the psalmist exuberantly invites listeners to praise God: "Lord, how majestic is your name in all the earth!" (v. 1). Why? Because of the jaw-dropping wonders of creation:

> I consider your heavens,
> the work of your fingers,
> the moon and the stars,
> which you have set in place. (v. 3)

Thankfulness is a natural response to God's power and provision, an accurate acknowledgment of who He is and what He has given us. And this right understanding of God leads to a right understanding of ourselves. Amazed by God's vast creation, the psalmist asks, "What is mankind that you are mindful of them, human beings that you care for them?" (v. 4). The psalmist recognizes our fragility and dependence on God, and marvels at the privilege and responsibility God has given humanity to care for His beautiful world (vv. 6–8).

In another part of the Bible, in the New Testament, we see another kind of gratitude: Paul's thankfulness for his fellow believers in Christ. "I thank my God every time I remember you," he wrote to the church in Philippi (Philippians 1:3). He goes on to explain why: "I always pray with joy because of your partnership in the gospel" (vv. 4–5). Paul was grateful for coworkers in spreading the message of Jesus, that he wasn't alone in the work. Feeling isolated would've made sense, as Paul was in prison when he wrote this letter (v. 13). But in his gratitude, Paul realized the truth—he was surrounded by a community.

Paul shows us another important aspect of biblical gratitude here: It doesn't depend on our circumstances. In fact, Paul told early Christians to practice gratitude in all things (Philippians 4:6; 1 Thessalonians 5:18). Throughout the most horrific events recorded in the Bible—from the destruction of Jerusalem to Job losing virtually everything he loved—we see God's people practicing what Paul preached and praising God for His faithfulness (Lamentations 3:22–24; Job 1:21). Even when we can't see any good in our circumstances, we too can cling to hope and thank God that He is working in all things for our good (Romans 8:28; see Genesis 50:20).

The 366 daily readings in this devotional are about gratitude in all its different forms: thankfulness, praise, celebration, worship, thanksgiving. Through these stories and biblical insights from a diverse company of *Our Daily Bread* writers, you will see many ways we can express gratitude in our walk with God. A "Practice Gratitude Today" prompt at the end of each devotion helps you show your gratefulness to God every day.

You will notice repeated themes, key Scripture verses, and gratitude prompts as you journey through the year with this devotional. As with other biblical habits, gratitude is not "one and done." I can't choose gratitude one day and then expect to automatically recognize God's goodness the next day. Whether the devotions encourage you to enjoy creation's beauty, reflect on God's faithfulness in the past, or celebrate your friends and loved ones, returning to the same themes and practices helps establish (or reestablish) gratitude as a learned skill that you can take with you beyond this year.

My prayer for you is the same that Paul prayed for the church in Thessalonica: "Rejoice always, pray continually, give thanks in all circumstances; for this is God's will for you in Christ Jesus" (1 Thessalonians 5:16–18).

Joel Armstrong
General Editor

Every Breath

EZEKIEL 37:1–3, 7–10, 14

I will put breath in you.
Ezekiel 37:6

When Tee Unn came down with a rare autoimmune disease that weakened all his muscles and nearly killed him, he realized that being able to breathe was a gift. For more than a week, a machine had to pump air into his lungs every few seconds, which was a painful part of his treatment.

Tee Unn made a miraculous recovery, and today he reminds himself not to complain about life's challenges. "I'll just take a deep breath," he says, "and thank God I can."

How easy it is to focus on things we need or want, and forget that sometimes the smallest things in life can be the greatest miracles. In Ezekiel's vision (Ezekiel 37:1–14), God showed the prophet that only He could give life to dry bones. Even after tendons, flesh, and skin had appeared, "there was no breath in them" (v. 8). It was only when God gave them breath that they could live again (v. 10).

This vision illustrated God's promise to restore Israel from devastation. It also reminds me that anything I have, big or small, is useless unless God gives me breath.

How about thanking God for the simplest blessings in life today? Amid the daily struggle, let's stop occasionally to take a deep breath, and "let everything that has breath praise the Lord" (Psalm 150:6).

Leslie Koh

Practice Gratitude Today

Spend a full minute breathing in and out deeply. Feel your lungs expand and contract with each life-giving breath. Thank God for giving you breath and life.

Thanks-Living

PSALM 23

Surely your goodness and love will follow
me all the days of my life.
Psalm 23:6

Wanting to mature in her spiritual life and become more thankful, Sue started what she called a Thanks-Living jar. Each evening she wrote on a small piece of paper one thing she thanked God for and dropped it in the jar. Some days she had many praises; other difficult days she struggled to find one. At the end of the year, she emptied her jar and read through all of the notes. She found herself thanking God again for everything He had done. He had given simple things like a beautiful sunset or a cool evening for a walk in the park, and other times He had provided grace to handle a difficult situation or answered a prayer.

Sue's notes of God's faithfulness reminded me of what the psalmist David says he experienced. God refreshed him with "green pastures" and "quiet waters" (Psalm 23:2). He gave him guidance, protection, and comfort (vv. 3–4). David concluded, "Surely your goodness and love will follow me all the days of my life" (v. 6).

I'm going to make a Thanks-Living jar this year. Maybe you'd like to as well. I think we'll see we have many reasons to thank God—including His gifts of friends and family and His provisions for our physical, spiritual, and emotional needs. We'll see that the goodness and love of God follow us all the days of our lives. *Anne Cetas*

Practice Gratitude Today

Start a Thanks-Living jar. Your daily praises can be small or big, simple or profound.

The Perfect Gift

ROMANS 11:33–12:2

Offer your bodies as a living sacrifice, holy and pleasing to God—this is your true and proper worship.
Romans 12:1

The weeks after Christmas are the busiest time of year in the United States for merchandise returns as people trade unwanted gifts for what they really want. Yet you probably know a few people who always seem to give the perfect gift. How do they know just what another person values and what is right for the occasion? The key to successful gift giving is not money; it's listening to others and taking an interest in what they enjoy and appreciate.

This is true for family and friends. But what about God? Is there anything meaningful or valuable that we can give to God? Is there anything He doesn't already have?

Romans 11:33–36, a song of praise to God for His great wisdom, knowledge, and glory, is followed by a call to give ourselves to Him. "Therefore, I urge you, brothers and sisters, in view of God's mercy, to offer your bodies as a living sacrifice, holy and pleasing to God—this is your true and proper worship" (12:1). Instead of being shaped by the world around us, we are to be "transformed by the renewing of [our] mind" (v. 2).

What's the best gift we can give to God today? In gratitude, humility, and love we can give ourselves completely to Him—heart, mind, and will. It's just what the Lord is longing to receive from each of us.

David McCasland

Practice Gratitude Today

How can you give your heart, mind, and will to God today? Let the gift of yourself be your thanks to God for calling you, having mercy on you, and giving you new life in Jesus.

Give Thanks to God

LUKE 24:28–35

When he was at the table with them, he took bread,
gave thanks, broke it and began to give it to them.
Luke 24:30

My friend hurried from her stressful job at the hospital, wondering what she would prepare for dinner before her husband returned from his equally demanding job. She had made chicken on Sunday and served leftovers on Monday. Then they had yet another round of chicken—this time baked—on Tuesday. She found two pieces of fish in the freezer, but she knew the fillets weren't her husband's favorite. Not finding anything else she could prepare in just a few minutes, she decided the fish would have to do.

As she placed the dish on the table, she said somewhat apologetically to her husband who had just arrived home, "I know this isn't your favorite." Her husband looked up and said, "Honey, I'm just happy we have food on the table."

His attitude reminds me of the importance of being grateful and thankful for our daily provisions from God—whatever they are. Giving thanks for our daily bread, or meals, models Jesus's example. When He ate with two disciples after His resurrection, Christ "took bread, gave thanks, [and] broke it" (Luke 24:30). He thanked His Father as He had earlier when He'd fed the five thousand with five "loaves and two small fish" (John 6:9). When we give thanks for our daily meals and for other provisions, our gratitude reflects Jesus's ways and honors our heavenly Father. Let's give thanks to God today. *Katara Patton*

Practice Gratitude Today

Choose a meal today to slow down and savor each bite. Pay attention to the flavors, textures, and smells. Thank God for providing the food on your table.

Fighting Life's Dragons

COLOSSIANS 2:9–15

Having disarmed the powers and authorities, he made a public spectacle of them, triumphing over them by the cross.
Colossians 2:15

Have you ever fought a dragon? If you answered no, Eugene Peterson disagrees with you. In *A Long Obedience in the Same Direction*, he wrote, "Dragons are projections of our fears, horrible constructions of all that might hurt us. . . . A peasant confronted by a magnificent dragon is completely outclassed." Peterson's point? Life is filled with dragons: the life-threatening health crisis, the sudden job loss, the failed marriage, the estranged prodigal child. These dragons are the supersize dangers and frailties of life that we're inadequate to fight alone.

But in those battles, we have a Champion. Not a fairy-tale champion—the ultimate Champion who has fought on our behalf and conquered the dragons that seek to destroy us. Whether they're dragons of our own failures or the spiritual enemy who desires our destruction, our Champion is greater, allowing Paul to write of Jesus, "Having disarmed the powers and authorities, he made a public spectacle of them, triumphing over them by the cross" (Colossians 2:15). The destructive forces of this broken world are no match for Him!

The moment we realize that the dragons of life are too big for us is the moment we can begin to rest in Christ's rescue. We can confidently say, "But thanks be to God! He gives us the victory through our Lord Jesus Christ" (1 Corinthians 15:57). *Bill Crowder*

Practice Gratitude Today

What difficulty or challenge feels too big for you today? Talk with God about it, and thank Him for triumphing over all the powers of evil, sin, and death on the cross.

Someone to Celebrate

MATTHEW 2:1–12

Come, let us bow down in worship, let us
kneel before the LORD our Maker.
Psalm 95:6

Many manger scenes depict the wise men, or magi, visiting Jesus in Bethlehem at the same time as the shepherds. But according to the gospel of Matthew, the only place in Scripture where their story is found, the magi showed up later. Jesus was no longer a baby in the manger but perhaps as much as two years old (2:16). Matthew 2:11 tells us, "On coming to the house, they saw the child with his mother Mary, and they bowed down and worshiped him. Then they opened their treasures and presented him with gifts of gold, frankincense and myrrh."

Realizing that the magi's visit happened later than we may think provides a helpful reminder as we begin a new year. Jesus is always worthy of worship. When the holidays are past and we head back to life's everyday routines, we still have Someone to celebrate.

Jesus Christ is Immanuel, "God with us" (Matthew 1:23), in every season. He has promised to be with us "always" (28:20). Because He is always with us, we can worship Him in our hearts every day and trust that He will show Himself faithful in the years to come. Just as the magi sought Him, may we seek Him too and worship Him wherever we are. *James Banks*

Practice Gratitude Today

Have you put away the manger scene and other Christmas decorations already? What is one decoration you can leave out a while longer to remind yourself to be thankful all year for Jesus's birth?

The Art of a Grateful Heart

PSALM 118:1–14, 26–29

Give thanks to the Lord, for he is good; his love endures forever.
Psalm 118:1

On our wedding day, Martie and I gladly vowed to be faithful "in good times as well as in bad, in sickness as well as in health, for richer or for poorer." In a way it may seem strange to include vows about the bleak reality of bad times, sickness, and poverty on a cheerful wedding day. But it underscores the fact that life often has bad times.

So what are we to do when we face life's inevitable difficulties? Paul urges us on behalf of Christ to "give thanks in all circumstances" (1 Thessalonians 5:18). As difficult as that may sound, there is good reason why God encourages us to embrace a spirit of gratitude. Gratitude is grounded in the truth that our Lord "is good" and "his love endures forever" (Psalm 118:1). He is present with us and strengthens us in the midst of trouble (Hebrews 13:5–6), and He lovingly uses our trials to grow our character into His likeness (Romans 5:3–4).

When life hits us with hard times, choosing to be grateful focuses our attention on the goodness of God and gives us the strength to make it through our struggles. With the psalmist, we can sing, "Give thanks to the Lord, for he is good; his love endures forever" (Psalm 118:29).

Joe Stowell

Practice Gratitude Today

What struggle or difficulty is life hitting you with today? Pause in prayer to thank God for His presence, strength, and love, and ask Him to use your trials to make you more like Christ.

Snow Muse

JOB 36:26–29; 37:5–7

He says to the snow, "Fall on the earth," and to the rain shower, "Be a mighty downpour."
Job 37:6

Named for a tough blue-collar neighborhood in Cincinnati, Ohio, the grassroots musical group Over the Rhine sings about a transformation that took place each year in the city. "Whenever we'd get our first real snowfall of the year, it felt like something sacred was happening," explains band cofounder Linford Detweiler. "Like a little bit of a fresh start. The city would slow down and grow quiet."

If you've experienced a heavy snowfall, you understand how it can inspire a song. A magical quietness drapes the world as snow conceals grime and grayness. For a few moments, winter's bleakness brightens, inviting our reflection and delight.

Elihu, the one friend of Job's who may have had a helpful view of God, noted how creation commands our attention. "God's voice thunders in marvelous ways," he said (Job 37:5). "He says to the snow, 'Fall on the earth,' and to the rain shower, 'Be a mighty downpour'" (v. 6). Such splendor can interrupt our lives, demanding a sacred pause. "So that everyone he has made may know his work, he stops all people from their labor," Elihu observed (v. 7).

Nature sometimes seizes our attention in ways we don't like. Regardless of what happens to us or what we observe around us, each moment—magnificent, menacing, or mundane—can inspire our worship. The poet's heart within us craves the holy hush. *Tim Gustafson*

Practice Gratitude Today

Depending on where you live, you may be able to step outside to enjoy snowfall today. Otherwise, find a video online. Allow the quietness of the falling snow to envelop you, and praise God for His creative power.

Food in the Cupboard

MATTHEW 6:25–34

Do not worry about your life, what you will eat or drink; or about your body, what you will wear.
Matthew 6:25

My friend Marcia, the director of the Jamaica Christian School for the Deaf, recently illustrated an important way to look at things. In a newsletter article she titled "A Blessed Start," she pointed out that for the first time in seven years the school began the new year with a surplus. And what was that surplus? A thousand dollars in the bank? No. Enough school supplies for the year? No. It was simply this: a month's supply of food in the cupboard.

When you're in charge of feeding thirty hungry kids on a shoestring budget, that's big! She accompanied her note with the verse 1 Chronicles 16:34, "Give thanks to the LORD, for he is good; his love endures forever."

Year after year Marcia trusts God to provide for the children and staff at her school. She never has much—whether it's water or food or school supplies. Yet she is always grateful for what God sends, and she is faithful to believe that He will continue to provide.

As we begin a new year, do we have faith in God's provision? To do so is to take our Savior at His word when He said, "Do not worry about your life. . . . Do not worry about tomorrow" (Matthew 6:25, 34).

Dave Branon

Practice Gratitude Today

What level of physical health, financial stability, or emotional well-being do you think you need to feel secure? Pray and thank God that He has given you enough for today.

Who Is He?

PSALM 24

Who is he, this King of glory? The LORD Almighty—he is the King of glory.
Psalm 24:10

On our way home from our honeymoon, my husband and I waited to check in our luggage at the airport. I nudged him and pointed to a man standing a few feet away.

My spouse squinted. "Who is he?"

I excitedly rattled off the actor's most notable roles, then walked up and asked him to take a photo with us. Twenty-four years later, I still enjoy sharing the story of the day I met a movie star.

Recognizing a famous actor is one thing, but there's Someone more important I'm thankful to know personally. "Who is this King of glory?" (Psalm 24:8). The psalmist David points to the Lord Almighty as Creator, Sustainer, and Ruler of all. He sings, "The earth is the LORD's, and everything in it, the world, and all who live in it; for he founded it on the seas and established it on the waters" (vv. 1–2). In awestruck wonder, David proclaims that God is above all yet intimately approachable (vv. 3–4). We can know Him, be empowered by Him, and trust Him to fight on our behalf, as we live for Him (v. 8).

God provides opportunities for us to declare Him as the only Famous One truly worth sharing with others. As we reflect His character, those who don't recognize Him can have more reasons to ask, "Who is He?" Like David, we can point to the Lord with awestruck wonder and tell His story!

Xochitl Dixon

Practice Gratitude Today

What attributes, acts, or roles best characterize God for you? Today, tell someone about something God has done or an aspect of His character that you are thankful for.

Locked into Love

ROMANS 8:31–39

Give thanks to the LORD, for he is good; his love endures forever.
Psalm 106:1

Recently the city of Paris removed forty-five tons of padlocks from the railings of the Pont des Arts pedestrian bridge. As a romantic gesture, couples would etch their initials onto a lock, attach it to the railing, click it shut, and throw the key into the River Seine.

After this ritual was repeated thousands of times, the bridge could no longer bear the weight of so much love. Eventually the city, fearing for the integrity of the bridge, removed the love locks.

The locks were meant to symbolize everlasting love, but human love does not always last. The closest of friends may offend each other and never resolve their differences. Family members may argue and refuse to forgive. A husband and wife may drift so far apart that they can't remember why they once decided to marry. Human love can be fickle.

But there is one constant and enduring love—the love of God. "Give thanks to the LORD, for he is good; his love endures forever," proclaims Psalm 106:1. The unfailing and everlasting nature of God's love is found throughout Scripture. And the greatest proof of this love is the death of His Son so that those who put their faith in Him can live eternally. And nothing will ever separate us from His love (Romans 8:38–39).

Fellow believers, we are locked into God's love forever.

Cindy Hess Kasper

Practice Gratitude Today

Recall a time when human love failed you. Bring that pain to God in prayer, and thank Him that His everlasting love will never fail you.

Remember to Sing

PSALM 147:1–7

How good it is to sing praises to our God.
Psalm 147:1

Nancy Gustafson, a retired opera singer, was devastated when she visited her mother and observed her decline from dementia. Her mom no longer recognized her and barely spoke. After several monthly visits, Nancy had an idea. She started singing to her. Her mother's eyes lit up at the musical sounds, and she began singing too—for twenty minutes! Then Nancy's mom laughed, joking they were "The Gustafson Family Singers." The dramatic turnaround suggested the power of music, as some therapists conclude, to evoke lost memories. Singing old favorites has also been shown to boost mood, reduce falls, lessen visits to the emergency room, and decrease the need for sedative drugs.

More research is underway on a music-memory link. Yet, as the Bible reveals, the joy that comes from singing is a gift from God—and it's real. "How good it is to sing praises to our God, how pleasant and fitting to praise him!" (Psalm 147:1).

Throughout the Scriptures, in fact, God's people are urged to lift their voices in songs of praise to Him. "Sing to the Lord, for he has done glorious things" (Isaiah 12:5). "He put a new song in my mouth, a hymn of praise to our God. Many will see and fear the Lord and put their trust in him" (Psalm 40:3). Our singing inspires us and also those who hear it. May we all remember: our God is great and worthy of praise.

Patricia Raybon

Practice Gratitude Today

Sing a favorite worship song to God, thanking Him for the gift of music. Consider singing along with a recording or with a friend or fellow believer in Jesus.

God Sees You

GENESIS 16:9–16

"You are the God who sees me," for [Hagar] said,
"I have now seen the One who sees me."
Genesis 16:13

"Get down!" my friend said firmly to her son after he climbed onto the church pew and waved his hands. "I want the pastor to see me," he innocently replied. "If I don't stand up, he won't see me."

While standing on the pews is probably not encouraged in most churches, my friend's son had a good point. Standing and waving his hands was certainly one way to be seen and to capture the pastor's attention.

When we're trying to get God's attention, we don't have to worry about being seen by Him. God sees each of us all the time. He's the same One who revealed Himself to Hagar when she was probably at the lowest, loneliest, most frustrating time in her life. She'd been used as a pawn and given to Abram by his wife, Sarai, to produce a son (Genesis 16:3). And when she did get pregnant, Abram allowed his wife to mistreat Hagar: "Sarai mistreated Hagar; so she fled from her" (v. 6).

The runaway slave found herself alone, pregnant, and miserable. Yet in the midst of her desperation in the wilderness, God compassionately sent an angel to speak to her. The angel told her that God had "heard of [her] misery" (v. 11). She responded by saying, "You are the God who sees me" (v. 13).

What a realization—especially in the midst of the wilderness. God saw Hagar and had compassion. And no matter how tough things are, He sees you. *Katara Patton*

Practice Gratitude Today

What circumstance, wound, or dream in your life feels like it's unseen by God? Talk with Him about it, and thank Him that He sees you and knows your pain.

God Made Them All

PSALM 104:24–35

How many are your works, LORD! In wisdom you made them all.
Psalm 104:24

My three-year-old son, Xavier, squeezed my hand as we entered the Monterey Bay Aquarium in California. Pointing to a life-size sculpture of a humpback whale suspended from the ceiling, he said, "Enormous." His wide-eyed joy continued as we explored each exhibit. We laughed as the otters splish-splashed during feeding time. We stood in silence in front of a large glass aquarium window, mesmerized by the golden-brown jellyfish dancing in the electric blue water. "God made every creature in the ocean," I said, "just like He made you and me." Xavier whispered, "Wow."

In Psalm 104, the psalmist acknowledged God's abounding creation and sang, "In wisdom you made them all; the earth is full of your creatures" (v. 24). He declared, "There is the sea, vast and spacious, teeming with creatures beyond number—living things both large and small" (v. 25). He proclaimed God's generous and satisfying provision for all He created (vv. 27–28). He also affirmed that God determined the days of each one's existence (vv. 29–30).

We can join the psalmist in singing this declaration of devotion: "I will sing to the LORD all my life; I will sing praise to my God as long as I live" (v. 33). Every creature that exists, from the big to the small, can lead us to praise because God made them all. *Xochitl Dixon*

Practice Gratitude Today

Spend a few minutes observing a living creation, whether a pet or a houseplant, a wild creature outside or in an online video. Praise God for His awe-inspiring creativity.

God Focus

1 TIMOTHY 6:6–11

Godliness with contentment is great gain.
1 Timothy 6:6

When I was shopping for engagement rings, I spent many hours looking for exactly the right diamond. I was plagued by the thought, *What if I miss the best one?*

According to economic psychologist Barry Schwartz, my chronic indecision indicates that I am what he calls a *maximizer*, in contrast to a *satisficer*. A satisficer makes choices based on whether something is adequate for their needs. Maximizers? We have a need to always make the best choice (guilty!). The potential outcome of our indecision in the face of many choices? Anxiety, depression, and discontent. In fact, sociologists have coined a phrase for this phenomenon: fear of missing out.

We won't find the words *maximizer* or *satisficer* in Scripture, of course. But we do find a similar idea. In 1 Timothy, Paul challenged Timothy to find value in God rather than the things of this world. The world's promises of fulfillment can never fully deliver. Paul wanted Timothy to instead root his identity in God: "Godliness with contentment is great gain" (6:6). Paul sounds like a satisficer when he adds, "But if we have food and clothing, we will be content with that" (v. 8).

When I fixate on the myriad ways the world promises fulfillment, I usually end up restless and unsatisfied. But when I focus on God and relinquish my compulsive urge to maximize, my soul moves toward genuine contentment and rest.

Adam R. Holz

Practice Gratitude Today

What choice, deadline, or event do you feel stressed about today? Thank God that His provision and love don't depend on anything you do.

Good for You

PROVERBS 24:13–14

Wisdom is like honey for you: If you
find it, there is a future hope.
Proverbs 24:14

People the world over spent an estimated $133.6 billion on chocolate in 2024. The number is staggering, yet at the same time not all that surprising. Chocolate, after all, tastes delicious and we enjoy consuming it. So the world rejoiced collectively when the sweet treat was found to have significant health benefits as well. Chocolate contains flavonoids that help safeguard the body against aging and heart disease. Never has a prescription for health been so well received or heeded (in moderation, of course!).

Solomon suggested there's another "sweet" worthy of our investment: wisdom. He recommended his son eat honey "for it is good" (Proverbs 24:13) and compared its sweetness to wisdom. The person who feeds on God's wisdom in Scripture finds it not only sweet to the soul but beneficial for teaching and training, equipping us for "every good work" we'll need to accomplish in life (2 Timothy 3:16–17).

Wisdom is what allows us to make smart choices and understand the world around us. And it's worth investing in and sharing with those we love—as Solomon wished to do for his son. We can feel good about feasting on God's wisdom in the Bible. It's a sweet treat that we can enjoy without limit—in fact, we're encouraged to! God, thank You for the sweetness of Your Scriptures! *Kirsten Holmberg*

Practice Gratitude Today

Spend time today reading the Bible, perhaps in a book known for its wisdom, such as Proverbs or James. Thank God for the sweetness of His wisdom.

Is There Hope?

ROMANS 8:31–39

If God is for us, who can be against us?
Romans 8:31

Edward Payson (1783–1827) led an extremely difficult life. The death of his younger brother shook him to the core. He struggled with bipolar disorder, and he was affected by extreme migraine headaches for days. If this wasn't enough, a fall from a horse led to paralysis of his arm, and he almost died from tuberculosis. Surprisingly, his response wasn't one of despair and hopelessness. His friends said that before Edward passed away, his joy was intense. How could that be?

In his letter to the believers in Rome, the apostle Paul expressed his complete confidence in the reality of God's love regardless of circumstances. He asked with boldness, "If God is for us, who can be against us?" (Romans 8:31). If God gave His very own Son, Jesus, to save us, then He will provide everything we need to finish this life well. Paul listed seven seemingly unbearable situations that he himself faced: trouble, hardship, persecution, famine, nakedness, danger, and the sword (v. 35). He didn't imply that Christ's love would stop bad things from happening. But Paul said that "in all these things we are more than conquerors through him who loved us" (v. 37).

Through the uncertainty of this world, God can be trusted completely, because we know that nothing, absolutely nothing, "will be able to separate us from the love of God that is in Christ Jesus our Lord" (v. 39). *Estera Pirosca Escobar*

Practice Gratitude Today

What feels unbearable or hopeless today? Honestly share your pain with God—then praise Him that nothing you experience can separate you from His never-ending love.

Greedy Grasping

ECCLESIASTES 4:4–8

Better one handful with tranquillity than two
handfuls with toil and chasing after the wind.
Ecclesiastes 4:6

In the ancient fable "The Boy and the Filberts," a boy sticks his hand into a jar of nuts and grabs a great fistful. But his hand is so full that it gets stuck in the jar. Unwilling to lose even a little of his bounty, the boy begins to weep. Eventually, he is counseled to let go of some of the nuts so the jar will let go of his hand. Greed can be a hard boss.

The wise teacher of Ecclesiastes illustrates this moral with a lesson on hands and what they say about us. He compared and contrasted the lazy with the greedy when he wrote: "Fools fold their hands and ruin themselves. Better one handful with tranquillity than two handfuls with toil and chasing after the wind" (4:5–6). While the lazy procrastinate until they're ruined, those who pursue wealth come to realize their efforts are "meaningless—a miserable business!" (v. 8).

According to the teacher, the desired state is to relax from the toil of greedy grasping in order to find contentment in what truly belongs to us. For that which is ours will always remain. As Jesus said, "What good is it for someone to gain the whole world, yet forfeit their soul?" (Mark 8:36).

Remi Oyedele

Practice Gratitude Today

What do you need to let go of today so you can be more content with what you have? Thank God that He has already given you enough in Christ.

Owner or Steward?

PSALM 50:7–15

Every animal of the forest is mine.
Psalm 50:10

"Am I an owner or a steward?" The CEO of a multibillion-dollar company asked himself that question as he weighed what was best for his family. Concerned about the temptations that can come with vast wealth, he didn't want to burden his heirs with that challenge. So he gave up his personal stake in the company. Recognizing that everything he owns belongs to God helped him make his decision to allow his family to earn a living in exchange for work while also using future profits to fund Christian ministry.

In Psalm 50:10, God tells His people, "Every animal of the forest is mine, and the cattle on a thousand hills." As the Creator of all things, God owes us nothing and needs nothing from us. "I have no need of a bull from your stall or of goats from your pens," He says (v. 9). He generously provides everything that we have and use as well as the strength and the ability to earn a living. Because He does, as the psalm shows us, He is worthy of our heartfelt worship.

God owns everything. But because of His goodness, He even chose to give Himself, entering into a relationship with any who turn to Him. Jesus "did not come to be served, but to serve, and to give his life as a ransom for many" (Mark 10:45). When we value the Giver over the gifts and serve Him with them, we are blessed to delight in Him forever.

James Banks

Practice Gratitude Today

What is one possession, talent, or privilege you think of as something you earned for yourself? Pause to thank God for providing you with that thing.

Tell of God's Goodness

PSALM 66:5–12, 16–20

Let me tell you what he has done for me.
Psalm 66:16

Testimony time was the segment in our church service when people shared how God had been at work in their lives. Auntie—or Sister Langford as she was known by others in our church family—was known for packing lots of praise into her testimonies. On the occasions when she shared her conversion story, one could expect her to take up a good bit of the service. Her heart gushed with praise to God who had graciously changed her life!

Similarly, the testimony of the writer of Psalm 66 is packed with praise as he testifies about what God had done for His people. "Come and see what God has done, his awesome deeds for mankind!" (v. 5). His deeds included miraculous rescue (v. 6), preservation (v. 9), and testing and discipline that resulted in His people being brought to a better place (vv. 10–12). While there are experiences of God that we have in common with other believers in Jesus, there are also things unique to our individual journeys. Have there been times in your life when God has particularly made Himself known to you? Those are worth sharing with others who need to hear how He's worked in your life. "Come and hear, all you who fear God; let me tell you what he has done for me" (v. 16). *Arthur Jackson*

Practice Gratitude Today

What has God done for you that you are particularly grateful for in this life season? Whether in person or by text, tell someone about God's goodness to you today.

God's Transforming Word

2 TIMOTHY 3:10–17

You have known the Holy Scriptures, which are able to make you wise for salvation through faith in Christ Jesus.
2 Timothy 3:15

When Kristin wanted to buy a special book for Xio-Hu, her Chinese husband, the only one she could find in Chinese was a Bible. Although neither of them was a believer in Christ, she hoped he would appreciate the gift anyway. At first sight of the Bible, he was angry, but eventually he picked it up. As he read, he became persuaded by the truth in its pages. Upset at this unforeseen development, Kristin started to read the Scriptures in order to refute Xio-Hu. To her surprise, she also came to faith in Jesus through being convinced by what she read.

The apostle Paul knew the transforming nature of Scripture. Writing from prison in Rome, he urged Timothy, whom he mentored, to "continue in what you have learned" because "from infancy you have known the Holy Scriptures" (2 Timothy 3:14–15). In the original language, the Greek for "continue" has the sense of "abiding" in what the Bible reveals. Knowing that Timothy would face opposition and persecution, Paul wanted him to be equipped for the challenges; he believed his protégé would find strength and wisdom in the Bible as he spent time pondering its truth.

God through His Spirit brings Scripture alive to us. As we dwell in it, He changes us to be more like Him. Even as He did with Xio-Hu and Kristin.

Amy Boucher Pye

Practice Gratitude Today

How has the Bible transformed you or someone you know? Praise God for how His Spirit works and speaks through His Word.

This Is the Day

PSALM 118:19–29

This is the day the LORD has made. We will rejoice and be glad in it.
Psalm 118:24 NLT

In 1940, Dr. Virginia Connally, age twenty-seven, braved opposition and criticism to become the first female physician in Abilene, Texas. A few months before her hundredth birthday in 2012, the Texas Medical Association presented her with its Distinguished Service Award, Texas's highest physician honor. Between those two landmark events, Dr. Connally enthusiastically embraced a passion for spreading the gospel around the world through her many medical mission trips while living a life of service to God and to others—one day at a time.

Dr. Connally's pastor, Phil Christopher, said, "Every day for her is a gift." He recalled a letter in which she wrote, "Every tour, trip, effort, I wonder if this will be my last and ultimate? Only God knows. And this is enough."

The psalmist wrote, "This is the day the LORD has made. We will rejoice and be glad in it" (Psalm 118:24 NLT). So often we focus on the disappointments of yesterday or the uncertainties of tomorrow and miss God's matchless gift to us: today!

Dr. Connally said of her journey with Christ, "As you live a life of faith, you're not looking for the results. I was just doing the things that God planted in my life and heart."

God made today. Let's celebrate it and make the most of every opportunity to serve others in His name. *David McCasland*

Practice Gratitude Today

Today is a gift from God. What can you do today to show your gratitude to God for giving you another day?

Children of God

EPHESIANS 4:32–5:10

Follow God's example, therefore, as dearly loved children and walk in the way of love.
Ephesians 5:1–2

I once spoke at a secular conference for childless couples. Heartbroken over their infertility, many attendees despaired of their future. Having walked the childless path too, I tried to encourage them. "You can have a meaningful identity without becoming parents," I said. "I believe you are fearfully and wonderfully made, and there's new purpose for you to find."

A woman later approached me in tears. "Thank you," she said. "I've felt worthless being childless and needed to hear that I'm fearfully and wonderfully made." I asked the woman if she was a believer in Jesus. "I walked away from God years ago," she said. "But I need a relationship with Him again."

Times like this remind me how profound the gospel is. Some identities, like "mother" and "father," are hard for some to attain. Others, like those based on a career, can be lost through unemployment. But through Jesus we become God's "dearly loved children" (Ephesians 5:1)—an identity that can never be stolen. And then we can "walk in the way of love" (v. 2)—a life purpose that transcends any role or employment status.

All human beings are "fearfully and wonderfully made" (Psalm 139:14), and those who follow Jesus become children of God (John 1:12–13). Once in despair, that woman left in hope—about to find an identity and purpose bigger than this world can give. *Sheridan Voysey*

Practice Gratitude Today

What is a cherished identity you've lost, or an identity you long to have but haven't achieved? Thank God that no matter what else you are, you are a beloved child of God.

Extravagant Love

1 PETER 2:11–12

They may see your good deeds and glorify God.
1 Peter 2:12

My seatmate on the flight told me she was nonreligious and had immigrated to a town that was home to numerous Christians. When she mentioned that most of her neighbors went to church, I asked about her experience. She said she could never repay their generosity. When she brought her disabled father to her new country, her neighbors built a ramp to her house and donated a hospital bed and medical supplies. She said, "If being a Christian makes one so kind, everyone should be a Christian."

Exactly what Jesus hoped she'd say! He told His disciples, "Let your light shine before others, that they may see your good deeds and glorify your Father in heaven" (Matthew 5:16). Peter heard Christ's command and passed it on: "Live such good lives among the pagans that, though they accuse you of doing wrong, they may see your good deeds and glorify God" (1 Peter 2:12).

Our neighbors who don't have faith in Jesus may not understand what we believe and why we believe it. Don't sweat it, as long as there's one more thing they can't understand: the extravagance of our love. My seatmate marveled that her Christian neighbors continue to care for her even though she isn't, in her words, "one of them." She knows she's loved, for Jesus's sake, and she gives thanks to God. She may not yet believe in Him, but she's grateful that others do. *Mike Wittmer*

Practice Gratitude Today

Recall a time when your church community reflected the generosity of Christ to you. Thank God for your fellow believers, and consider how you can reflect Christ's generosity to someone else today.

Growing Gratitude

ROMANS 11:33–36

For from him and through him and for him are all things.
Romans 11:36

Would you like to cultivate a greater sense of gratitude? George Herbert, a seventeenth-century British poet, encourages readers toward that goal in his poem "Gratefulness": "Thou that hast given so much to me, give one thing more: a grateful heart."

Herbert recognized the only thing he needed in order to be thankful was simply an awareness of the blessings God had already given him.

The Bible declares Christ Jesus as the source of all blessing in Romans 11:36: "For from him and through him and for him are all things." "All things" encompasses both the extravagant and the mundane, everyday gifts in our lives. Everything we receive in life comes directly from our heavenly Father (James 1:17), and He willingly gives us those gifts out of His love for us.

To expand my awareness of God's blessings in my life, I am learning to cultivate a heart that acknowledges the source of all the joys I experience each day, but especially the ones I often take for granted. Today those included a crisp morning to run, the anticipation of an evening with friends, a stocked pantry so I could make French toast with my daughters, the beauty of the world outside my window, and the aroma of freshly brewed coffee.

What is the "so much" that God has already given to you? Opening our eyes to those blessings will help us to develop grateful hearts.

Lisa M. Samra

Practice Gratitude Today

Name some of the simple blessings you have today that you might normally take for granted. Thank God for His generosity, and ask Him to give you a grateful heart.

Learning from the Redwoods

ISAIAH 65:17–66:2

As the days of a tree, so will be the days of my people.
Isaiah 65:22

North America's coastal redwoods are some of the biggest trees in the world. The tallest on record, Hyperion, soars 380 feet into the air.

During a visit to California's Muir Woods National Park, I was surprised and overwhelmed by the enormity of those redwoods. Trees as tall as a thirty-story building seemed to press me into the forest floor while drawing my thoughts upward.

The memory of what I felt at the base of some of the tallest and oldest trees in the world has left me with lingering thoughts about their origin. Those redwoods, like the family tree of our own humanity, are rooted in a Creator who is infinitely and eternally greater than His creation.

The prophet Isaiah caught a glimpse of this God. In a vision that mingled the wonders of a messianic kingdom with the promise of a new heaven and earth, he describes one who makes the skies His throne and the earth His footstool (Isaiah 66:1).

Yet Isaiah saw something even more overwhelming. He saw a great God who wants His people to "be glad and rejoice forever in what [He] will create" (65:18). In response, let's bow before Him in humble adoration (66:2).

Mart DeHaan

Practice Gratitude Today

Recall a natural wonder or beautiful part of creation you saw in the past. Why does that memory stick with you? Praise God for His creativity and power, and the beauty of His works.

The Language of the Cross

ROMANS 5:1–10

God demonstrates his own love for us in this: While we were still sinners, Christ died for us.
Romans 5:8

Pastor Tim Keller said, "Nobody ever learns who they are by being told. They must be shown." In a sense, it's one application of the adage "Actions speak louder than words." Spouses show their mates that they're appreciated by listening to them and loving them. Parents show their children they're valued by lovingly caring for them. Coaches show athletes they have potential by investing in their development. And on it goes. By the same token, a different kind of action can show people painful things that communicate much darker messages.

Of all the action-based messages in the universe, there's one that matters most. When we want to be shown who we are in God's eyes, we need look no further than His actions on the cross. In Romans 5:8, Paul wrote, "God demonstrates his own love for us in this: While we were still sinners, Christ died for us." The cross shows us who we are: those whom God so loved that He gave His one and only Son for us (John 3:16).

Against the mixed messages and confusing actions of broken people in a broken culture, the message of God's heart rings clear. Who are you? You're the one so loved by God that He gave His Son for your rescue. Consider the price He paid for you and the wonderful reality that, to Him, you were always worth it. *Bill Crowder*

Practice Gratitude Today

Read one of the gospel accounts of Jesus's crucifixion (Matthew 27; Mark 15; Luke 23; John 19). Thank God for what He did for you, because He loves you.

Prayers on La Playa

PSALM 148

Let them praise the name of the Lord,
for his name alone is exalted.
Psalm 148:13

During a trip to celebrate our twenty-fifth anniversary, my husband and I read our Bibles on the beach. As vendors passed and called out the prices of their wares, we thanked each one but didn't buy anything. One vendor, Fernando, smiled wide at my rejection and insisted we consider buying gifts for friends. After I declined his invitation, Fernando packed up and began walking away, still grinning. "I pray God will bless your day," I said.

Fernando turned toward me and said, "He has! Jesus changed my life." Fernando knelt between our chairs. "I feel His presence here." He then shared how God had delivered him from drug and alcohol abuse more than fourteen years earlier.

My tears flowed as he recited entire poems from the book of Psalms and prayed for us. Together, we praised God and rejoiced in His presence . . . on *la playa*.

Psalm 148 is a prayer of praise. The psalmist encourages all of creation to "praise the name of the Lord, for at his command [everything was] created" (v. 5). "His name alone is exalted; his splendor is above the earth and the heavens" (v. 13).

Though God invites us to bring our needs before Him and to trust that He hears and cares for us, He also delights in prayers of grateful praise wherever we are. Even on the beach. *Xochitl Dixon*

Practice Gratitude Today

Where is a place in your daily life that you don't normally stop to pray? Take time today to pray in that place, thanking God for the relationships, responsibilities, or opportunities in that part of your life.

God Works in Mud

GENESIS 2:1–7

The LORD God formed a man from the dust of the ground and breathed into his nostrils the breath of life, and the man became a living being.
Genesis 2:7

In a 1950s novel, there is a scene where four village men confess their sins to one another. One of the men, Michelis, cries out, "How can God let us live on the earth? Why doesn't He kill us to purify creation?" "Because, Michelis," one of the men answered, "God is a potter; He works in mud."

This is literally what the Lord did in Genesis. The sovereign Creator formed and shaped humanity by unique design. This process involved fashioning a man from the dust of the ground. The word "formed" in Genesis 2:7 describes the work of an artist. Like a potter, molding and fashioning mud into a pot or some other earthen vessel, so the Lord God formed humanity from clay.

God's work with dust and mud continued by breathing into the man the breath of life, changing his form into a living soul. This made the man a spiritual being, with a capacity to serve and fellowship with the Lord.

After Adam and Eve sinned, God continued working in and with mud, sending His Son, Jesus, to die for humanity and then regenerating those who receive Him so that we can enjoy fellowship with Him. In gratitude, let's use our hands to do good works for His glory.

Marvin Williams

Practice Gratitude Today

Spend a few minutes observing someone—a spouse, child, friend, or yourself in a mirror. Thank God that His Spirit is living in and working through these muddy creations.

Love's Long Reach

PSALM 139:1–10

Oh, the depth of the riches of the wisdom
and knowledge of God!
Romans 11:33

Mary Lee was a sixteen-foot, thirty-five-hundred-pound great white shark tagged by oceanographers off the east coast of the United States. The transmitter attached to her dorsal fin was tracked by satellite when she surfaced. For five years Mary Lee's movements were observed online by everyone from researchers to surfers, up and down the coast. She was tracked for nearly forty thousand miles until one day her signal stopped—probably because the battery on her transmitter expired.

Human knowledge and technology reach only so far. Those following Mary Lee lost track of her, but you and I can never evade God's awareness throughout every moment of our lives. David prayed, "Where can I go from your Spirit? Where can I flee from your presence? If I go up to the heavens, you are there; if I make my bed in the depths, you are there" (Psalm 139:7–8). "Such knowledge is too wonderful for me," he exclaims gratefully (v. 6).

God chooses to know us because He loves us. He cares enough not only to observe our lives but also to enter into them and make them new. He drew near through Christ's life, death, and resurrection, so we could know Him in return and love Him for eternity. We can never go beyond the reach of God's love. *James Banks*

Practice Gratitude Today

When or where have you felt like you were beyond the reach of God's love? Talk with Him about it. Thank Him that no matter where you are or what you're feeling, God's love is with you.

Biblical Prescription

PROVERBS 17:19–22

A cheerful heart is good medicine, but a
crushed spirit dries up the bones.
Proverbs 17:22

Greg and Elizabeth have a regular joke night with their four school-age children. Each child brings several jokes they've read or heard (or made up themselves!) during the week to tell at the dinner table. This tradition has created joyful memories of fun shared around the table. Greg and Elizabeth even noticed the laughter was healthy for their children, lifting their spirits on difficult days.

The benefit of joyful conversation around the dinner table was observed by C. S. Lewis, who wrote, "The sun looks down on nothing half so good as a household laughing together over a meal."

The wisdom of fostering a joyful heart is found in Proverbs 17:22, where we read, "A cheerful heart is good medicine, but a crushed spirit dries up the bones." The proverb offers a "prescription" to stimulate health and healing: allowing our hearts to be filled with joy, a medicine that costs little and yields great results.

We all need this biblical prescription. When we bring joy into our conversations, it can put a disagreement into perspective. It can help us to experience peace, even after a stressful test at school or a difficult day at work. Laughter among family and friends can create a safe place where we both know and feel that we're loved.

Do you need to incorporate more laughter into your life as "good medicine" for your spirit? Remember, you have encouragement from Scripture to cultivate a cheerful heart. *Lisa M. Samra*

Practice Gratitude Today

Share a joke, meme, or funny video with someone you like to laugh with. Ask them to send one back. Thank God for the gift of laughter.

Flourishing Like a Flower

PSALM 103:13–22

The life of mortals is like grass, they
flourish like a flower of the field.
Psalm 103:15

My youngest grandson is only two months old, yet every time I see him, I notice little changes. Recently, as I cooed to him, he looked up at me and smiled! And suddenly I began crying. Perhaps it was joy mixed with remembering my own children's first smiles, which I witnessed so long ago, and yet it feels like just yesterday. Some moments are like that—inexplicable.

In Psalm 103, David penned a poetic song that praised God while also reflecting on how quickly the joyful moments of our lives pass by: "The life of mortals is like grass, they flourish like a flower of the field; the wind blows over it and it is gone" (vv. 15–16).

But despite acknowledging the brevity of life, David describes the flower as flourishing, or thriving. Although each individual flower blossoms swiftly, its fragrance and color and beauty bring great joy in the moment. And even though an individual flower can be quickly forgotten—"its place remembers it no more" (v. 16)—by contrast we have the assurance that "from everlasting to everlasting the Lord's love is with those who fear him" (v. 17).

We, like flowers, can rejoice and flourish in the moment; but we can also celebrate the truth that the moments of our lives are never truly forgotten. God holds every detail of our lives, and His everlasting love is with His children forever! *Alyson Kieda*

Practice Gratitude Today

Recall some cherished memories from a life season, friendship, or community in your past. Thank God that you had those experiences and memories—and that He remembers them too.

Hope That Holds

HABAKKUK 3:11–19

I will rejoice in the Lord, I will be joyful in God my Savior.
Habakkuk 3:18

"I know Daddy's coming home because he sent me flowers." Those were my seven-year-old sister's words to our mother when Dad was missing in action during wartime. Before Dad left for his mission, he preordered flowers for my sister's birthday, and they arrived while he was missing. But she was right: Dad did come home—after a harrowing combat situation. And decades later she still keeps the vase that held the flowers as a reminder to always hold on to hope.

Sometimes holding on to hope isn't easy in a broken, sinful world. Daddies don't always come home, and children's wishes sometimes go unfulfilled. But God gives hope in the most difficult circumstances. In another time of war, the prophet Habakkuk predicted the Babylonian invasion of Judah (Habakkuk 1:6) but still affirmed that God is always good (vv. 12–13). Remembering God's kindness to His people in the past, Habakkuk proclaimed: "Though the fig tree does not bud and there are no grapes on the vines, though the olive crop fails and the fields produce no food, though there are no sheep in the pen and no cattle in the stalls, yet I will rejoice in the Lord, I will be joyful in God my Savior" (3:17–18).

Some commentators believe Habakkuk's name means "to cling." We can cling to God as our ultimate hope and joy even in trials because He holds on to us and will never let go. *James Banks*

Practice Gratitude Today

Like a vase of flowers, what object do you own that reminds you of the hope you have in God? Display it in your home where you will see it often in the coming days and weeks.

The Great Creator-Healer

PSALM 139:1–16

I praise you because I am fearfully and wonderfully made.
Psalm 139:14

A few years ago, I had a rather serious skiing accident and severely tore the muscles in one of my legs. In fact, my doctor told me that the tear caused excessive bleeding. The healing process was slow, but during that time of waiting I found myself in awe of our great Creator.

I've wrinkled a few car fenders in my lifetime and dropped more than one dish. They've always stayed broken. Not so with my leg. As soon as the tearing of my muscles occurred, the internal healing mechanisms that Christ created in my body went to work. Invisibly, down deep in my throbbing leg, the medics of His marvelous design were mending the tear. Before long, I was up and running again with a whole new sense of what the psalmist meant when he said that we are "fearfully and wonderfully made" (Psalm 139:14), and my heart was filled with praise.

Sometimes it takes an injury or a sickness to remind us of the masterful design that we carry around in our bodies. So the next time you face an unwanted interruption—no matter its cause—focus your attention on Jesus's wonderful love and let Him lift your heart to grateful worship in the midst of the pain. *Joe Stowell*

Practice Gratitude Today

Recall a past injury or illness that your body overcame because of its miraculous healing capabilities. Thank God for the body He's given you.

Pray Always

1 THESSALONIANS 5:16–22

Pray continually.
1 Thessalonians 5:17

"I got an 84 on the test!"

I felt my teen's excitement as I read her message on my phone. She'd just started attending classes at a high school and was using her phone during lunch. My mama heart leaped, not just because my daughter had done well on a challenging test but because she was choosing to communicate it to me. She wanted to share her good news with me!

Realizing that her text had made my day, I later thought about how God must feel when I reach out to Him. Is He as pleased when I talk to Him? Prayer is how we communicate with God and something we're told to do "continually" (1 Thessalonians 5:17). Talking with Him reminds us that He's with us through the good and the bad. Sharing our news with God, even though He already knows all about us, is helpful as it shifts our focus and helps us think about Him. Isaiah 26:3 says, "You will keep in perfect peace those whose minds are steadfast, because they trust in you." We have peace awaiting us when we turn our attention to God.

Regardless of what we face, may we continually speak with God and keep in touch with our Creator and Savior. Whisper a prayer and remember to rejoice and "give thanks." After all, Paul says, this is "God's will" for us (1 Thessalonians 5:18). *Katara Patton*

Practice Gratitude Today

Today, whenever you have news, good or bad, first turn to God and tell Him about it before you share it with your spouse, friend, or colleague.

Gracias!

1 CHRONICLES 16:7–10, 23–36

Give praise to the Lord.
1 Chronicles 16:8

When I visited Mexico, I wished I knew how to speak Spanish. I could say *gracias* (thank you), *muy bien* (very good), and *hola* (hello). But that was about it. I grew tired of just saying *gracias* to everyone who talked with me or did something for me.

But we should never grow tired of giving words of thanks to God. David knew the importance of saying thanks. After he became king over Israel and had a tent constructed to house the ark of the covenant (where God's presence dwelt), he appointed some of the Levites "to extol, thank, and praise the Lord" (1 Chronicles 16:4). Many people remained there to offer sacrifices and give thanks to God daily (vv. 37–38).

David also committed to Asaph and his associates a song of thanks (vv. 8–36). His psalm gave thanks for what the Lord had done: "his wonderful acts" (v. 9), "his miracles, and the judgments he pronounced" (v. 12), and His salvation (v. 35). David's song also gave praise for who the Lord is: good, merciful, and holy (vv. 34–35).

Like David, we should never grow tired of saying *gracias* to God for who He is and for all He's done for us. Take time today to offer your sacrifice of praise to Him. *Anne Cetas*

Practice Gratitude Today

Find a way outside of your usual practice of worship to say thanks to God. Choose a posture of prayer, a song, or a creative expression of praise that is new to you.

Leave a Little Behind

LEVITICUS 23:15–22

Leave them for the poor and for the foreigner residing among you.
Leviticus 23:22

Pennies, nickels, dimes, quarters, and occasionally a half-dollar. That's what you'd find on the nightstand beside his bed. He'd empty his pockets each evening and leave the contents there, because he knew eventually they'd come to visit—*they* being his grandchildren. Over the years the kids learned to visit his nightstand as soon as they arrived. He could have put all that spare change in a coin bank or even stored it away in a savings account. But he didn't. He delighted in leaving it there for the little ones, the precious guests in his home.

A similar mindset is expressed in Leviticus 23 when it comes to bringing in the harvest from the land. God, via Moses, told the people something quite counterintuitive: not to "reap to the very edges of your field or gather the gleanings of your harvest" (v. 22). Essentially, He said, "Leave a little behind." This instruction reminded the people that God was behind the harvest in the first place, and that He used His people to provide for those with few resources—foreigners in the land.

Such thinking is definitely not the norm in our world. But it's exactly the kind of mindset that will characterize the grateful sons and daughters of God. He delights in a generous heart. And that often comes through you and me. *John Blase*

Practice Gratitude Today

How can you leave behind a little of what you have for someone else today? Thank God for the things He's given you, and that you have enough to share.

His Heart for All

MATTHEW 11:27–30

Come to me, all you who are weary.
Matthew 11:28

Nine-year-old Dan Gill arrived with his best friend, Archie, at their classmate's birthday party. When the mother of the birthday boy saw Archie, however, she refused him entry. "There aren't enough chairs," she insisted. Dan offered to sit on the floor to make room for his friend, who was Black, but the mother said no. Dejected, Dan left their presents with her and returned home with Archie, the sting of his friend's rejection searing his heart.

Now, decades later, Dan is a schoolteacher who keeps one empty chair in his classroom. When students ask why, he explains it's his reminder to "always have room in the classroom for anyone."

A heart for all people can be seen in Jesus's welcoming life: "Come to me, all you who are weary and burdened, and I will give you rest" (Matthew 11:28). This invitation may seem to contradict the "first to the Jew" scope of Jesus's ministry (Romans 1:16). But the gift of salvation is for all people who place their faith in Jesus. "This is true for everyone who believes," Paul wrote, "no matter who we are" (3:22 NLT).

We rejoice then at Jesus's invitation to all: "Take my yoke upon you and learn from me, for I am gentle and humble in heart, and you will find rest for your souls" (Matthew 11:29). For all seeking His rest, His open heart awaits.

Patricia Raybon

Practice Gratitude Today

In prayer, thank God for inviting you into rest and new life through Christ. Then consider how you can invite someone else into a place or opportunity where they may have been previously unwelcome.

Happy Thanksgiving

PHILIPPIANS 4:4–7

In every situation, by prayer and petition, with thanksgiving, present your requests to God.
Philippians 4:6

A study by psychologist Robert Emmons divided volunteers into three groups that each made weekly entries in journals. One group wrote five things they were grateful for. One described five daily hassles. And a control group listed five events that had impacted them in a small way. The results of the study revealed that those in the gratitude group felt better about their lives overall, were more optimistic about the future, and reported fewer health problems.

Giving thanks has a way of changing the way we look at life. Thanksgiving can even make us happier.

The Bible has long celebrated the benefits of giving thanks to God, as doing so reminds us of His character. The Psalms repeatedly call God's people to give Him thanks because "the Lord is good and his love endures forever" (100:5) and because of His "unfailing love" and "wonderful deeds" (107:8, 15, 21, 31).

As the apostle Paul closed his letter to the Philippians—the letter itself a kind of thank-you note to a church that had supported him—he linked thankful prayers with the peace of God "which transcends all understanding" (4:7). When we focus on God and His goodness, we find that we can pray with thanksgiving in every situation. Giving thanks brings us a peace that uniquely guards our hearts and minds and changes the way we look at life. A heart full of gratitude nurtures a spirit of joy.

Elisa Morgan

Practice Gratitude Today

What are five things that happened in the past week that you're thankful for? Praise God for these good things in your life.

Every Grief

REVELATION 21:1–6

He will wipe every tear from their eyes.
Revelation 21:4

"I measure every Grief I meet," the nineteenth-century poet Emily Dickinson wrote. "With narrow, probing, eyes – I wonder if It weighs like Mine – Or has an Easier size." The poem is a moving reflection on how people carry the unique ways they've been wounded throughout their lives. Dickinson concludes, almost hesitantly, that her only solace is the "piercing Comfort" of seeing at Calvary her own wounds reflected in the Savior's: "Still fascinated to presume that Some – are like my own –."

The book of Revelation describes Jesus, our Savior, as a "Lamb, looking as if it had been slain" (5:6; see v. 12), His wounds still visible. He recieved those wounds by taking upon Himself the sin and despair of His people (1 Peter 2:24–25), so that they might have new life and hope.

And Revelation describes a future day when the Savior will "wipe every tear" from each of His children's eyes (21:4). Jesus won't minimize their pain but truly see and care for each person's unique grief—while inviting them into the new, healing realities of life in His kingdom, where there is "'no more death' or mourning or crying or pain" (v. 4). Where healing water will flow "without cost from the spring of the water of life" (v. 6; see 22:2).

Because our Savior has carried our every grief, we can find rest and healing in His kingdom. *Monica La Rose*

Practice Gratitude Today

Compassionately consider the grief and pain of your own life. Talk with God about it. Then thank Him that He knows your grief completely, and will one day wipe every tear from your eyes.

Heaven Is Singing

REVELATION 19:1–8

They cried: "Amen, Hallelujah!"
Revelation 19:4

Joy was apparent in their voices as the high school choir sang the Argentinian song "El Cielo Canta Alegría." I was enjoying the performance but couldn't understand the lyrics because I don't know Spanish. But it wasn't long until I recognized a familiar word as the choir began to jubilantly declare, "Aleluya!" Repeatedly, I heard "Aleluya," a declaration of praise to God that sounds similar in most languages around the world. Eager to know the background of the song, I went online after the concert and discovered the title means "Heaven Is Singing for Joy."

In a celebratory passage in Revelation 19, we're given a glimpse of the reality expressed in that choral song—all of heaven rejoicing! In the apostle John's vision of the future in the last book of the New Testament, he saw an enormous gathering of people and angelic creatures in heaven declaring gratitude to God. John wrote that the chorus of voices celebrated God's power that overcame evil and injustice, His reign over the whole earth, and eternal life with Him forever. Over and over again, all the inhabitants of heaven declare, "Hallelujah!" (vv. 1, 3, 4, 6), or "Praise God!"

One day people "from every tribe and language and people and nation" (5:9) will declare God's glory. And with joy all our voices in every different language will shout together, "Hallelujah!"

Lisa M. Samra

Practice Gratitude Today

Search online for a Christian worship song in a language you don't understand. Listen to it, thanking God that His kingdom includes people from every tribe, language, people, and nation.

Read Backward

REVELATION 21:1–7

Those who are victorious will inherit all this, and I will be their God and they will be my children.
Revelation 21:7

I confess that I sometimes read the end of a book before I read the beginning. Doing so allows me to know which characters live and which characters don't. When I know how it will turn out, I'm able to relax and thoroughly enjoy the story and the characters.

In a similar way, reading the final book of the Bible, Revelation, can be an encouragement and comfort for followers of Jesus. Time and again, Christians are called to be victorious overcomers (1 John 4:4; 5:4; Revelation 2:7, 11, 17, 26; 3:5, 12, 21). We can be overcomers now and will be for all eternity.

As the apostle John talks about the revealing of the new heaven and the new earth in Revelation (21:1), he describes what the final victory will look like for those who have received Jesus as Savior. At that time, we will see the end of death, tears, sorrow, and pain (v. 4). The Lord declares: "Those who are victorious will inherit all this, and I will be their God and they will be my children" (v. 7). He will dwell with us (v. 3), and He will make "everything new" (v. 5).

When the trials of today seem more daunting than your strength, let the Lord show you the end of the story when you will be in His presence forever!

Randy Kilgore

Practice Gratitude Today

What feels too difficult for you today? Thank Jesus that He has secured the end of the story—and that He is making everything new.

A Debtor

2 CORINTHIANS 5:12–17

Christ's love compels us.
2 Corinthians 5:14

As a young man, Robert Robinson (1735–1790) enjoyed getting into trouble with his friends, so the stories go. At age seventeen, though, he heard a sermon by George Whitefield from Matthew 3:7 and realized his need for salvation in Christ. The Lord changed Robinson's life, and he became a preacher. He also wrote several hymns, including his best-known "Come, Thou Fount of Every Blessing."

Lately I've been pondering God's amazing grace toward us and the last stanza of that hymn: "O to grace how great a debtor daily I'm constrained to be!" The hymn brings to mind the apostle Paul's words: "Christ's love compels [or constrains] us . . . that those who live should no longer live for themselves but for him who died for them and was raised again" (2 Corinthians 5:14–15).

We can't earn God's love and grace. But because He has lavished it on us, how can we help but love Him in return by living for Him! I'm not exactly sure what that looks like, but it must include drawing near to Him, listening to His Word, serving Him, and obeying Him out of gratitude and love.

As debtors, we are called to live each day for Jesus who gave Himself for us.

Anne Cetas

Practice Gratitude Today

Jesus said, "Whoever has my commands and keeps them is the one who loves me" (John 14:21). How can you show your gratitude for God's grace today by following his command to love those around you?

Unapologetic Tears

LUKE 7:36–44

As she stood behind him at his feet weeping,
she began to wet his feet with her tears.
Luke 7:38

"I'm sorry," Karen said, apologizing for her flowing tears. After the death of her husband, she stretched herself to care for her teenage kids. When men from her church provided a weekend camping excursion to entertain them and give her a break, Karen wept with gratitude, apologizing over and over for her tears.

Why do so many of us apologize for our tears? Simon, a Pharisee, invited Jesus to dinner. In the middle of the meal, as Jesus reclined at the table, a woman who had lived a sinful life brought an alabaster jar of perfume. "As she stood behind [Jesus] at his feet weeping, she began to wet his feet with her tears. Then she wiped them with her hair, kissed them and poured perfume on them" (Luke 7:38). Unapologetically, this woman freely expressed her love and then unwound her hair to dry Jesus's feet. Overflowing with gratitude and love for Jesus, she topped off her tears with perfumed kisses—actions that contrasted with those of the proper but coldhearted host.

Jesus's response? He praised her exuberant expression of love and proclaimed her "forgiven" (vv. 44–48).

We may be tempted to squelch tears of gratitude when they threaten to overflow. But God made us emotional beings, and we can use our feelings to honor Him. Like the woman in Luke's gospel, let's unapologetically express our love for our good God who provides for our needs and freely receives our thankful response. *Elisa Morgan*

Practice Gratitude Today

When you think of what God has done for you, what emotions do you feel? Bring those emotions to God in prayer, thanking Him that He created you to feel His love deeply.

"Love You—Whole World"

1 JOHN 4:7–19

God is love. Whoever lives in love lives
in God, and God in them.
1 John 4:16

My three-year-old niece, Jenna, has an expression that never fails to melt my heart. When she really loves something, be it banana cream pie, jumping on the trampoline, or playing Frisbee, she'll proclaim, "I love it—whole world!" ("whole world" accompanied with a dramatic sweep of her arms).

Sometimes I wonder, When's the last time I've dared to love like that? With nothing held back, completely unafraid?

"God is love," John wrote repeatedly (1 John 4:8, 16), perhaps because the truth that God's love is the deepest foundation of reality—not our anger, fear, or shame—is hard for us grown-ups to get. The world divides us into camps based on what we're most afraid of—and all too often we join in, ignoring or villainizing the voices that challenge our preferred vision of reality.

Yet amid the deception and power struggles, the truth of God's love remains, a light that shines in the darkness, inviting us to learn the path of humility, trust, and love (1:7–9; 3:18). For no matter what painful truths the light uncovers, we can know that we'll still be loved (4:10, 18; Romans 8:1).

When Jenna leans over and whispers to me, "I love you—whole world!" I whisper back, "I love *you* whole world!" And I'm grateful for a gentle reminder that every moment I'm held in limitless love and grace.

Monica La Rose

Practice Gratitude Today

Who loves you? Your family? Your friends? Your church community? Thank God for the people who love you—and for how their love points you to His perfect and limitless love.

Full Attention

1 THESSALONIANS 5:12–28

Rejoice always, pray continually, give thanks in all circumstances.
1 Thessalonians 5:16–18

Technology today seems to demand our constant attention. The modern "miracle" of the internet gives us the amazing capacity to access humanity's collective learning in the palm of our hand. But for many, such constant access can come at a cost.

Linda Stone coined the phrase "continual partial attention" to describe the modern impulse to always need to know what's happening "out there," to make sure we're not missing anything. If that sounds like it could produce chronic anxiety, you're right!

Although the apostle Paul struggled with different reasons for anxiety, he knew our souls are wired to find peace in God. Which is why, in a letter to new believers who'd endured persecution (1 Thessalonians 2:14), Paul concluded by urging the believers to "rejoice always, pray continually, give thanks in all circumstances" (5:16–18).

Praying "continually" might seem pretty daunting. But then, how often do we check our phones? What if we instead let that urge be a prompt to talk to God? To say thank you, lift up a prayer request, or praise Him?

More important, what if we learned to exchange a need to always be in the know for continual, prayerful rest in God's presence? Through relying on Christ's Spirit, we can learn to give our heavenly Father our continual full attention as we make our way through each day.

Adam Holz

Practice Gratitude Today

Spend a few minutes alone in silence, resting in God's presence and giving Him your full attention. At the end of your time, thank Him for always giving you His full attention.

Charity Island

PSALM 107:23–32

The Lord is good, a refuge in times of trouble.
He cares for those who trust in him.
Nahum 1:7

Charity Island is the largest island in Saginaw Bay in the Michigan waters of Lake Huron. For many years the island has provided a lighthouse for navigational aid and a safe harbor for those sailing these waters. The island received its name because sailors believed it was there "through the charity of God."

Sometimes in life we have to navigate through seas of troubling circumstances. Like those sailors we need guidance and a place of safety; we might wish for our own Charity Island. The psalmist understood that God is the one who can bring tranquility to troubled waters and guide us to safe harbors. He wrote, "He stilled the storm to a whisper; the waves of the sea were hushed. They were glad when it grew calm, and he guided them to their desired haven" (Psalm 107:29–30).

While no one asks for the storms of life, they can multiply our appreciation for the guidance and refuge God provides. He offers the light of His Spirit and His Word to guide us. It is the safe harbor of His love that we long for. He alone can be our ultimate Charity Island.

Dennis Fisher

Practice Gratitude Today

What trouble or difficulty are you navigating today? Thank God that His Spirit is guiding you even amid the challenges.

A Full Life

DEUTERONOMY 8:7–18

Out of his fullness we have all received grace
in place of grace already given.
John 1:16

During the celebration of Chinese New Year, it is customary to use certain words in print and conversation. One word is often used by itself. It is the word *full*, meaning "abundance of," and it is used to wish someone material prosperity for the year ahead.

Moses told the Israelites about the wealth and prosperity in the land of Canaan before they entered it (Deuteronomy 8:7–9). They would have everything they needed and more. But he warned them of the danger of forgetting that God, the one who had brought them out of Egypt and protected them along the way, had given them that abundance (v. 11). Thus Moses commanded them, "Remember the LORD your God, for it is he who gives you the ability to produce wealth" (v. 18).

"Wealth," of course, is not just material things. Everything you have is from God. Our Lord Jesus told His disciples, "I have come that [you] may have life, and have it to the full" (John 10:10).

We too may be tempted to forget that it's the Lord who has blessed us and met our needs. Our lives will be full, abundant, and satisfying only when we are connected to Jesus Christ. *C. P. Hia*

Practice Gratitude Today

Where is your life full? Perhaps you are experiencing wealth in your friendships, your work, your relationship with God, or your health. Thank God for the fullness He's given you today.

A Debt of Gratitude

ROMANS 16:1–16

They risked their lives for me. Not only I but all the churches of the Gentiles are grateful to them.
Romans 16:4

Dave Randlett was someone of whom I can say, "Because of him, my life will never be the same." Dave became a mentor to me when I was a new follower of Jesus in my college years. He not only invested time in me but took risks by giving me opportunities to learn and grow in ministry. Dave was God's instrument to give me the opportunity to be a student preacher and travel with a college music team. As a result, he helped shape and prepare me for a life of teaching God's Word. I'm glad I was able to express thanks to him on a number of occasions before he went to be with the Lord.

Just as I am thankful for Dave's influence in my life, the apostle Paul was grateful for Aquila and Priscilla, who served the Lord with him. He said, "They risked their lives for me." In gratitude, he thanked them, as did "all the churches of the Gentiles" (Romans 16:4).

You too may have people in your life who have taken risks by giving you opportunities to serve or who have greatly influenced you spiritually. Perhaps pastors, ministry leaders, friends, or family members have given of themselves to move you further along for Christ. The question is, Have you thanked them?

Bill Crowder

Practice Gratitude Today

Who has provided you with significant opportunities and helped you develop your relationship with God? Reach out today to thank that person.

Celebrating Creativity

GENESIS 1:1–21

God said, "Let the water teem with living creatures."
Genesis 1:20

A rarely seen jellyfish waltzed with the currents, four thousand feet deep in the ocean near Baja, California. Its body shone with fluorescent shades of blue, purple, and pink, bright against the backdrop of black water. Elegant tentacles waved gracefully with each pulse of its bell-shaped hood. As I watched the amazing footage of the *Halitrephes maasi* jellyfish on the National Geographic video, I reflected on how God chose the specific design of this beautiful, gelatinous creature. He also fashioned the other two thousand types of jellyfish that scientists have identified so far.

Though we acknowledge God as Creator, do we slow down long enough to truly consider the profound truth revealed in the first chapter of the Bible? Our amazing God brought forth light and life into the creatively diverse world He crafted with the power of His word. He designed "the great creatures of the sea and every living thing with which the water teems" (Genesis 1:21). Scientists have discovered only a fraction of the wondrous creatures the Lord created in the beginning.

God also intentionally sculpted each person in the world, giving purpose to every day of our lives before we drew our first breaths (Psalm 139:13–16). As we celebrate the Lord's creativity, we can also rejoice over the many ways He helps us imagine and create with Him and for His glory.

Xochitl Dixon

Practice Gratitude Today

Find a video online of a creature or natural wonder from a part of the world far from where you live. Praise God for His limitless creativity, and for inviting you to steward the world and cocreate with Him.

Rewired by Gratitude

PSALM 103:1–8, 17

Praise the Lord, my soul, and forget not all his benefits.
Psalm 103:2

After being diagnosed with a brain tumor, Christina Costa noticed how much of the talk around facing cancer is dominated by the language of fighting. She found that this metaphor quickly started to feel exhausting. She "didn't want to spend over a year at war with [her] own body." Instead, what she found most helpful were daily practices of gratitude—for the team of professionals caring for her and for the ways her brain and body were showing healing. She experienced firsthand that no matter how difficult the struggle, practices of gratitude can help us resist depression and "wire our brains to help us build resilience."

Costa's powerful story reminded me that practicing gratitude isn't just something believers do out of duty. Although it's true that God deserves our gratitude, expressing our gratitude is also profoundly good for us. When we lift up our hearts to say, "Praise the Lord, my soul, and forget not all his benefits" (Psalm 103:2), we're reminded of the countless ways God is at work—assuring us of forgiveness, working healing in our bodies and hearts, letting us experience "love and compassion" and countless "good things" in His creation (vv. 3–5).

While not all suffering will find complete healing in this lifetime, our hearts can always be renewed by gratitude, for God's love is with us "from everlasting to everlasting" (v. 17). *Monica La Rose*

Practice Gratitude Today

What aspect of your life feels exhausting, difficult, or negative? Tell God about one thing you can be thankful for amid that challenge.

Hope Blossoms

ISAIAH 35:1–4

The desert and the parched land will be glad;
the wilderness will rejoice and blossom.
Isaiah 35:1

In the city of Philadelphia, when weedy vacant lots were cleaned up and brightened with beautiful flowers and trees, nearby residents also brightened in overall mental health. This proved especially true for those who struggled economically.

"There's a growing body of evidence that green space can have an impact on mental health," said Dr. Eugenia South, "and that's particularly important for people living in poorer neighborhoods." South, a faculty member at the University of Pennsylvania's Perelman School of Medicine, is coauthor of a study on the subject.

The downtrodden people of Israel and Judah found fresh hope in the prophet Isaiah's vision of their beautiful restoration by God. Amid all the doom and judgment Isaiah foretold, this bright promise took root: "The desert and the parched land will be glad; the wilderness will rejoice and blossom. Like the crocus, it will burst into bloom; it will rejoice greatly and shout for joy" (Isaiah 35:1–2).

No matter our situation today, we too can rejoice in the beautiful ways our heavenly Father restores us with fresh hope, including through His creation. When we feel down, reflecting on His glory and splendor will bolster us. "Strengthen the feeble hands, steady the knees that give way," Isaiah encouraged (v. 3).

Can a few flowers rekindle our hope? A prophet said yes. So does our hope-giving God. *Patricia Raybon*

Practice Gratitude Today

Spend time enjoying a green space today, in person if possible, or online. Thank God for the hope of creation—that He created all things and is sovereign over them.

Adoption

EPHESIANS 1:3–12

He chose us in him. . . . He predestined us for adoption to sonship through Jesus Christ.
Ephesians 1:4–5

My wife, Marlene, and I have been married for over forty-five years. When we were first dating, we had a conversation I have never forgotten. She told me that at six months old she had been adopted. When I asked her if she ever wondered about who her real parents were, she responded, "My mom and dad could have selected any of a number of other babies that day, but they chose me. They adopted me. They are my real parents."

That strong sense of identification and gratitude she has for her adoptive parents should also mark our relationship with God. As followers of Christ, we have been born from above through faith in Him and have been adopted into the family of God. Paul wrote, "He chose us in him before the creation of the world to be holy and blameless in his sight. In love he predestined us for adoption to sonship through Jesus Christ, in accordance with his pleasure and will" (Ephesians 1:4–5).

Notice the nature of this transaction. We have been chosen by God and adopted as His sons and daughters. Through adoption, we have a radically new relationship with God. He is our beloved Father!

May this relationship stir our hearts to worship Him—our Father—with gratitude.

Bill Crowder

Practice Gratitude Today

Consider the long, difficult process some parents go through to adopt children. God's adoption process started before the creation of the world. Thank Him for being your loving, generous, and patient Father.

The Perfect Sentence

EXODUS 3:13–18

Who among the gods is like you, LORD? Who is like you—
majestic in holiness, awesome in glory, working wonders?
Exodus 15:11

As a young girl writing in my diary, my secret ambition was to compose the perfect sentence. I wondered what it would look and sound like. Perhaps it would include a strong verb and colorful adjectives.

My pursuit of the perfect sentence will never be satisfied, but I have found a statement of perfection in Exodus 3:14. When the Lord God called Moses from the burning bush, He told Moses that he had been chosen to bring God's people out of bondage in Egypt (v. 10). Moses, who was anxious about this responsibility, wondered what to say if the Israelites doubted him and asked who he was representing.

The Lord replied, "I AM WHO I AM" (v. 14). By using His unique name, God offered Moses a glimpse of His eternal nature in one sentence. You might say it's a statement of perfection!

Bible commentator Matthew Henry writes this about God's description of Himself: "He is self-existent: he has his being of himself. . . . He is eternal and unchangeable, and always the same, yesterday, to-day, and for ever. . . . He is faithful and true to all his promises, unchangeable in his word as well as in his nature."

God says, "I AM WHO I AM." He and His name are perfect. In reverence we are to bow before Him.

Anne Cetas

Practice Gratitude Today

In your own words, write out a description of who God is. Then thank Him for all His attributes.

Confession and Thanksgiving

NEHEMIAH 9:32–37

Even while they were . . . enjoying your great goodness to them . . . , they did not serve you.
Nehemiah 9:35

During a Sunday worship service, our congregation said this prayer of confession in unison: "Gracious God, like many believers before us, we complain when things do not go our way. We want abundance of everything rather than what is sufficient to sustain us. We would rather be elsewhere than where we are at the moment. We would rather have the gifts You give to others than what You provide for us. We would rather have You serve us than serve You. Forgive our lack of gratitude for what You give."

Abundance is no guarantee of gratefulness or thanksgiving. Prosperity may even turn our hearts away from the Lord.

When a group of Jewish exiles returned from Babylon with Nehemiah to rebuild the walls of Jerusalem, they gathered to confess their sins and those of their fathers. They prayed: "Our kings, our leaders, our priests and our ancestors did not follow your law. . . . Even while they were in their kingdom, enjoying your great goodness to them in the spacious and fertile land you gave them, they did not serve you or turn from their evil ways" (Nehemiah 9:34–35). In recognizing their sin, they saw God's "great goodness" more clearly.

Confession is a powerful prelude to a prayer of thanksgiving. Obedience is the amen.

David McCasland

Practice Gratitude Today

Reread the prayer of confession above, praying the words to God. Then add your own confession, including confession for groups or communities you are part of. Thank God for His faithfulness to forgive.

Who Am I?

1 CHRONICLES 29:14–20

But who am I, and who are my people, that we should be able to give as generously as this?
1 Chronicles 29:14

When I was a member of the leadership team for a local ministry, part of my job was to invite others to join us as group discussion leaders. My invitations described the time commitment required and outlined the ways leaders would need to engage with their small group participants, both in meetings and during regular phone calls. I was often reluctant to impose on other people, aware of the sacrifice they'd be making to become a leader. And yet sometimes their reply would completely overwhelm me: "I'd be honored." Instead of citing legitimate reasons to decline, they described their gratitude to God for all He'd done in their lives as their reason for being eager to give back.

When the time came to give resources toward building a temple for God, David had a similar response: "Who am I, and who are my people, that we should be able to give as generously as this?" (1 Chronicles 29:14). David's generosity was driven by gratitude for God's involvement in his life and with the people of Israel. His response speaks of his humility and his acknowledgment of God's goodness toward "foreigners and strangers" (v. 15).

Our giving to God's work—whether in time, talent, or treasure—reflects our gratitude to the one who gave to us to begin with. All that we have comes from His hand (v. 14); in response, we can give gratefully to others.

Kirsten Holmberg

Practice Gratitude Today

How can you give of your time, talent, or treasure to benefit someone else today? Thank God that as He has generously given to you, so you can give to others.

Being Glad

PSALM 30

The LORD has done it this very day; let
us rejoice today and be glad.
Psalm 118:24

One of my favorite childhood books was *Pollyanna*, the story of the optimistic young girl who always found something to be glad about—even when bad things happened.

I was reminded recently of that literary friend when my real-life friend fell and broke her arm while riding her bicycle. Marianne told me how thankful she was that she was able to ride all the way back home and how grateful she was that she wouldn't need to have surgery. It was her left arm (she's right-handed), so she would still be able to work. And wasn't it great, she marveled, that she had good bones, so her arm should heal fine? And wasn't it wonderful that it hadn't been any worse?

Whew! Marianne is an example of someone who has learned to rejoice in spite of trouble. She has a confidence that God will care for her—no matter what.

Suffering eventually touches us all. And in times of difficulty, thankfulness is usually not our first response. But I think God is pleased when we find reasons to be thankful (1 Thessalonians 5:16–18). As we realistically look for the good despite our bad circumstances, we can be grateful that God is holding us close. It is when we trust in His goodness that we find gladness. *Cindy Hess Kasper*

Practice Gratitude Today

What difficulty are you currently experiencing? Realistically consider what good you can see in the midst of that struggle. Thank God that He is close to you, even in suffering.

God Understands

PSALM 147:1–11

Great is our Lord and mighty in power;
his understanding has no limit.
Psalm 147:5

After a recent move, Mabel's seven-year-old son, Ryan, fussed as he prepared to attend a summer camp at his new school. Mabel encouraged him, assuring him that she understood change was hard. But one morning, Ryan's out-of-character grumpiness seemed excessive. With compassion, Mabel asked, "What's bothering you, Son?"

Staring out of the window, Ryan shrugged. "I don't know, Mom. I just have too many feelings."

Mabel's heart ached as she comforted him. Desperate for a way to help him, she shared that the move was hard for her too. She assured Ryan that God would stay close, that He knew everything, even when they couldn't understand or voice their frustrations. "Let's set up a visit with your friends before school starts," she said. They made plans, grateful that God understands even when His children have "too many feelings."

The writer of Psalm 147 experienced overwhelming emotions and recognized the benefits of praising the all-knowing Maker and Sustainer of all, the Healer of physical and emotional wounds (vv. 1–6). He praised God for the ways He provides and "delights in those who fear him, who put their hope in his unfailing love" (v. 11).

When we're struggling to make sense of our ever-changing emotions, we don't have to feel alone or discouraged. We can rest in the unconditional love and unlimited understanding of our unchanging God.

Xochitl Dixon

Practice Gratitude Today

Look online for a feelings wheel, chart, or list, then identify the different emotions you are feeling today. Thank God that His understanding and unfailing love don't depend on your feelings.

Out of the Trap

1 TIMOTHY 6:6–10

I have learned the secret of being content.
Philippians 4:12

The Venus flytrap comes from a small area of sandy wetlands not far from our home in North Carolina. These plants are fascinating to watch because they're carnivorous.

Venus flytraps release a sweet-smelling nectar into colorful traps that resemble open flowers. When an insect crawls inside, triggering sensors along the outer rim, the trap clamps shut in less than a second—capturing its victim. The trap then closes further and emits enzymes that consume its prey over time, giving the plant nutrients not provided by the sandy soil.

God's Word tells of another trap that can capture unexpectedly. The apostle Paul warned his protégé Timothy: "Those who want to get rich fall into temptation and a trap and into many foolish and harmful desires that plunge people into ruin and destruction. . . . Some people, eager for money, have wandered from the faith and pierced themselves with many griefs" (1 Timothy 6:9–10).

Money and material things may promise happiness, but when they take first place in our lives, we walk on dangerous ground. We avoid this trap by living with thankful, humble hearts focused on God's goodness to us through Jesus: "godliness with contentment is great gain" (v. 6).

The temporary things of this world never satisfy like God can. True, lasting contentment is found only through our relationship with Him.

James Banks

Practice Gratitude Today

What do you feel like you need more money to buy, so you can finally be happy? Talk with God about it. Thank Him for giving you what you have today.

Never Alone

JOHN 14:15–18

He will give you another advocate to help you and
be with you forever—the Spirit of truth.
John 14:16–17

While writing a Bible guide for pastors in Indonesia, a writer friend grew fascinated with that nation's culture of togetherness. Called *gotong royong*—meaning "mutual assistance"—the concept is practiced in villages, where neighbors may work together to repair someone's roof or rebuild a bridge or path. In cities too my friend said, "People always go places with someone else—to a doctor's appointment, for example. It's the cultural norm. So you're never alone."

Worldwide, believers in Jesus rejoice in knowing we also are never alone. Our constant and forever companion is the Holy Spirit, the third person of the Trinity. Far more than a loyal friend, the Spirit of God is given to every follower of Christ by our heavenly Father to "help you and be with you forever" (John 14:16).

Jesus promised God's Spirit would come after His own time on earth ended. "I will not leave you as orphans," Jesus said (v. 18). Instead, the Holy Spirit—"the Spirit of truth" who "lives with you and will be in you"—indwells each of us who receives Christ as Savior (v. 17).

The Holy Spirit is our Helper, Comforter, Encourager, and Counselor—a constant companion in a world where loneliness can afflict even connected people. May we forever abide in His comforting love and help.

Patricia Raybon

Practice Gratitude Today

Who can you ask to be with you through something you aren't looking forward to today? If they can't be with you physically, perhaps they can pray for you or text you. Thank God that He is always with you.

How to Reflect Christ

COLOSSIANS 1:25–27

God has chosen to make known . . . the glorious riches of this mystery, which is Christ in you, the hope of glory.
Colossians 1:27

Thérèse of Lisieux was a joyful and carefree child—until her mother died when she was just four years old. She became timid and easily agitated. But many years later on Christmas Eve, all of that changed. After celebrating the birth of Jesus with her church community, she experienced God releasing her from her fear and giving her joy. She attributed the change to the power of God leaving heaven and becoming a man, Jesus, and dwelling in her through Him.

What does it mean for Christ to dwell within us? It's a mystery, said Paul to the Colossian church. It's one that God "kept hidden for ages and generations" (Colossians 1:26), but which He disclosed to God's people. To them God revealed "the glorious riches of this mystery, which is Christ in you, the hope of glory" (v. 27). Because Christ now dwelled in the Colossians, they experienced the joy of new life. No longer were they enslaved to the old self of sin.

If we've asked Jesus to be our Savior, we too live out this mystery of His dwelling in us. Through His Spirit, He can release us from fear, as He did Thérèse, and grow within us the fruit of His Spirit, such as joy, peace, and self-control (Galatians 5:22–23).

Let's give thanks for the wonderful mystery of Christ within us.

Amy Boucher Pye

Practice Gratitude Today

What are you afraid of today? Thank Jesus for making His home inside of you. Ask Him to fill your life with signs of His presence—love, joy, peace, patience, kindness, gentleness, and faithfulness.

Thankful for Monday

ECCLESIASTES 2:17–25

A person can do nothing better than to . . .
find satisfaction in their own toil.
Ecclesiastes 2:24

I used to dread Mondays. Sometimes, when I got off the train to head to a previous job, I'd sit at the station for a while, trying to delay reaching the building, if only for a few minutes. My heart would beat fast as I worried over meeting deadlines and managing the moods of a temperamental boss.

For some of us, it can be especially difficult to start another dreary workweek. We may be feeling overwhelmed or underappreciated in our job. King Solomon described the toil of work when he wrote: "What do people get for all the toil and anxious striving with which they labor under the sun? All their days their work is grief and pain" (Ecclesiastes 2:22–23).

While the wise king didn't give us a cure-all for making work less stressful or more rewarding, he did offer us a change in perspective. No matter how difficult our work is, he encourages us to "find satisfaction" in it with God's help (v. 24). Perhaps it will come as the Holy Spirit enables us to display Christlike character. Or as we hear from someone who's been blessed through our service. Or as we remember the wisdom God provided to deal with a difficult situation. Though our work may be difficult, our faithful God is there with us. His presence and power can light up even gloomy days. With His help, we can be thankful for Monday.

Poh Fang Chia

Practice Gratitude Today

What is one thing you find satisfying about your daily work? Share your answer with a colleague or friend today.

God's Timing

GENESIS 8:1–5, 13–18

I trust in you, LORD. . . . My times are in your hands.
Psalm 31:14–15

Mag had been looking forward to her planned trip to another country. But, as was her usual practice, she prayed about it first. "It's just a holiday," a friend remarked. "Why do you need to consult God?" Mag, however, believed in committing everything to Him. This time, she felt Him prompting her to cancel the trip. She did, and later—when she would have been there—an epidemic broke out in the country. "I feel like God was protecting me," she notes.

Noah too relied on God's protection as he and his family waited in the ark for nearly two months after the flood subsided. After being cooped up for more than ten months, he must have been eager to get out. After all, "the water had dried up from the earth" and "the ground was dry" (Genesis 8:13). But Noah didn't just rely on what he saw; instead, he left the ark only when God told him to (vv. 15–19). He trusted that God had good reason for the extended wait—perhaps the ground wasn't completely safe yet.

As we pray about the decisions in our life, using our God-given faculties and waiting for His leading, we can trust in His timing, knowing that our wise Creator knows what is best for us. As the psalmist declared, "I trust in you, LORD. . . . My times are in your hands" (Psalm 31:14–15).

Leslie Koh

Practice Gratitude Today

What part of your life is not going according to your timetable? Talk with God about it, and thank Him that you can trust His timing.

Life to the Full

JOHN 10:7–15

The thief comes only to steal and kill and destroy; I have come that they may have life, and have it to the full.
John 10:10

The year was 1918, near the end of World War I, and photographer Eric Enstrom was putting together a portfolio of his work. He wanted to include one that communicated a sense of fullness in a time that felt quite empty to so many people. In his now much-loved photo, an old bearded man sits at a table with his head bowed and his hands clasped in prayer. On the surface before him there is only a book, spectacles, a bowl of gruel, a loaf of bread, and a knife. Nothing more, but also nothing less.

Some might say the photograph reveals scarcity. But Enstrom's point was quite the opposite: here is a full life, one lived in gratitude, one you and I can experience as well regardless of our circumstances. Jesus announced the good news in John 10: "life . . . to the full" (v. 10). We do a grave disservice to such good news when we equate "full" with "many things." The fullness Jesus spoke of isn't measured in worldly categories like riches or real estate but rather by a heart, mind, soul, and strength brimming in gratitude that the Good Shepherd gave "his life for the sheep" (v. 11) and cares for us and our daily needs. This is a full life—enjoying relationship with God—that's possible for every one of us.

John Blase

Practice Gratitude Today

Choose a daily necessity to pay attention to: a glass of water, the clothes you're wearing, a slice of bread. As you enjoy that daily necessity, thank God for His provision and presence in your life.

A Grateful Response

DANIEL 6:1–10

[Daniel] prayed, giving thanks to his
God, just as he had done before.
Daniel 6:10

Raw fish and rainwater. An Australian sailor named Timothy survived on only those provisions for three months. Marooned on his storm-damaged catamaran, he was losing hope—bobbing twelve hundred miles from land in the Pacific Ocean. But then the crew of a Mexican tuna boat spotted his ailing boat and rescued him. Later, the thin and weather-beaten man declared, "To the captain and fishing company that saved my life, I'm just so grateful!"

Timothy gave thanks following his ordeal, but the prophet Daniel revealed a grateful heart before, during, and after a crisis. Having been exiled to Babylon from Judah with other Jews (Daniel 1:1–6), Daniel had risen in power only to be threatened by other leaders who wanted him dead (6:1–7). His foes got the king of Babylon to sign a decree stating that anyone who prayed "to any god" except the king himself would be "thrown into the lions' den" (v. 7). What would Daniel, a man who loved and served the one true God, do? He "got down on his knees and prayed, giving thanks to . . . God, just as he had done before" (v. 10). He gave thanks, and his grateful heart was rewarded as God spared his life and brought him honor (vv. 26–28).

As the apostle Paul wrote, may God help us "give thanks in all circumstances" (1 Thessalonians 5:18). Whether we're facing a crisis or have just come through one, a grateful response honors Him and helps keep our faith afloat.

Tom Felten

Practice Gratitude Today

In prayer, thank God for bringing you through a past difficulty. Then thank Him for being with you in the middle of a challenge you are currently facing.

Fighting Off Jealousy

1 CORINTHIANS 3:1–10

Since there is jealousy and quarreling among you, are you not worldly? Are you not acting like mere humans?
1 Corinthians 3:3

The story is told of two shopkeepers who were bitter rivals. They spent each day keeping track of each other's business. If one got a customer, he would smile triumphantly at his rival.

One night an angel appeared to one of the shopkeepers in a dream and said, "I will give you anything you ask, but whatever you receive, your competitor will receive twice as much. What is your desire?" The man frowned and then said, "Strike me blind in one eye." Now that's jealousy of the worst kind!

The self-destructive emotion of jealousy had the potential of tearing apart the Corinthian church. These believers had received the gospel but had not allowed the Holy Spirit to change their hearts. As a result, they became jealous of one another, which led to a divided community. Paul identified their jealousy as a sign of immaturity and worldliness (1 Corinthians 3:3). These believers were not acting like people who had been transformed by the gospel.

One of the clearest indicators that the Holy Spirit is working in our lives is our contentment and our thankfulness for what we have. Then, instead of experiencing jealousy, we are able to genuinely celebrate the gifts and blessings of others. *Marvin Williams*

Practice Gratitude Today

Make a list of gifts and abilities you're grateful your friends have. Thank one of your friends today, telling them how they have helped you with their gifts.

Blessing in the Tears

MATTHEW 5:1–12

Blessed are those who mourn.
Matthew 5:4

I received an email from a young man in England, a son who explained that his father (only sixty-three) was in the hospital in critical condition, hanging on to life. Though we'd never met, his dad's work and mine shared many intersections. The son, trying to cheer his father, asked me to send a video message of encouragement and prayer. Deeply moved, I recorded a short message and a prayer for healing. I was told that his dad watched the video and gave a hearty thumbs-up. Sadly, a couple days later, I received another email telling me that he had died. He held his wife's hand as he took his final breath.

My heart broke. Such love, such devastation. The family lost a husband and father far too soon. Yet it's surprising to hear Jesus insist that it's precisely those who grieve who are blessed: "Blessed are those who mourn" (Matthew 5:4). Jesus isn't saying suffering and sorrow are good but rather that God's mercy and kindness pour over those who need it most. Those overcome by grief due to death or even their own sinfulness are most in need of God's attention and consolation—and Jesus promises us "they will be comforted" (v. 4).

God steps toward us, His loved children (v. 9). He blesses us in our tears.

Winn Collier

Practice Gratitude Today

What are you grieving today? Tell Jesus about it. Then thank Him for knowing what it feels like to cry over loss (John 11:35) and for being with you in your grief.

Unshakable Faith

MATTHEW 6:19–24

Life does not consist in an abundance of possessions.
Luke 12:15

Kevin walked into the nursing facility after his dad passed away to pick up his belongings. The staff handed him two small boxes. He said he realized that day that it really didn't take an abundance of possessions to be happy.

His dad, Larry, had been carefree and always ready with a smile and an encouraging word for others. The reason for his happiness was another "possession" that didn't fit into a box: an unshakable faith in his Redeemer, Jesus.

Jesus urges us to "store up . . . treasures in heaven" (Matthew 6:20). He didn't say we couldn't own a home or buy a car or save for the future or have things. But He urged us to examine the focus of our hearts. Where was Larry's focus? On loving God by loving others. He would wander up and down the halls where he lived, greeting and encouraging those he met. If someone was in tears, he was there with a comforting word or listening ear or heartfelt prayer. His mind was focused on living for God's honor and the good of others.

We might want to ask ourselves if we could be happy with fewer things that clutter and distract us from the more important matters of loving God and others. "Where [our] treasure is, there [our] heart will be also" (v. 21). What we value is reflected in how we live.

Anne Cetas

Practice Gratitude Today

Find three things in your home you no longer use that you can give away or donate and then do that. Thank God for providing you with your possessions—and for bringing you joy that doesn't depend on material things.

Totally Clean

1 JOHN 1:1–10

If we confess our sins, he is faithful and just and will forgive us our sins and purify us from all unrighteousness.
1 John 1:9

A friend was updating me on his past year—a year in which he had received ongoing medical treatment for cancer. The smile on his face was a powerful testimony to the good news he had just received. He said that at his one-year checkup the doctor announced that the test results all pointed to one thing: "You are totally clean!" What a difference two words can make! To my friend, "totally clean" meant every trace of the disease that had threatened his life only months before had been wiped from his body. We rejoiced to hear that he was totally clean!

King David, after his sexual failure with Bathsheba, longed for a similar thing to happen in his heart. Hoping for the stains of his sin to be washed away, he cried out, "Create in me a pure heart, O God, and renew a steadfast spirit within me" (Psalm 51:10). The good news for him and for us is that our sins can be taken care of. When we need cleansing, John's familiar words bring hope: "If we confess our sins, he is faithful and just and will forgive us our sins and purify us from all unrighteousness" (1 John 1:9).

We can't cleanse our own hearts; only God can do that. If we confess our sins to Him, He promises to make us totally clean! *Bill Crowder*

Practice Gratitude Today

What sin, past or present, makes you feel unclean, damaged, or contaminated? Thank God that in His faithfulness and grace, through the blood of Jesus, He has made you totally clean.

Joy and Wisdom

ECCLESIASTES 8:14–17

I commend the enjoyment of life, because there is nothing better for a person under the sun than to eat and drink and be glad.
Ecclesiastes 8:15

Sweetly fragrant cherry tree blossoms flood Japan with exquisite pale and vibrant pinks every spring, delighting the senses of residents and tourists alike. The short-lived nature of the blossoms cultivates a keen awareness in the Japanese to savor the beauty and scent while they linger: the very brevity of the experience heightens the poignancy of it. They call this deliberate enjoyment of something that will change quickly *mono no aware.*

As humans, it's understandable that we'd want to seek and prolong feelings of joy. Yet the reality that life is riddled with hardship means we must cultivate the ability to view both pain and pleasure through a lens of faith in a loving God. We needn't be overly pessimistic, nor should we fashion ourselves an unrealistically sunny outlook on life.

The book of Ecclesiastes offers a helpful model for us. Though this book is sometimes thought to be a catalog of negative statements, the same King Solomon who wrote that "everything is meaningless" (1:2) also encouraged his readers to find joy in the simple things in life: "There is nothing better for a person under the sun than to eat and drink and be glad" (8:15).

Joy comes when we ask God to help us "know wisdom" and learn to observe "all that God has done" (8:16–17) in both beautiful seasons and difficult ones (3:11–14; 7:13–14), knowing that neither is permanent on this side of heaven. *Kirsten Holmberg*

Practice Gratitude Today

What is something available to you today that may not be later because of its season, window of opportunity, or expiration date? Make time today to enjoy it, thanking God for it.

In All Circumstances

1 THESSALONIANS 5:16–18

Give thanks in all circumstances; for this is
God's will for you in Christ Jesus.
1 Thessalonians 5:18

In our suburb we complain about the constant power outages. They can hit three times in a week and last up to twenty-four hours, plunging the neighborhood into darkness. The inconvenience is hard to bear when we cannot use basic household appliances.

Our Christian neighbor often asks, "Is this also something to thank God for?" She is referring to 1 Thessalonians 5:18: "Give thanks in all circumstances; for this is God's will for you in Christ Jesus." We always say, "Yes, of course, we thank God in all things." But the half-hearted manner in which we say it is contradicted by our grumbling every time the power goes off.

One day, however, our belief in thanking God in all circumstances took on new meaning. I returned from work to find our neighbor visibly shaken as she cried, "Thank Jesus the power was off. My house would have burned down, and my family and I would have perished!"

A refuse-collection truck had hit the electricity pole in front of her house and brought down the high-tension cables right over several houses. Had there been power in the cables, fatalities would have been likely.

The difficult circumstances we face can make it hard to say, "Thanks, Lord." But we can be thankful to our God who sees in every situation an opportunity for us to trust Him—whether or not we see His purpose.

Lawrence Darmani

Practice Gratitude Today

Recall a difficult time in your past that, after the fact, you could see how God used it for good in your life. Thank God that He can use your current challenges to bring you closer to Him and increase your trust in Him.

Front-Porch Relief

PHILIPPIANS 4:10–20

I have learned the secret of being content
in any and every situation.
Philippians 4:12

On a particularly hot day, eight-year-old Carmine McDaniel wanted to make sure his neighborhood mail carrier stayed cool and hydrated. So he left a cooler filled with a sports drink and water bottles on their front step. The family security camera recorded the mail carrier's reaction: "Oh man, water and Gatorade. Thank God; thank you!"

Carmine's mom says, "Carmine feels that it's his duty to supply the mailman with a cool beverage even if we're not home."

This story warms our hearts, but it also reminds us that there is One who will "meet all your needs," as the apostle Paul phrased it (Philippians 4:19). Though Paul was languishing in jail and uncertain about his future, he expressed joy for the Christians in Philippi because God had met his needs through their financial gift to him. The Philippian church was not wealthy, but they were generous, giving to Paul and others out of their poverty (see 2 Corinthians 8:1–4). As the Philippians had met Paul's needs, so God would meet theirs, "according to the riches of his glory in Christ Jesus" (Philippians 4:19).

God often sends vertical help through horizontal means. Put another way, He sends us what we need through the help of others. When we trust Him for what we need, we learn, as Paul did, the secret of true contentment (vv. 12–13). *Marvin Williams*

Practice Gratitude Today

Make time today to do a small act of kindness for someone who isn't expecting it. Thank God for the ways He's provided for you through the kindness of others.

At the King's Table

2 SAMUEL 9:6–13

So Mephibosheth ate at David's table like one of the king's sons.
2 Samuel 9:11

"He'll live," the vet announced, "but his leg will have to be amputated." The stray mutt my friend had brought in had been run over by a car. "Are you the owner?" There would be a hefty surgery bill, and the puppy would need care as it recovered. "I am now," my friend replied. Her kindness has given that dog a future in a loving home.

Mephibosheth saw himself as a "dead dog," unworthy of favor (2 Samuel 9:8). Being lame in both feet due to an accident (4:4), he was dependent on others to protect and provide for him. Furthermore, after the death of his grandfather, King Saul, he probably feared that David, the new king, would kill all enemies and rivals to the throne, as was the common practice of the time.

Yet, out of love for his friend Jonathan, David ensured that Jonathan's son Mephibosheth would always be safe and cared for as his own son (9:7). In the same way, we who were once God's enemies, marked for death, have been saved by Jesus and given a place with Him in eternity. That's what it means to eat at the banquet in the kingdom of God that Luke describes in his gospel (Luke 14:15). Here we are—the sons and daughters of the King! What extravagant, undeserved kindness we've received! Let's draw near to God in gratitude and joy. *Karen Kwek*

Practice Gratitude Today

Sit at a table and imagine that you are at the banquet of God's kingdom. Thank Jesus for inviting you to His feast, and for the many blessings He secured for you through His death and resurrection.

How to Bloom

1 PETER 1:1–9

Rejoice inasmuch as you participate in the sufferings of Christ.
1 Peter 4:13

My family and I live in an apartment, so our flower garden consists of what we can grow in indoor pots. For a long time our plants would not flower despite watering and fertilizing. Then we discovered that the soil had to be raked and turned over if the plants were to bloom. Now our potted plants are a pure joy to look at with their healthy leaves and blooming flowers.

Sometimes we need a little raking and turning in our own lives to make us bloom. Writing to the harassed believers in his day, Peter said, "Dear friends, do not be surprised at the fiery ordeal that has come on you to test you, as though something strange were happening to you. But rejoice inasmuch as you participate in the sufferings of Christ" (1 Peter 4:12–13).

Like the soil in our potted plants, these Christians were having their lives "turned over." God's purpose in doing that was to allow their faith to result in praise and glory to Him at the revelation of Jesus Christ (1:7).

God wants to loosen the things that can choke our lives and prevent us from radiating joy. To do this, He sometimes has to allow pain and trouble—trials that help stir up the soil of our lives. If this is what you are experiencing today, rejoice. Surrender to His touch and grow a joy and fruitfulness you never imagined possible. *C. P. Hia*

Practice Gratitude Today

Where is your life being turned over today? Talk with God about the pain you are experiencing—and thank Him that He can use these trials to make you more like Jesus.

Kingdom Motivation

MARK 10:28–31; JOHN 10:9–10

I have come that they may have life, and have it to the full.
John 10:10

When I stopped by to visit my sister's family, my nephews eagerly showed me their new chore system, a set of Choropoly boards. Each colorful electronic board keeps track of their chores. A job well done means the kids can hit a green button, which adds points to their "spending" account. A misdeed like leaving the back door open results in a fine being deducted from the total. Since a high-points total leads to exciting rewards such as computer time—and misdeeds deduct from that total—my nephews are now unusually motivated to do their work and to keep the door closed!

The ingenious system had me joking that I wished I had such an exciting motivational tool. But of course God has given us motivation. Rather than simply commanding obedience, Jesus has promised that a life of following Him, while costly, is also a life of abundance: "life . . . to the full" (John 10:10). Experiencing life in His kingdom is worth "a hundred times" the cost—now and eternally (Mark 10:29–30).

We can rejoice in the fact that we serve a generous God, one who does not reward and punish as we deserve. He generously accepts our weakest efforts—even welcoming and rewarding latecomers to His kingdom as generously as old-timers (see Matthew 20:1–16). In light of this reality, let us joyfully serve Him today. *Monica La Rose*

Practice Gratitude Today

How can you love and serve God today? Thank Him that you have His example of how He lavishes His life, grace, and generosity on those He loves.

Thanks for Being You!

PSALM 100

Enter his gates with thanksgiving.
Psalm 100:4

When I served as my mom's live-in caregiver at a cancer center, I got to know Lori, another caregiver who lived down the hallway from us with her husband, Frank. I would chat, laugh, vent, cry, and pray with Lori in the shared living areas. We enjoyed supporting each other as we cared for our loved ones.

One day, I missed the free shuttle that took residents to buy groceries. Lori offered to drive me to the store later that evening. With grateful tears, I accepted her offer. "Thanks for being you," I said. I truly appreciated her for who she was as a person, not just for what she did for me as a friend.

Psalm 100 demonstrates an appreciation of God for who He is, not simply for all He does. The psalmist invites "all the earth" to "worship the Lord with gladness" (vv. 1–2), being confident in knowing "the Lord is God" (v. 3). Our Maker invites us into His presence to "give thanks to him and praise his name" (v. 4). Yes, the Lord remains worthy of our ongoing thankfulness because He "is good," His "love endures forever," and His "faithfulness continues through all generations" (v. 5).

God will always be the Creator and Sustainer of the universe and our intimately loving Father. He deserves our genuine, joy-filled gratitude.

Xochitl Dixon

Practice Gratitude Today

Reflect on God's unchanging character, without focusing specifically on how He has been faithful in your life. Worship God for who He is.

Sharing Excitement for Christ

ROMANS 12:9–16

Never be lacking in zeal, but keep your spiritual fervor, serving the Lord.
Romans 12:11

The first time we met our neighbor Henry, he pulled a well-worn Bible out of a bag he'd been carrying. Eyes sparkling, he asked if we'd like to discuss Scripture. We nodded and he flipped to some highlighted passages that he excitedly explained. He showed us a notebook full of his observations. With a humble grin, he announced he'd also created a computer presentation full of other related information.

Henry went on to tell us how he'd come from a difficult family situation and then, alone and at his worst, he accepted Jesus's death and resurrection as the foundation of his faith (Acts 4:12). His life had changed as the Spirit helped him follow the Bible's principles. Although Henry had committed his life to God years ago, his enthusiasm was fresh and powerful.

Henry's zeal inspired me, someone who had walked with Jesus many years, to consider my spiritual passion. The apostle Paul wrote: "Never be lacking in zeal, but keep your spiritual fervor, serving the Lord" (Romans 12:11). That seems like a tall order, unless I'm allowing Scripture to nurture in me an ongoing thankfulness for all that God has done for me.

Unlike the emotional highs and lows we experience in life, zeal for God comes from an ever-expanding relationship with Him. The more we learn about Him, the more precious He becomes and the more His goodness floods our souls and spills out into the world.

Jennifer Benson Schuldt

Practice Gratitude Today

How can you share your excitement for God with someone else today? In prayer, let your excitement deepen as you thank God for His goodness, faithfulness, and love for you.

How Deserving Are We?

DEUTERONOMY 9:1–6

It is not because of your righteousness that the LORD your God is giving you this good land to possess.
Deuteronomy 9:6

I remember the day our secondhand refrigerator finally broke down. As a young newlywed employed by a Christian ministry, I didn't have much money to spend on repairs. Not knowing where to turn for reliable help, I called a friend in the electrical business. He assured me that he would handle the problem. Later that evening, I found a brand-new refrigerator in our kitchen. I asked myself, "What did I do to deserve such help?"

It's easy to think we deserve the help that others graciously give us. When we're successful, we tend to assume that we deserve our possessions. Success goes to our head. It makes us proud and can even turn us away from God.

In Deuteronomy 9, we read of God's reminder to Israel about the reason they would be successful. God wanted His people to remember that He was leading them into the land to fulfill His purpose and promises. They would succeed because of Him, not because of their own righteousness (vv. 4–5). He knew they would be tempted to become ungrateful after they were prospering in the promised land.

Ungratefulness is a temptation for us today as well. If our endeavors are successful, let's make sure we are thankful to God for His goodness, help, and protection.

Albert Lee

Practice Gratitude Today

What do you feel you deserve because of your success, hard work, or determination? Thank God for the abilities, possessions, and help that all come from His generous hand.

Look to the Skies

PSALM 19:1–9

The heavens declare the glory of God.
Psalm 19:1

Alex Smalley wants everyone to wake up earlier—or perhaps pause more at day's end. Why? To gaze at sunrises and sunsets. Those fleeting moments are the most beautiful, awe-inspiring times of the day, according to Smalley, the lead researcher of a British study on awe-inducing weather effects. Even more than blue skies or glittering nightscapes, a stunning sunrise or sunset can improve mood, increase positive emotions, and decrease stress. Smalley says, "When you see something vast and overwhelming or something that produces this feeling of awe, your own problems can feel diminished and so you don't worry so much about them."

His findings on wonder echo those of the prophet Jeremiah: "Ah, Sovereign Lord, you have made the heavens and the earth by your great power and outstretched arm. Nothing is too hard for you" (Jeremiah 32:17).

King David also beheld God's creation: "The heavens declare the glory of God; the skies proclaim the work of his hands" (Psalm 19:1). As for the sun, "it rises at one end of the heavens and makes its circuit to the other; nothing is deprived of its warmth" (v. 6). Therefore, writes David, "the law of the Lord is perfect, refreshing the soul" (v. 7). God's glorious creation reflects the all-powerful Creator. Why not take time today to look to the skies and marvel in Him! *Patricia Raybon*

Practice Gratitude Today

Make time today to enjoy either sunrise or sunset. If that isn't possible, find a video online of a sunrise or sunset. Thank God for His power and creativity, and the beauty of His creation.

Longing for Spring

ECCLESIASTES 3:1–13

There is nothing better for people than to be happy and to do good while they live.
Ecclesiastes 3:12

It's been a long, cold winter, and I am eager for warm weather. I'm tired of seeing bare trees and lifeless brown leaves covering the ground. I long to see wildflowers poke through the dead leaves and to watch the woods turn green once more.

Yet even as I anticipate my favorite season, I hear my mother's voice saying, "Don't wish your life away."

If you're like me, you sometimes hear yourself saying, "When such and such happens, then I will . . ." Or, "If only so and so would do this, then I would . . ." Or, "I would be happy if . . ." Or, "I will be satisfied when . . ."

In longing for some future good, we forget that every day—regardless of the weather or our circumstances—is a gift from God to be used for His glory.

According to author Ron Ash, "We are where we need to be and learning what we need to learn. Stay the course because the things we experience today will lead us to where He needs us to be tomorrow."

In every season, there is a reason to rejoice and an opportunity to do good (Ecclesiastes 3:12). The challenge for each of us every day is to find something to rejoice about and some good to do—and then to do both.

Julie Ackerman Link

Practice Gratitude Today

What life circumstance, experience, or season do you wish you were done with? How can you slow down today to enjoy, or at least be grateful amid, that circumstance?

When Life Is Hard

PSALM 16

I say to the Lord, "You are my Lord; apart from you I have no good thing."
Psalm 16:2

Physically, mentally, and emotionally exhausted, I curled up in my recliner. Our family had followed God's leading and had moved from California to Wisconsin. After we arrived, our car broke down and we were without a vehicle for two months. Meanwhile, my husband's limited mobility after an unexpected back surgery and my chronic pain complicated our unpacking. We uncovered costly problems with our old, new-to-us home. Our senior dog suffered with health issues. And though our new pup brought great joy, raising a furry ball of energy was far more work than anticipated. My attitude soured. How was I supposed to have unshakable faith while traveling on a bumpy road of hardships?

As I prayed, God reminded me of the psalmist whose praise didn't depend on circumstances. David poured out his emotions, often with great vulnerability, and sought refuge in the presence of God (Psalm 16:1). Acknowledging God as Provider and Protector (vv. 5–6), David praised Him and followed His counsel (v. 7). David affirmed that he would "not be shaken" because he kept his eyes "always on the Lord" (v. 8). So he rejoiced and rested secure in the joy of God's presence (vv. 9–11).

We too can delight in knowing our peace doesn't depend on our present situation. As we thank our unchanging God for who He is and always will be, His presence will fuel our steadfast faith.

Xochitl Dixon

Practice Gratitude Today

Bring your frustrations, difficulties, and fears to God in prayer. Thank Him that His presence is unchanging and that His peace doesn't depend on your circumstances.

God's Moves

EXODUS 12:24–28

It is the Passover sacrifice to the LORD, who passed over the houses of the Israelites in Egypt and spared our homes.
Exodus 12:27

I love a good game of Scrabble. After one particular game, my friends named a move after me—calling it a "Katara." I'd been trailing the entire game, but at the end of it—with no tiles left in the bag—I made a seven-letter word. This meant the game was over, and I received fifty bonus points as well as all the points from my opponents' leftover tiles, moving me from last place to first. Now whenever we play and someone is trailing, they remember what happened and hold out hope for a Katara.

Remembering what happened in the past has the power to lift our spirits and give us hope. And that's exactly what the Israelites did when they celebrated Passover. The Passover commemorates what God did for the Israelites when they were in Egypt, oppressed by Pharaoh and his crew (Exodus 1:6–14). After they cried out to God, He delivered the people in a mighty way. He told them to put blood on their doorposts so the death angel would "pass over" their firstborn people and animals (12:12–13). Then they would be kept safe from death.

Centuries later, believers in Jesus regularly take Communion as we remember His sacrifice on the cross—providing what we needed to be delivered from sin and death (1 Corinthians 11:23–26). Remembering God's loving acts in the past gives us hope for today. *Katara Patton*

Practice Gratitude Today

Communion, like the Passover feast, is a physical, sensory reminder of God's faithfulness in the past. What physical experience, object, or meal can you enjoy today to remind you of God's faithfulness?

A New Name

JOHN 1:35–42

Jesus looked at him and said, ". . . You will be called Cephas" (which, when translated, is Peter).
John 1:42

In the article "Leading by Naming," Mark Labberton wrote about the power of a name. He said: "I can still feel the impact of a musical friend who one day called me 'musical.' No one had ever called me that. I didn't really play an instrument. I was no soloist. Yet . . . I instantly felt known and loved. . . . [He] noticed, validated, and appreciated something deeply true about me."

Perhaps this is what Simon felt when Jesus renamed him. After Andrew was convinced that Jesus was the Messiah, he immediately found his brother Simon and brought him to Jesus (John 1:41–42). Jesus peered into his soul and validated and appreciated something deeply true about Simon. Yes, Jesus saw the failure and impetuous nature that would get him into trouble. But more than that He saw the potential of Simon to become a leader in the church. Jesus named him Cephas, Aramaic for Peter—a "rock" (John 1:42; see Matthew 16:18).

And so it is with us. God sees our pride, anger, and lack of love for others, but He also knows who we are in Christ. He calls us justified and reconciled (Romans 5:9–10); forgiven, holy, and beloved (Colossians 2:13; 3:12); chosen and faithful (Revelation 17:14). Remember how God sees you and seek to let that define who you are.

Marvin Williams

Practice Gratitude Today

What weakness, failure, or sin do you feel defined by? Talk with God about it. Thank Him that He sees you as His forgiven, chosen, and beloved child.

The Story Isn't Over

MATTHEW 6:9–13

Your kingdom come, your will be done,
on earth as it is in heaven.
Matthew 6:10

When British drama *Line of Duty* concluded, record numbers watched to see how its fight against organized crime would end. But many viewers were left disappointed when the finale implied that evil would ultimately win. "I wanted the bad guys brought to justice," one fan said. "We needed that moral ending."

Sociologist Peter Berger once noted that we hunger for hope and justice—hope that evil will one day be overcome and that those who caused it will be made to face their crimes. A world where the bad guys win goes against how we know the world should work. Without probably realizing it, those disappointed fans were expressing humanity's deep longing for the world to be made right again.

In the Lord's Prayer, Jesus is realistic about evil. It exists not only between us, requiring forgiveness (Matthew 6:12), but on a grand scale, requiring deliverance (v. 13). This realism, however, is matched with hope. There's a place where evil doesn't exist—heaven—and that heavenly kingdom is coming to earth (v. 10). One day God's justice will be complete, His "moral ending" will come, and evil will be banished for good (Revelation 21:4).

So when the real-life bad guys win and disappointment sets in, let's remember this: until God's will is done "on earth as it is in heaven" (Matthew 6:10), there is always hope—because the story isn't over.

Sheridan Voysey

Practice Gratitude Today

Pray the words of the Lord's Prayer, remembering that Christians all over the world pray this prayer together. Thank God that on earth as in heaven, He will make everything new (Revelation 21:5).

Prompted to Pray

1 THESSALONIANS 5:12–18

Rejoice always, pray continually, give thanks in all circumstances; for this is God's will for you in Christ Jesus.
1 Thessalonians 5:16–18

A coworker once told me that her prayer life had improved because of our manager. I was impressed, thinking that our difficult leader had shared some spiritual nuggets with her and influenced how she prayed. I was wrong—sort of. My coworker and friend went on to explain: "Every time I see him coming, I start praying." Her time of prayer had improved because she prayed more before each conversation with him. She knew she needed God's help in her challenging work relationship with her manager and she called out to Him more because of it.

My coworker's practice of praying during tough times and interactions is something I've adopted. It's also a biblical practice found in 1 Thessalonians when Paul reminds the believers in Jesus to "pray continually, give thanks in all circumstances" (5:17–18). No matter what we face, prayer is always the best practice. It keeps us connected with God and invites His Spirit to direct us (Galatians 5:16) rather than having us rely on our human inclinations. This helps us "live in peace with each other" (1 Thessalonians 5:13) even when we face conflicts.

As God helps us, we can rejoice in Him, pray about everything, and give thanks often. And those things will help us live in even greater harmony with our brothers and sisters in Jesus. *Katara Patton*

Practice Gratitude Today

What is a challenging conversation, task, or interaction you're not looking forward to today? Pray beforehand, thanking God for His presence and the guidance of His Spirit.

Out of the Darkness

PSALM 77:1–15

I cried out to God for help. . . . What god is as great as our God?
Psalm 77:1, 13

I don't know what desperate situation gripped Asaph, the writer of Psalm 77, but I've heard, and made, similar laments. Over the past dozen years since I lost my daughter, many others who have experienced the loss of a loved one have shared with me heartbreaking sentiments like these:

Crying out to God (v. 1). Stretching empty arms heavenward (v. 2). Experiencing troubling thoughts about God because of horrible circumstances (v. 3). Enduring unspeakable trouble (v. 4). Cowering under the feeling of being cast aside (v. 7). Fearing failed promises (v. 8). Fearing a lack of mercy (v. 8).

But a turnaround occurs for Asaph in verse 10 through a recollection of God's great works. Thoughts turn to God's love. To memories of what He has done. To His marvelous deeds of old. To the comfort of God's faithfulness and mercy. To reminders of God's wonders and greatness. To His strength and redemption.

Despair is real in this life, and answers do not come easily. Yet in the darkness—as we remember God's glory, majesty, power, and love—our despair can slowly subside. Like Asaph, we can rehearse God's acts, especially the salvation He brought through Jesus, and we can return to where we once were—resting gratefully in His mighty love.

Dave Branon

Practice Gratitude Today

What trouble, despair, or failure do you face today? Reach out to a fellow Jesus follower and ask them how God has been faithful to them in the past. Thank God that He is faithful to you as well.

For Our Health

1 CHRONICLES 16:7–14

Give praise to the Lord.
1 Chronicles 16:8

According to a prominent Duke University Medical Center researcher, "If thankfulness were a drug, it would be the world's best-selling product with [health benefits] for every major organ system."

For some, being thankful means simply living with a sense of gratitude—taking time to recognize and focus on the things we have instead of the things we wish we had. The Bible takes the idea of thankfulness to a deeper level. The act of giving thanks causes us to recognize the One who provides our blessings (James 1:17).

David knew that God was responsible for the safe delivery of the ark of the covenant in Jerusalem (1 Chronicles 15:26). As a result, he penned a song of gratitude that centered on God instead of simply expressing his delight in an important event. The ballad began: "Give praise to the Lord, proclaim his name; make known among the nations what he has done" (16:8). David's song went on to rejoice in God's greatness, highlighting God's salvation, creative power, and mercy (vv. 25–36).

Today we can be truly thankful by worshiping the Giver instead of the gifts we enjoy. Focusing on the good things in our lives may benefit our bodies, but directing our thanks to God benefits our souls.

Jennifer Benson Schuldt

Practice Gratitude Today

List as many of God's gifts to you today as you can think of. Thank God for His goodness to you—and that your body, heart, and soul were meant to be in grateful relationship with Him.

Serve and Be Served

PHILIPPIANS 4:10–19

You were concerned, but you had no opportunity to show it.
Philippians 4:10

Marilyn had been ill for many weeks, and many people had encouraged her through this difficult time. *How will I ever repay all their kindnesses?* she worried. Then one day she read the words of a written prayer: "Pray that [others] will develop humility, allowing them not only to serve, but also to be served." Marilyn suddenly realized there was no need to balance any scale, but just to be thankful and allow others to experience the joy of serving.

In Philippians 4, the apostle Paul expressed his gratitude for all those who shared "in [his] troubles" (v. 14). He depended on people to support him as he preached and taught the gospel. He understood that the gifts provided for him when he was in need were simply an extension of people's love for God: "[Your gifts] are a fragrant offering, an acceptable sacrifice, pleasing to God" (v. 18).

It may not be easy to be the one on the receiving end—especially if you've usually been the first one to help other people. But with humility, we can allow God to gently care for us by a variety of means when we need help.

Paul wrote, "My God will meet all your needs" (v. 19). It was something he had learned during a life of trials. God is faithful and His provision for us has no limits.

Cindy Hess Kasper

Practice Gratitude Today

Where could you use help today? Reach out to someone in your life who may be able to support you. Praise God that He created His people to be in community.

Ending Envy

ROMANS 6:11–14

Each one should test their own actions. Then they can take pride in themselves alone, without comparing themselves to someone else.
Galatians 6:4

The famous French artist Edgar Degas is remembered worldwide for his paintings of ballerinas. Less known is the envy he expressed of his friend and artistic rival Édouard Manet, another master painter. Said Degas of Manet, "Everything he does he always hits off straightaway, while I take endless pains and never get it right."

It's a curious emotion, envy—listed by the apostle Paul among the worst traits, alongside "greed and depravity . . . envy, murder, strife, deceit and malice" (Romans 1:29). It results from foolish thinking—from worshiping idols instead of worshiping God (v. 28).

Author Christina Fox says that when envy develops among believers, it's "because our hearts have turned from our one true love." In our envy, she said, "we are chasing after the inferior pleasures of this world instead of looking to Jesus. In effect, we've forgotten whose we are."

Yet there's a remedy. Turn back to God. "Offer every part of yourself to him," Paul wrote (Romans 6:13)—your work and life especially. In another of his letters Paul wrote, "Each one should test their own actions. Then they can take pride in themselves alone, without comparing themselves to someone else" (Galatians 6:4).

Thank God for His blessings—not just things but the freedom of His grace. Seeing our own God-given gifts, we find contentment again.

Patricia Raybon

Practice Gratitude Today

What is a gift, life circumstance, or privilege someone else has that you are envious of? Confess this to God, and ask Him to make you more aware of the gifts He has given you.

Heart of Joy

JOHN 15:1–11

I have told you this so that my joy may be in you and that your joy may be complete.
John 15:11

While waiting at the gate area of Singapore's Changi Airport to board my flight, I noticed a young family—mom, dad, and son. The area was crowded, and they were looking for a place to sit. Suddenly, the little boy began loudly singing "Joy to the World." He was about six years old, so I was pretty impressed that he knew all the words.

What captured my attention even more was the look on the boy's face—his beaming smile matched the words he was singing as he proclaimed to everyone at the gate the joy of the Christ who has come.

This joy is not limited to exuberant children nor should it be confined to the Christmas season. The overflowing joy of knowing Christ's presence in our lives was one of the themes of Jesus's final teaching with His disciples the night before He died on the cross. He told them of His extravagant love for them—that He loved them as the Father loved Him (John 15:9). After sharing what this eternal relationship looks like, Jesus said, "I have told you this so that my joy may be in you and that your joy may be complete" (v. 11).

What a promise! Through Jesus Christ our hearts can be filled with joy—real joy!

Bill Crowder

Practice Gratitude Today

How can you express the joy you have in Jesus's extravagant love today? Thank God that your joy depends on Jesus's work on the cross, not your circumstances.

Plans and Providence

JAMES 4:13–17

If it is the Lord's will, we will live and do this or that.
James 4:15

In 2000, an upstart company operating on a movie-rental-by-mail system offered to sell their company for $50 million to Blockbuster, the king of home movies and video game rentals at that time. Netflix had roughly 300,000 subscribers, while Blockbuster had millions and millions of them. Blockbuster passed on the opportunity to purchase their little competitor. The result? Today Netflix has more than 180 million subscribers and is worth nearly $200 billion. As for Blockbuster, well . . . it went bust. None of us can predict the future.

We're tempted to believe that we're in control of our lives and that our plans for the future will succeed. But James says, "You are a mist that appears for a little while and then vanishes" (James 4:14). Life is brief, quick, and more fragile than we often realize. Planning is necessary, but the sin of presumption is in the assumption that we're in control. That's why James warns us not to "boast in [our] arrogant schemes," for "all such boasting is evil" (v. 16).

The way to avoid this sinful practice is through grateful participation with God. Gratitude reminds us that He's the source of "every good and perfect gift" (1:17). Then when we come to God, we ask Him not to simply bless our present and future plans but to help us join Him in what He's doing. This is what it means to pray, "If it is the Lord's will" (4:15). *Glenn Packiam*

Practice Gratitude Today

Make a list of future plans you will be disappointed if they don't happen. Take that list to God in prayer, thanking Him that He is in control and working out the details of your life to make you more like Christ.

Thanks Journal

PSALM 117

Praise the LORD, all you nations; extol him, all you peoples.
Psalm 117:1

When I was a new believer in Jesus, a spiritual mentor encouraged me to keep a thanks journal. It was a little booklet I carried with me everywhere I went. Sometimes I would record a thanksgiving right away. Other times, I would pen it at the end of the week during a time of reflection.

Taking note of praise items is a good habit—one I'm considering reestablishing in my life. It would help me to be mindful of God's presence and grateful for His provision and care.

In the shortest of all the psalms, Psalm 117, the writer encourages everyone to praise the Lord because "great is his love toward us" (v. 2).

Think about it: How has the Lord shown His love toward you today, this week, this month, and this year? Don't just look for the spectacular. His love is seen in the ordinary, everyday circumstances of life. Then consider how He has shown His love toward your family, your church, and others. Let your mind soak up the extent of His love for all of us.

The psalmist added that "the faithfulness of the LORD endures forever" (v. 2). In other words, He will *continue* to love us! So we will continue to have many things to praise God for in the coming days. As His dearly loved children, may praising and thanking God characterize our lives!

Poh Fang Chia

Practice Gratitude Today

Write down ways that God has shown His love to you, to your family, to your friends or church family, and to all people. Thank Him that He will continue to love you for all your days.

Who We Are

PSALM 100

You are . . . God's special possession, that you may declare the praises of him who called you out of darkness into his wonderful light.
1 Peter 2:9

In her autobiography, Corrie ten Boom described her and her sister Betsie's horrific time in a Nazi concentration camp in the early 1940s. On one occasion they were forced to take off their clothes during an inspection. Corrie stood in line feeling defiled and forsaken. Suddenly, she remembered that Jesus had hung naked on the cross. Struck with wonder and worship, Corrie whispered to her sister, "Betsie, they took His clothes too." Betsie gasped and said, "Oh, Corrie . . . and I never thanked Him."

It is easy for us to live thanklessly in a world that is full of trouble, struggles, and woes. On any given day we can find many reasons to complain. However, Psalm 100 exhorts God's people to be glad, joyful, and thankful, for "it is he who made us, and we are his; we are his people, the sheep of his pasture" (v. 3). As we remember who we are, we can respond in thanksgiving. For even in the worst of times, we can remember Christ's love and sacrifice for us.

Don't let the brutality of the world take away your thankful heart. Remember you are God's child, and He has shown you His goodness and mercy through His work on the cross. *Albert Lee*

Practice Gratitude Today

Where do you see brutality, crisis, or horror in the world today? Talk with God about it. Thank Him for experiencing the violence and horror of the cross in order to win the victory over sin and death.

Hungry for God

JEREMIAH 15:15–21

When your words came, I ate them; they
were my joy and my heart's delight.
Jeremiah 15:16

A new believer in Jesus was desperate to read the Bible. However, he'd lost his eyesight and both hands in an explosion. When he heard about a woman who read Braille with her lips, he tried to do the same—only to discover that the nerve endings of his lips had also been destroyed. Later, he was filled with joy when he discovered that he could feel the Braille characters with his tongue! He had found a way to read and enjoy the Scriptures.

Joy and delight were the emotions the prophet Jeremiah experienced when he received God's words. "When your words came, I ate them," he said, "they were my joy and my heart's delight" (Jeremiah 15:16). Unlike the people of Judah who despised God's words (8:9), Jeremiah had been obedient and rejoiced in them. His obedience, however, also led to the prophet being rejected by his own people and persecuted unfairly (15:17).

Some of us may have experienced something similar. We once read the Bible with joy, but obedience to God led to suffering and rejection from others. Like Jeremiah, we can bring our confusion to God. He answered Jeremiah by repeating the promise He gave him when He first called him to be a prophet (vv. 19–21; see 1:18–19). God reminded him that He never lets His people down. We can have this same confidence too. He's faithful and will never abandon us.

Poh Fang Chia

Practice Gratitude Today

How can you taste Scripture in a fresh way today? Perhaps listen to an audio version, read it aloud, read it with others, or copy a passage in your journal. Thank God for the truth and joy of His Word.

Release from Slavery

EXODUS 6:1–8

I will free you from being slaves to them.
Exodus 6:6

"You are like Moses, leading us out from slavery!" Jamila exclaimed. As a bonded brick-kiln worker in Pakistan, she and her family (and her parents before her) suffered because of the exorbitant amount they owed the kiln owner. Barely able to survive, they used much of their earnings just to pay off the interest. But when they received a gift from a nonprofit agency that released them from their debt, they felt tremendous relief. In thanking the agency's representative for their freedom, Jamila, a Christian, pointed to the example of God's release of Moses and the Israelites from slavery.

The Israelites had been oppressed by the Egyptians for hundreds of years, laboring under harsh conditions. They cried out to God, asking for help (Exodus 2:23). But their workload increased, for the new Pharaoh ordered them not only to make bricks but also to gather the straw for the bricks (5:6–8). When the Israelites again cried out against the oppression, God again promised to be their God (6:7). No longer would they be slaves, for He would redeem them with "an outstretched arm" (v. 6).

Under God's direction, Moses led the Israelites out of Egypt (Exodus 14). Today God still delivers us, for through the outstretched arms of His Son Jesus on the cross, we are set free from a far greater enslavement to the sin that once controlled us. We're no longer slaves but free!

Amy Boucher Pye

Practice Gratitude Today

What sin, wound, or behavior do you feel enslaved to today? Praise God that through Jesus's life, death, and resurrection, He has set you free from bondage to sin.

Grief Overturned

JOHN 20:11–18

I have seen the Lord!
John 20:18

According to Jim and Jamie Dutcher, filmmakers known for their knowledge of wolves, when happy, wolves wag their tails and romp about. But after the death of a pack member, they grieve for weeks. They visit the place where the pack member died, showing grief by their drooping tails and mournful howls.

Grief is a powerful emotion that we've all experienced, particularly at the death of a loved one or a treasured hope. Mary Magdalene experienced it. She had belonged to Christ's supporters and traveled with Him and His disciples (Luke 8:1–3). But His cruel death on a cross separated them now. The only thing left for Mary to do for Jesus was to finish anointing His body for burial—a task the Sabbath had interrupted. But imagine how Mary felt upon arriving at the tomb and finding not a lifeless, broken body but a living Savior! Though she hadn't at first recognized the man standing before her, the sound of her name spoken by Him told her who He was—Jesus! Instantly, grief turned to joy. Mary now had joyful news to share: "I have seen the Lord!" (John 20:18).

Jesus entered our dark world to bring freedom and life. His resurrection is a celebration of the fact that He accomplished what He set out to do. Like Mary, we can celebrate Christ's resurrection and share the good news that He's alive. Alleluia! *Linda Washington*

Practice Gratitude Today

Spend a few minutes in quietness pondering Jesus's resurrection. Remember both the grief of the cross and the love that brought Jesus to save His creation—including you.

A Big Deal

ISAIAH 58:6–9

This is the kind of fasting I want: . . . Let the oppressed go free, and remove the chains that bind people.
Isaiah 58:6 NLT

A family member needed help with his December rent. To his family, the request felt like a burden—especially with their own unexpected expenses at year's end. But they dug into their savings, grateful for God's provision—and blessed by their relative's gratitude.

He handed them a thank-you card filled with grateful words. "There you go again . . . doing nice things, probably passing it off as no big deal."

Helping others is a big deal, however, to God. The prophet Isaiah made that point to the nation of Israel. The people were fasting but still quarreling and fighting. Instead, said Isaiah: "Free those who are wrongly imprisoned; lighten the burden of those who work for you. . . . Share your food with the hungry, and give shelter to the homeless. Give clothes to those who need them, and do not hide from relatives who need your help" (Isaiah 58:6–7 NLT).

Such a sacrifice, said Isaiah, shares God's light but also heals our own brokenness (v. 8). As the family helped their relative, they looked hard at their own finances, seeing ways they could manage better all year. This was God's promise for being generous: "Your godliness will lead you forward, and the glory of the Lord will protect you from behind" (v. 8 NLT). In the end, giving to their kin blessed them more. And God? He already gave His all—with love. *Patricia Raybon*

Practice Gratitude Today

Who needs your generosity today, even though it feels inconvenient? Thank God that in giving to others, you can contribute to God's vision for how His world is supposed to be.

I'm Alive

EPHESIANS 2:1–10

As for you, you were dead in your transgressions and sins.
Ephesians 2:1

Laura Brooks, a fifty-two-year-old mother of two, didn't know it but she was one of twelve thousand people whose names are incorrectly entered each year into the government database as dead. She wondered what was wrong when she stopped receiving disability checks, and her loan payments and her rent checks bounced. She went to the bank to clear up the issue, but the representative told her that her accounts had been closed because she was dead! Obviously, they were mistaken.

The apostle Paul was not mistaken when he said that the Ephesian believers were at one point dead—spiritually dead (Ephesians 2:5). They were dead in the sense that they were separated from God, enslaved to sin, and condemned under the wrath of God. What a state of hopelessness!

Yet God in His goodness took action to reverse this condition for them and for us. The living God "who gives life to the dead" (Romans 4:17) poured out His rich mercy and great love by sending His Son Jesus to this earth. Through Christ's death and resurrection, we are made alive (Ephesians 2:4–5).

When we believe in the death and resurrection of Jesus Christ, we go from death to life. Now we live to rejoice in His goodness!

Marvin Williams

Practice Gratitude Today

What is your experience with death? Have you lost loved ones, coworkers, community members, or pets? Thank God that He has brought you from death to life through Jesus Christ.

With All My Art

EXODUS 35:30–35

[The Lord] has filled him with the Spirit of
God . . . to make artistic designs.
Exodus 35:31–32

"Why plant flowers? You can't eat them," said my father-in-law after witnessing my spring ritual of filling pots with fragrant and colorful treasures from the garden store. Jay's dad is an engineer—a practical sort of person. He can make anything work, but making it beautiful is not a priority. He values function over form, usefulness over aesthetics.

God created us with different gifts. Engineers who work for the glory of God design things that make life easier. The Lord also created artists, who make life more pleasant by creating beautiful things for the glory of God and the enjoyment of others.

When we think of art in worship, we usually think of music. But other art forms have long had a role in glorifying God. The calling of Bezalel demonstrates God's regard for fine art (Exodus 35:30–35). God commissioned him to beautify the first official place of worship: the tabernacle. God's purpose for the arts, says Gene Edward Veith, is "to glorify God and to manifest beauty."

When artistic talent is enlivened by the Spirit of God, it becomes an act of worship that then can become a witness to point people to Christ. God has greatly enriched our lives with beauty. And we in turn express our gratitude by displaying His glory in our art.

Julie Ackerman Link

Practice Gratitude Today

How can you make something beautiful today to the glory of God? As you make something a little more pleasant or appealing, thank God that He made His creation both functional and beautiful.

He Watches over Us

PSALM 33:8–22

From his dwelling place he watches all who live on earth.
Psalm 33:14

As a young man I read the novel *Nineteen Eighty-Four* by George Orwell, which made famous the phrase "Big Brother is watching you." In this imaginary society, all aspects of life are under surveillance.

Today, there are an estimated 5.2 million closed-circuit video cameras in the UK alone! London is saturated with them. These cameras watch lobbies and sidewalks for security reasons. They even monitor traffic.

Psalm 33 tells us that God is also watching from on high (v. 14). He not only sees images and activities but discerns thoughts and motives. As creator God, when He speaks, it will be done (v. 9). His eternal purposes march on unhindered (vv. 10–11). Earthly obstacles are mere stepping stones to Him. Though many depend on military strength for deliverance and safety, their hope is in vain (vv. 16–17).

Yet we who fear the Lord need not flee from this awesome God. The psalmist affirms, "The eyes of the Lord are on those who fear him, on those whose hope is in his unfailing love. . . . He is our help and our shield" (vv. 18, 20).

The eye of the Lord may be fearsome, but we who trust in Him rejoice. He is not an intrusive Big Brother but our loving heavenly Father who watches over us. *Albert Lee*

Practice Gratitude Today

What part of your life makes you feel anxious, exposed, or fearful knowing that God sees it? Thank God that He is a loving Father who watches over you with mercy and love.

How to Enjoy Things

ECCLESIASTES 5:13–20

When God gives someone . . . the ability . . . to accept their lot and be happy in their toil—this is a gift of God.
Ecclesiastes 5:19

In his book *Daring to Draw Near*, Dr. John White wrote that several years earlier God had made it possible for him to acquire a lovely home with many luxuries. His feelings about the house fluctuated dramatically.

When he reminded himself that it was a gracious gift from God, he felt joy and thanksgiving. But when he compared it with those of his friends, he would feel proud because he had such a fine house—and his joy would evaporate. His home would actually become a burden. All he could see were the many hedges and trees to care for and the endless odd jobs to do. White said, "While vanity clouds my eyes and burdens my heart, gratitude clears my vision and lightens my load."

The writer of Ecclesiastes saw God at every turn in the enjoyment of material things. The power to eat the fruits of our labors and even the strength to receive and rejoice in them is from Him (5:18–19).

From beginning to end, all of life is a continuous gift-giving by God. We deserve nothing. He owes us nothing. Yet He gives us everything. If we remember this, we need not feel selfish or guilty. Whatever material blessings we have are gifts from our gracious God.

Dennis DeHaan

Practice Gratitude Today

Do you have luxuries, surpluses, or opportunities that others don't? What can you do today to remind yourself that these are all gifts from God—and to enjoy them in a way that brings Him glory?

Deeper Love

1 PETER 4:7–11

God demonstrates his own love for us in this: While we were still sinners, Christ died for us.
Romans 5:8

When they first met, Edwin Stanton snubbed United States president Abraham Lincoln personally and professionally—even referring to him as a "long-armed creature." But Lincoln appreciated Stanton's abilities and chose to forgive him, eventually appointing Stanton to a vital cabinet position during the Civil War. Stanton later grew to love Lincoln as a friend. It was Stanton who sat by Lincoln's bed throughout the night after the president was shot at Ford's Theater and whispered through tears on his passing, "Now he belongs to the ages."

Reconciliation is a beautiful thing. The apostle Peter pointed followers of Jesus there when he wrote, "Above all, love each other deeply, because love covers over a multitude of sins" (1 Peter 4:8). Peter's words cause me to wonder if he was thinking of his own denial of Jesus (Luke 22:54–62) and the forgiveness Jesus offered him (and us) through the cross.

The deep love Jesus demonstrated through His death on the cross frees us from the debt for our sins and opens the way for our reconciliation with God (Colossians 1:19–20). His forgiveness empowers us to forgive others as we realize we can't forgive in our own strength and as we ask Him to help us. When we love others because our Savior loves them and forgive because He has forgiven us, God gives us strength to let go of the past and walk forward with Him into beautiful new places of grace.

James Banks

Practice Gratitude Today

Who do you need to forgive today? (Remember, reconciliation is not always possible, within your control, or safe during this life.) Thank God that you can love and forgive because He loves and forgives you.

Joy in the Meaningless

ECCLESIASTES 2:1–11

When I surveyed all that my hands had done and what I had toiled to achieve, everything was meaningless, a chasing after the wind.
Ecclesiastes 2:11

James Ward, the creator of the blog *I Like Boring Things*, launched a conference called the Boring Conference. It's a one-day celebration of the mundane, the ordinary, and the overlooked. In the past, speakers have addressed seemingly meaningless topics like sneezing, sounds that vending machines make, and inkjet printers of 1999. Ward knows the topics may be boring, but the speakers can take a mundane subject and make it interesting, meaningful, and even joyful.

Several millennia ago, Solomon, the wisest of kings, launched his own search for joy in the meaningless and mundane. He pursued work, bought flocks, built wealth, acquired singers, and constructed buildings (Ecclesiastes 2:4–9). Some of these pursuits were honorable and some were not. Ultimately, in his pursuit of meaning, the king found nothing but boredom (v. 11). Solomon maintained a worldview that didn't press beyond the limits of human experience to include God. In the end, however, he realized that he'd find joy in the mundane only when he remembered and worshiped God (12:1–7).

When we find ourselves in the whirlwind of tedium, let's launch our own daily mini conference, as we "remember [our] Creator" (v. 1)—the God who fills the mundane with meaning. As we remember and worship Him, we'll find wonder in the ordinary, gratitude in the mundane, and joy in the seemingly meaningless things of life. *Marvin Williams*

Practice Gratitude Today

What is a daily task you find boring? How can you make this task an opportunity to notice God's presence in your life and worship Him?

Put Down Your Burdens

MATTHEW 11:25–30

Come to me, all you who are weary and
burdened, and I will give you rest.
Matthew 11:28

A man driving his pickup truck on a country track saw a woman carrying a heavy load, so he stopped and offered her a lift. The woman expressed her gratitude and climbed into the back of the truck.

A moment later, the man noticed a strange thing: the woman was still holding on to her heavy load despite sitting in the vehicle! Astonished, he pleaded, "Please, madam, put down your load and take your rest. My truck can carry you and your stuff. Just relax."

What do we do with the load of fear, worry, and anxiety we often carry as we go through life's many challenges? Instead of relaxing in the Lord, I sometimes behave like that woman. Jesus said, "Come to me, all you who are weary and burdened, and I will give you rest" (Matthew 11:28), yet I've caught myself carrying burdens I should off-load onto Jesus.

We put down our burdens when we bring them to the Lord in prayer. The apostle Peter says, "Cast all your anxiety on [Jesus] because he cares for you" (1 Peter 5:7). Because He cares for us, we can rest and relax as we learn to trust Him. Instead of carrying the burdens that weigh us down and weary us, we can give them to the Lord and let Him carry them. *Lawrence Darmani*

Practice Gratitude Today

Make a list of the things you currently feel worried, afraid, or anxious about. Take them to God in prayer, thanking Him that you can cast your cares on Him because He cares for you.

Grieving and Grateful

JOB 1:13–22

The LORD gave and the LORD has taken away;
may the name of the Lord be praised.
Job 1:21

After my mom died, one of her fellow cancer patients approached me. "Your mom was so kind to me," she said, sobbing. "I'm sorry she died . . . instead of me."

"My mom loved you," I said. "We prayed God would let you see your boys grow up." Holding her hands, I wept with her and asked God to help her grieve peacefully. I also thanked Him for her remission that allowed her to continue loving her husband and two growing children.

The Bible reveals the complexity of grief when Job lost most everything, including all his children. Job grieved and "fell to the ground in worship" (Job 1:20). With a heartbreaking and hopeful act of surrender and expression of gratitude, he declared, "The LORD gave and the LORD has taken away; may the name of the LORD be praised" (v. 21). While Job would struggle mightily later through his grieving and God's rebuilding of his life, in this moment he accepted and even rejoiced in God's sovereignty over good and bad situations.

God understands the many ways we process and struggle with emotions. He invites us to grieve with honesty and vulnerability. Even when sorrow seems endless and unbearable, God affirms that He hasn't and won't change. With this promise, He comforts us and empowers us to be grateful for His presence. *Xochitl Dixon*

Practice Gratitude Today

What is one thing God has given you? What is one thing He's taken away from you? Praise God that His love and presence are unchanging through both joy and grief.

Exceedingly Better

1 CHRONICLES 17:1–15

He is the one who will build a house for me,
and I will establish his throne forever.
1 Chronicles 17:12

My birthday is the day after my mother's. As an adolescent, I would scramble to think of a gift that delighted my mom yet fit in my budget. She always received my purchases with appreciation, and on the following day, my birthday, she would present her gift to me. Without fail, her gift vastly outshone mine. Her intention wasn't to diminish what I'd given her; she simply gave generously from her resources, which far exceeded my own.

My desire to give to my mother reminds me of David's wish to build a home for God. Struck by the contrast between his palace and the tent where God revealed Himself, David longed to build God a temple. Instead of granting David's wish, God responded by giving David an exceedingly better gift. God promised not only that one of David's children (Solomon) would build the temple (1 Chronicles 17:11) but that He would build David a house, a dynasty. That promise began with Solomon but found its ultimate fulfillment in Jesus, whose throne was indeed established "forever" (v. 12). David wanted to give from his finite resources, but God promised something infinite.

Like David, may we always be moved to give to God out of gratitude and love. And may we always see how much more abundantly He has given to us in Jesus. *Kirsten Holmberg*

Practice Gratitude Today

In light of God's generosity to you, how can you be generous to someone today? Thank God that in giving to another, you can reflect His deep love and goodness to you.

The Secret

PHILIPPIANS 4:10–19

I have learned the secret of being content
in any and every situation.
Philippians 4:12

Sometimes I suspect my cat Heathcliff suffers from a bad case of FOMO (fear of missing out). When I come home with groceries, Heathcliff rushes over to inspect the contents. When I'm chopping vegetables, he stands up on his back paws, peering at the produce and begging me to share. But when I actually give Heathcliff whatever's caught his fancy, he quickly loses interest, walking away with an air of bored resentment.

But it would be hypocritical for me to be hard on my little buddy. In comical caricature, he reflects a bit of my own insatiable hunger for more, my assumption that now is never enough.

According to Paul, contentment isn't natural—it's learned (Philippians 4:11). On our own, we desperately pursue whatever we think will satisfy, moving on to the next thing the minute we realize it won't. Other times, our discontent takes the form of anxiously shielding ourselves from any and all suspected threats.

Ironically, sometimes it takes experiencing what we'd feared the most in order to stumble into real joy. Having experienced much of the worst life has to offer, Paul could testify firsthand to "the secret" (v. 12) of true contentment—the mysterious reality that as we lift up to God our longings for wholeness, we experience unexplainable peace (vv. 6–7), carried ever deeper into the depths of Christ's power, beauty, and grace.

Monica La Rose

Practice Gratitude Today

When have you achieved something you thought would bring you contentment—only to realize it still didn't feel like enough? Thank God that you can be content today in His love and presence.

Strengthened in Song

PSALM 59:1, 14–17

I will sing of your strength, in the morning I will sing of your love; for you are my fortress.
Psalm 59:16

When French villagers helped Jewish refugees hide from the Nazis during World War II, some sang songs in the dense forest surrounding their town—letting the refugees know it was safe to come out from hiding. These brave townspeople of Le Chambon-sur-Lignon had answered the call of local pastor André Trocmé and his wife, Magda, to offer wartime refuge to Jews on their windswept plateau known as La Montagne Protestante ("The Protestant Mountain"). Their musical signal became just one feature of the villagers' bravery that helped save up to three thousand Jews from almost certain death.

In another dangerous time, David sang when his enemy Saul sent nighttime assassins to his house. His use of music wasn't a signal; rather, it was his song of gratitude to God, his refuge. David rejoiced, "I will sing of your strength, in the morning I will sing of your love; for you are my fortress, my refuge in times of trouble" (Psalm 59:16).

Such singing isn't "whistling in the dark" during danger. Instead, David's singing conveyed his trust in almighty God. "You, God, are my fortress, my God on whom I can rely" (v. 17).

David's praise and the villagers' singing in Le Chambon-sur-Lignon offer an invitation to bless God today with our singing, making melody to Him despite the worries of life. His loving presence will respond, strengthening our hearts. *Patricia Raybon*

Practice Gratitude Today

What difficulty, challenge, or danger do you face today? Amid that circumstance, choose to sing or listen to a recording of a favorite worship song or hymn. Thank God for his ever-present faithfulness.

A Good Daddy

PSALM 63

On my bed I remember you; I think of you
through the watches of the night.
Psalm 63:6

When our son, Xavier, was younger, business trips often pulled my husband away from home. Though his father called often, there were rough nights when the calls alone didn't comfort Xavier. To help soothe our son when he felt he needed his dad, I'd pull out our photo albums as he prepared for bedtime. I'd point out the images that showed them spending time together and ask, "Do you remember this?"

Memory after memory encouraged our son, who often said, "I have a good daddy."

I understood Xavier's need to be reminded of his father's love when he couldn't see him. Whenever I'm going through tough or lonely times, I too long to know I'm loved, especially by my heavenly Father.

David proclaimed his deep yearning for God as he hid from his enemies in the desert (Psalm 63:1). Remembering his personal encounters with God's limitless power and satisfying love led him to praise (vv. 2–5). Through his most difficult nights, David could still rejoice in his dependable Father's loving care (vv. 6–8).

During our dark times, when we feel as if God's not there for us, we need reminders of who God is and how He's demonstrated His love. Reflecting on our personal experiences with Him, as well as His actions recorded in Scripture, can affirm the countless ways our good Abba Father loves us. *Xochitl Dixon*

Practice Gratitude Today

When was a time you experienced God's loving care in the past? Thank Him that even when it feels like He isn't with you, God is a good, present, and loving Father.

A Blessing Bowl

ROMANS 1:1–10

I thank my God every time I remember you.
Philippians 1:3

The familiar ping of an arriving email caught my attention while I wrote at my computer. Usually I try to resist the temptation to check every email but the subject line was too enticing: "You are a blessing."

Eagerly, I opened it to discover a faraway friend telling me she was praying for my family. Each week, she displays one Christmas card photo in her kitchen table "blessing bowl" and prays for that family. She wrote, "I thank my God every time I remember you" (Philippians 1:3), and then highlighted our efforts to share God's love with others—our "partnership in the gospel" (v. 5).

Through my friend's intentional gesture, the apostle Paul's words to the Philippians came trickling into my inbox, creating the same joy in my heart I suspect readers received from his first-century thank-you note. It seems Paul made it a habit to speak his gratitude to those who worked alongside him. A similar phrase opens many of his letters: "I thank my God through Jesus Christ for all of you, because your faith is being reported all over the world" (Romans 1:8).

In the first century, Paul blessed his co-laborers with a thank-you note of prayerfulness. In the twenty-first century, my friend used a blessing bowl to bring joy into my day. How might we thank those who serve in the mission of God with us today? *Elisa Morgan*

Practice Gratitude Today

Who are you grateful for today? Take time to thank them, whether in person or by email or text.

Two Portraits

JOHN 16:19–24

Now is your time of grief, but I will see you again and you will rejoice, and no one will take away your joy.
John 16:22

Clutching two framed photographs, the proud grandmother showed them to friends in the church foyer. The first picture was of her daughter back in her homeland of Burundi. The second was of her grandson, born recently to that daughter. But the daughter wasn't holding her newborn. She had died giving birth to him.

A friend approached and looked at the pictures. Reflexively, she reached up and held that dear grandmother's face in her hands. All she could say through her own tears was, "I know. I know."

And she did know. Two months earlier she had buried a son.

There's something special about the comfort of others who have experienced our pain. They know. Just before Jesus's arrest, He warned His disciples, "You will weep and mourn while the world rejoices." But in the next breath He comforted them: "You will grieve, but your grief will turn to joy" (John 16:20). In mere hours, the disciples would be devastated by Jesus's arrest and crucifixion. But their crushing grief soon turned to a joy they could not have imagined when they saw Him alive again.

Isaiah prophesied of the Messiah, "Surely he took up our pain and bore our suffering" (Isaiah 53:4). We have a Savior who doesn't merely know about our pain; He lived it. He knows. He cares. One day our grief will be turned into joy. *Tim Gustafson*

Practice Gratitude Today

What are you grieving today? Take your pain to Jesus in prayer, thanking Him that He experienced and understands the suffering of this world.

Human Race

MARK 6:7–13, 30–32

He said to them, "Come with me by yourselves
to a quiet place and get some rest."
Mark 6:31

The alarm clock goes off. Too early, it seems. But you have a long day ahead. You have work to do, appointments to keep, people to care for, or all this and more. Well, you are not alone. Each day, many of us rush from one matter to another. As someone has wittily suggested, "That's why we are called the human race."

When the apostles returned from their first mission trip, they had a lot to report. But Mark did not record Jesus's evaluation of the disciples' work; rather, Mark focused on His concern that they rest awhile. Jesus said, "Come with me by yourselves to a quiet place and get some rest" (6:31).

Ultimately, we find true rest through recognizing the presence of God and trusting Him. While we take our responsibilities seriously, we also recognize that we can relax our grip on our work and careers, our families and ministry, and give them over to God in faith. We can take time each day to tune out the distractions, put away the tense restlessness, and reflect in gratitude on the wonder of God's love and faithfulness.

So feel free to stop and take a breath. Get some real rest.

Poh Fang Chia

Practice Gratitude Today

Make time today to rest—even if you don't feel like there's any room in your schedule. As you rest, thank God that He is in control of everything so you don't have to be.

Gratitude on Earth Day

GENESIS 2:4–10, 15

The LORD God took the man and put him in the Garden of Eden to work it and take care of it.
Genesis 2:15

Earth Day is an annual event observed on April 22. In recent years, more than one billion people in about two hundred countries have taken part in educational and service activities. Each year, Earth Day is a reminder of the importance of caring for our amazing planet. But the mandate to care for the environment is far older than this annual event—it goes all the way back to creation.

In Genesis, we learn that God created the entire universe and formed the earth as a place for humans to dwell. Not only did He fashion the mountain peaks and lush plains, God also created the garden of Eden, a beautiful place providing food, shelter, and beauty for its inhabitants (Genesis 2:8–9).

After breathing life into His most important creation, humans, God placed them in this garden (vv. 8, 22) and gave them the responsibility "to work it and take care of it" (v. 15). After Adam and Eve were expelled from the garden, caring for God's creation became more difficult (3:17–19), but to this day God Himself cares for our planet and its creatures (Psalm 65:9–13) and asks us to do the same (Proverbs 12:10).

Whether we live in crowded cities or rural areas, we all have ways we can care for the areas God has entrusted to us. And as we tend the earth, may it be an act of gratitude to Him for this beautiful planet.

Lisa M. Samra

Practice Gratitude Today

What is one thing you can do today to care for the plants, animals, air, water, or soil around you? As you care for the bit of earth where you live, thank God for giving you a beautiful planet to call home.

Etch A Sketch Forgiveness

PSALM 103:7–13

As far as the east is from the west, so far has he removed our transgressions from us.
Psalm 103:12

The little red rectangular box was magical. As a kid, I could play with it for hours. When I turned one knob on the box, I created a horizontal line on its screen. Turn the other knob and voilà—a vertical line. When I turned the knobs together, I could make diagonal lines, circles, and creative designs. But the real magic came when I turned my Etch A Sketch toy upside down, shook it a little, and turned it right side up. A blank screen appeared, offering me the opportunity to create a new design.

God's forgiveness works much like that Etch A Sketch. He wipes away our sins, creating a clean canvas for us. Even if we remember wrongs we committed, God chooses to forgive and forget. He's wiped them out and doesn't hold our sins against us. He doesn't treat us according to our sinful actions (Psalm 103:10) but extends grace through forgiveness. We have a clean slate—a new life awaiting us when we seek God's forgiveness. We can be rid of guilt and shame because of His amazing gift to us.

The psalmist reminds us that our sins have been separated from us as far as the east is separated from the west (v. 12). That's as far away as you can get! In God's eyes, our sins no longer cling to us like a scarlet letter or a bad drawing. That's reason to rejoice and to thank God for His amazing grace and mercy.

Katara Patton

Practice Gratitude Today

Think of a recent sin you regret, or a sin whose consequences you still experience or think about. Thank God that He has forgiven you for your sins and removed them from you as far as the east is from the west.

Quiet Awe

PSALM 104:10–24

How many are your works, LORD! In wisdom you made them all; the earth is full of your creatures.
Psalm 104:24

My life often feels frenzied and hectic. I hurry from one appointment to the next, returning phone calls and checking items off my seemingly infinite to-do list while on my way. Out of sheer exhaustion one Sunday, I collapsed into the hammock in our backyard. My phone was inside, as were my children and husband. At first I planned to sit for just a moment or two, but in the undistracted stillness, I began to notice things that invited me to linger longer. I could hear the creak of the hammock swinging gently, the buzz of a bee in the nearby lavender, and the flap of a bird's wings overhead. The sky was a brilliant blue, and the clouds moved on the wind.

I found myself moved to tears in response to all God had made. When I slowed long enough to take in the many wonderful things within my eyesight and earshot, I was stirred to worship in gratitude for God's creative power. The writer of Psalm 104 was equally humbled by the work of God's hands, noting "you fill the earth with the fruit of your labor" (v. 13 NLT).

In the midst of a harried life, a quiet moment can remind us of God's creative might. He surrounds us with evidence of His power and tenderness; He made both the high mountains and branches for birds. "In wisdom [He] made them all" (v. 24). *Kirsten Holmberg*

Practice Gratitude Today

Spend a few minutes sitting still and observing the world around you, preferably outside. Thank God for the power and creativity evident in the beauty of His creation.

Followed by God's Goodness

PSALM 23

Surely your goodness and love will follow
me all the days of my life.
Psalm 23:6

At my first job during my high school years, I worked at a women's clothing store where a female security guard dressed as a shopper followed women she thought might steal the merchandise. Certain people fit profiles of those the store owners thought were suspicious. Others not considered a threat were left alone. I've been profiled in stores myself and followed, an interesting experience since I still recognize the tactic.

In sharp contrast, David declared he was followed by a divine blessing—God's goodness and mercy. These two gifts always stay close, following him not with suspicion but real love. The "twin guardian angels," as evangelist Charles Spurgeon described the pair, follow believers closely during both bleak days and bright. "The dreary days of winter as well as the bright days of summer. Goodness supplies our needs, and mercy blots out our sins."

As a onetime shepherd, David understood this intentional pairing of goodness and mercy as they're provided by God. Other things can follow believers—fear, worry, temptation, doubts. But "surely," David declares with undoubting certainty, God's kind goodness and loving mercy follow us always.

As David rejoiced, "Surely your goodness and love will follow me all the days of my life, and I will dwell in the house of the Lord forever" (Psalm 23:6). What an amazing gift to follow us home!

Patricia Raybon

Practice Gratitude Today

How have God's goodness and mercy followed you in the past? Thank Him that no matter your current anxieties, doubts, or temptations, surely His love is with you.

Community Memory

LUKE 22:14–23

He took bread, gave thanks and broke it, and gave it to them, saying, "This is my body given for you."
Luke 22:19

In his book *Restless Faith*, theologian Richard Mouw talks about the importance of remembering the lessons of the past. He quotes sociologist Robert Bellah, who said that "healthy nations must be 'communities of memory.'" Bellah extended that principle to other societal bonds such as families. Remembering is an important part of living in community.

The Scriptures teach the value of community memory as well. The Israelites were given the Passover feast to remind them of what God had done to rescue them from slavery in Egypt (Exodus 12:1–30). Still today, Jewish people around the world revisit that rich community memory every spring.

Passover holds great meaning for followers of Christ too, for Passover has always pointed to the work of the Messiah on the cross. It was during Passover, on the night before the cross, that Jesus established His own memorial table. Luke 22:19 records, "He took bread, gave thanks and broke it, and gave it to them, saying, 'This is my body given for you; do this in remembrance of me.'"

Every time we gather at the Lord's Table to celebrate Communion, we remember that Christ rescued us from slavery to sin and provided us with eternal life. May the rescuing love of Jesus remind us that His cross is worth remembering—together. *Bill Crowder*

Practice Gratitude Today

Be part of a community of memory today. Whether in person or over text, tell a fellow Christian about a time God provided for you in the past, and ask them to tell you how God has provided for them.

Jesus Our Rescuer

MATTHEW 1:18–25

You are to give him the name Jesus, because
he will save his people from their sins.
Matthew 1:21

What began as a normal cable-car ride across a Pakistani valley turned into a frightful ordeal. Shortly after the ride began, two supporting cables snapped, leaving eight passengers—including schoolchildren—suspended hundreds of feet in the air. The situation sparked an arduous twelve-hour rescue operation by the Pakistani military, who used zip lines, helicopters, and more to rescue the passengers.

Those well-trained rescuers are to be commended, but their work pales in comparison to the eternal work of Jesus, whose mission was to save and rescue us from sin and death. Prior to Christ's birth, an angel instructed Joseph to take Mary home because her pregnancy was from "the Holy Spirit" (Matthew 1:18, 20). Joseph was also told to name his son Jesus, because he would "save his people from their sins" (v. 21). Yet, while this name was common in the first century, only this child was qualified to be the Savior (Luke 2:30–32). Christ came at the right time to seal and secure the eternal salvation of all who repent and believe in Him.

We were all trapped in the cable car of sin and death, suspended over the valley of eternal separation from God. But in His love and grace, Jesus came to rescue us and bring us safely home to our heavenly Father. Praise Him!

Marvin Williams

Practice Gratitude Today

Reflect on how Jesus's life, death, and resurrection have transformed your life—past, present, and future. In prayer, praise Him for His love and grace.

An Open, Generous Heart

1 TIMOTHY 6:17–19

Be generous and willing to share.
1 Timothy 6:18

After Vicki's old car broke down with no option for repair, she started scraping together money for another vehicle. Chris, a frequent customer of the restaurant where Vicki works at the drive-through window, one day heard her mention she needed a car. "I couldn't stop thinking about it," Chris said. "I [had] to do something." So he bought his son's used car (his son had just put it up for sale), shined it up, and handed Vicki the keys. Vicki was shocked. "Who . . . does that?" she said in amazement and gratitude.

The Scriptures call us to live with open hands, giving freely as we can—providing what's truly best for those in need. As Paul says: "Command those who are rich in this present world . . . to do good, to be rich in good deeds" (1 Timothy 6:17–18). We don't merely perform a benevolent act here or there, but rather live out a cheerful spirit of giving. Bigheartedness is our normal way of life. "Be generous and willing to share," we're told (v. 18).

As we live with an open, generous heart, we don't need to fear running out of what we need. Rather, the Bible tells us that in our compassionate generosity, we're taking "hold of the life that is truly life" (v. 19). With God, genuine living means loosening our grip on what we have and giving to others freely.

Winn Collier

Practice Gratitude Today

How can you be generous to others today? As you give compassionately and freely, thank God that He has freely given you everything you have.

He Will Fight for You

PROVERBS 21:21–31

The horse is made ready for the day of battle,
but victory rests with the LORD.
Proverbs 21:31

The wounded horse was named Drummer Boy, one of 112 mounts carrying British soldiers into battle during the famed Charge of the Light Brigade. The animal showed such bravery and stamina that his assigned commander, Lieutenant Colonel de Salis, decided his horse deserved a medal as much as his valiant men. This was done even though their military action against enemy forces failed. Yet the cavalry's valor, matched by the courage of their horses, established the clash as one of Britain's greatest military moments, still celebrated today.

The confrontation, however, shows the wisdom of an ancient Bible proverb: "The horse is made ready for the day of battle, but victory rests with the LORD" (Proverbs 21:31). Scripture affirms this principle clearly. "For the LORD your God is the one who goes with you to fight for you against your enemies to give you victory" (Deuteronomy 20:4). Indeed, even against the sting of death, wrote the apostle Paul, "Thanks be to God! He gives us the victory through our Lord Jesus Christ" (1 Corinthians 15:57).

Knowing this, our task still is to be prepared for life's tough tests. To build a ministry, we study, work, and pray. To create beautiful art, we master a skill. To conquer a mountain, we secure our tools and build our strength. Then prepared, we're more than conquerors through Christ's strong love.

Patricia Raybon

Practice Gratitude Today

What enemy, task, or test do you face today? How can you prepare yourself for this challenge? Thank God that in every struggle, we are more than conquerors through His love and strength.

Begin Where You Are

PSALM 136:1–9

The heavens declare the glory of God; the skies proclaim the work of his hands.
Psalm 19:1

I came across a solitary flower growing in a meadow—a tiny purple blossom "wasting its sweetness in the desert air," to borrow from the poet Thomas Gray's wonderful line. I'm sure no one had seen this particular flower before, and perhaps no one would see it again. *Why this beauty in this place?* I thought.

Nature is never wasted. It daily displays the truth, goodness, and beauty of the One who brought it into being. Every day nature offers a new and fresh declaration of God's glory. Do I see Him through that beauty, or do I merely glance at it and shrug it off in indifference?

All nature declares the beauty of the One who made it. Our response can be worship, adoration, and thanksgiving—for the radiance of a cornflower, the splendor of a morning sunrise, the symmetry of a tree.

C. S. Lewis describes a walk in the forest on a hot summer day. He had just asked his friend how best to cultivate a heart of thankfulness toward God. His hiking companion turned to a nearby brook, splashed his face and hands in a little waterfall, and asked, "Why not begin with this?" Lewis said he learned a great principle in that moment: "Begin where you are."

A trickling waterfall, the wind in the willows, a baby robin, the blue sky, a tiny flower. Why not begin your thankfulness with this?

David Roper

Practice Gratitude Today

What part of God's creation do you see every day but tend to overlook? Perhaps it's weeds growing through the sidewalk, a family pet, or your own hands. Thank God for everyday displays of His glory.

Deal, or No Deal

LUKE 15:11–24

I am no longer worthy to be called your son;
make me like one of your hired servants.
Luke 15:19

If you're like me, you love a good deal. Not just bargain shopping, but when you manage to cut a great deal for yourself without giving anything up in return. If you can identify with these kinds of deals, you'll understand the prodigal son's scheme when he decided to return home.

There were three kinds of servants in those days: day workers who were paid on a day-to-day basis, hired servants who worked long hours on the estate but lived in town with their independence intact, and bond servants who lived on the estate and gave all of themselves to serving the family.

When the prodigal son hit rock bottom, it's interesting that his planned apology involved asking if he could be like a hired servant. Why not a grateful bond servant? Some commentators suggest that perhaps he was trying to negotiate a deal—a way to get a paycheck and keep his independence as well.

Often we approach God and essentially say, "I'll serve You—but You can't take away my freedom." It may seem like a good deal at the time, but God's deal is so much better. Just like the boy's father, His arms are ready and willing to receive repentant sinners as part of His family. There could be no better deal and no better way to serve Him!

Joe Stowell

Practice Gratitude Today

Where do you tend to believe that you know better than God how He should relate to you? Talk with Him about it, then thank Him that you are part of His family.

Give Thanks

1 THESSALONIANS 5:16–19

Give thanks in all circumstances; for this is
God's will for you in Christ Jesus.
1 Thessalonians 5:18

In Lansing, Michigan, during the winter, we don't get many sunny days. But last year God blessed us with one of those beautiful days, and it seemed that almost everyone was thanking God, except me. As I left my office, a man said, "What a wonderful day we're having. This is a gift from God!" To which I replied, "Yes, but we're getting snow later this week." What ingratitude!

In his letters, the apostle Paul helped his readers to develop a theology of gratitude. He wrote about thanksgiving more often than any other New Testament author. From the twenty-three times Paul used the word, we learn a few lessons about thanksgiving.

Thanksgiving was always directed toward God and never toward people. People are gifts from God, and Paul thanked God for their growth, love, and faith (1 Corinthians 1:4; 1 Thessalonians 1:2).

Thanksgiving is given through Jesus for everything (Colossians 3:15, 17). Paul believed followers of Jesus could be thankful for everything because God is sovereign, and He is working things out for the believers' good (1 Thessalonians 5:18).

May we intentionally be aware of God's gifts all around us and respond with gratitude. In response to God's gifts, it's natural to say, "Thank You, Lord."

Marvin Williams

Practice Gratitude Today

Some of God's greatest gifts are people. Who are the people you are most grateful are in your life? Thank God for the ways they are a blessing to you.

Abide with Me

HEBREWS 13:1–8

Keep your lives free from the love of money and be content with what you have, because God has said, "Never will I leave you; never will I forsake you."
Hebrews 13:5

One of the highlights of English football (soccer) each year is the final match of the annual FA Cup Final. For more than a hundred years, the day has been marked by excitement, festivity, and competition. But what fascinates me is how the game begins. It starts with the singing of the traditional hymn "Abide with Me."

At first that struck me as odd. What does that hymn have to do with football? As I thought about it, though, I realized that for the follower of Christ it has everything to do with sports, shopping, working, going to school, or anything else we do. Since there is no corner of our lives that should not be affected by the presence of God, the longing that He abide with us is actually the most reasonable thing we could desire. Of course, the presence of our heavenly Father is not something we need to plead for—it is promised to us. In Hebrews 13:5, we read, "God has said, 'Never will I leave you; never will I forsake you.'"

Not only is God's presence the key to our contentment, but it is also the promise that can give us wisdom, peace, comfort, and strength—no matter where we are or what we are doing. *Bill Crowder*

Practice Gratitude Today

Listen to a favorite recording of "Abide with Me" or look up the lyrics. Pray through the words, thanking God that He is always with you.

Why Me, God?

PSALM 13

How long, LORD? Will you forget me forever?
Psalm 13:1

Jim has been battling a motor neuron disease for more than a year. The neurons in his muscles are breaking down, and his muscles are wasting away. He's lost his fine-motor skills and is losing his ability to control his limbs. He can no longer button his shirt or tie his shoelaces, and using a pair of chopsticks has become impossible. Jim struggles with his situation and asks, *Why is God allowing this to happen? Why me?*

He's in good company with many other believers in Jesus who have brought their questions to God. In Psalm 13, David cries out, "How long, LORD? Will you forget me forever? How long will you hide your face from me? How long must I wrestle with my thoughts and day after day have sorrow in my heart?" (vv. 1–2).

We too can take our confusion and questions to God. He understands when we cry out "How long?" and "Why?" His ultimate answer is given to us in Jesus and His triumph over sin and death.

As we look at the cross and the empty tomb, we gain confidence to trust in God's "unfailing love" (v. 5) and rejoice in His salvation. Even in the darkest nights, we can "sing the LORD's praise, for he has been good to [us]" (v. 6). Through our faith in Christ, He's forgiven our sins, adopted us as His children, and is accomplishing His eternal good purpose in our lives.

Poh Fang Chia

Practice Gratitude Today

In prayer, honestly share your frustration, grief, or anguish with God. When you are ready, conclude by thanking Him for making you His in Christ.

God's Great Creation

PSALM 104:1–6, 10–23

The birds of the sky nest by the waters;
they sing among the branches.
Psalm 104:12

On a recent visit with some of our grandchildren, we enjoyed watching a webcam that focused on an eagle family in Florida. Every day we checked in on the mom, the dad, and the baby as they went about their daily routine in their nest high off the ground. Each day the parent birds kept a constant, protective vigil over the eaglet, bringing it fish from a nearby river for nourishment.

This little eagle family depicts one image the psalmist gave of God's magnificent creation in Psalm 104, which offers us an array of creation images, of scenes from the work of God's creative hand.

We see the majesty of God's creation in the sky, clouds, and wind (vv. 2–4).

We experience the creation of the earth itself—oceans, mountains, valleys (vv. 5–9).

We enjoy the glory of God's gift of land animals, birds, and crops (vv. 10–18).

We marvel at the cycles God created in our world—morning and night, darkness and light, work and rest (vv. 19–23).

What a glorious world God has fashioned with His hands for our enjoyment—and for His glory! "Praise the LORD, my soul" (v. 1). Each one of us can say "thank You" to God for all He has given us to appreciate and enjoy. *Dave Branon*

Practice Gratitude Today

Spend a few minutes enjoying an aspect of God's creation: the sky, land, water, animals, plants, or natural cycles of time. Thank God for giving you a wonderous creation to live in.

Just Enough

PROVERBS 30:7–9

Give me neither poverty nor riches, but
give me only my daily bread.
Proverbs 30:8

In the movie *Fiddler on the Roof,* the character Tevye talks honestly with God about His economics: "You made many, many poor people. I realize, of course, that it's no shame to be poor. But it's no great honor either! So, what would have been so terrible if I had a small fortune! . . . Would it have spoiled some vast, eternal plan—if I were a wealthy man?"

Many centuries before playwright Joseph Stein placed these honest words on Tevye's tongue, Agur lifted an equally honest but somewhat different prayer to God in the book of Proverbs. Agur asked God to give him neither poverty nor wealth—just his "daily bread" (Proverbs 30:8). He knew that having "too much" could make him proud and transform him into a practical atheist—denying the character of God. In addition, he asked God to not let him "become poor" because it might cause him to dishonor God's name by stealing from others (v. 9). Agur recognized God as his sole provider, and he asked Him for "just enough" to satisfy his daily needs. His prayer revealed a pursuit of God and the contentment that's found in Him alone.

May we have Agur's attitude, recognizing God as the provider of all we have. And as we pursue financial stewardship that honors His name, let's live in contentment before Him—the One who provides not only just enough but more than enough. *Marvin Williams*

Practice Gratitude Today

Make a list of things you have been able to spend money on in the past days or weeks, especially things you consider daily necessities. Thank God for what He has provided.

Forever Love

PSALM 136:1–9

And so we know and rely on the love God has for us. God is love.
1 John 4:16

Years ago, my four-year-old son gave me a framed wooden heart mounted on a metal plate with the word *forever* painted in its center. "I love you forever, Mommy," he said.

I thanked him with a hug. "I love you more."

That priceless gift still assures me of my son's never-ending love. On tough days, God uses that sweet present to comfort and encourage me as He affirms that I'm deeply loved.

The frame also reminds me of the gift of God's everlasting love, as expressed throughout His Word and confirmed by His Spirit. We can trust God's unchanging goodness and sing grateful praises that confirm His enduring love, as the psalmist does (Psalm 136:1). We can exalt the Lord as greater than and above all (vv. 2–3) as we reflect on His endless wonders and unlimited understanding (vv. 4–5). The God who loves us forever is the conscious and caring Maker of the heavens and earth, who maintains control of time itself (vv. 6–9).

We can rejoice because the everlasting love the psalmist sang about is the same continuing love our all-powerful Creator and Sustainer pours into the lives of His children today. No matter what we're facing, the One who made us and remains with us strengthens us by asserting that He loves us unconditionally and completely. Thank You, God, for the countless reminders of Your endless and life-transforming love!

Xochitl Dixon

Practice Gratitude Today

What reminds you of God's never-ending love? Perhaps it's a Bible passage, song, aspect of creation, or favorite memory. Spend a few minutes with that reminder, thanking God for who He is.

The Miracle of White Snow

ISAIAH 1:15–20

Though your sins are like scarlet, they shall be as white as snow.
Isaiah 1:18

In the seventeenth century, Sir Isaac Newton used a prism to study how light helps us see different colors. He found that when light passes through an object, the object appears to possess a specific color. While a single ice crystal looks translucent, snow is made up of many ice crystals smashed together. When light passes through all of the crystals, snow appears to be white.

The Bible mentions something else that has a certain color—sin. Through the prophet Isaiah, God confronted the sins of the people of Judah and described their sin as "like scarlet" and as "red as crimson." But God promised they would "be as white as snow" (Isaiah 1:18). How? Judah needed to turn away from wrongdoing and seek God's forgiveness.

Thanks to Jesus, we have permanent access to God's forgiveness. Jesus called Himself "the light of the world" and said whoever follows Him "will never walk in darkness, but will have the light of life" (John 8:12). When we confess our sins, God forgives us and we're seen through the light of Christ's sacrifice on the cross. This means that God sees us as He sees Jesus—blameless.

We don't have to wallow in the guilt and shame of what we've done wrong. Instead, we can hold on to the truth of God's forgiveness, which makes us "white as snow." *Linda Washington*

Practice Gratitude Today

Have you continued to punish yourself for a sin, mistake, or unhealthy pattern that you've confessed to God? Talk with Him about it, thanking Him that He sees you as He sees Jesus.

Thankful Hearts

LUKE 17:11–19

Has no one returned to give praise to God except this foreigner?
Luke 17:18

Hansle Parchment was in a predicament. He caught the bus to the wrong place for his semifinal in the Tokyo Olympics and was left stranded with little hope of getting to the stadium on time. But thankfully he met Trijana Stojkovic, a volunteer helping out at the games. She gave him some money to take a taxi. Parchment made it to the semifinal on time and eventually clinched the gold medal in the 110-meter hurdle. Later, he went back to find Stojkovic and thanked her for her kindness.

In Luke 17 we read of the Samaritan leper who came back to thank Jesus for healing him (vv. 15–16). Jesus had entered a village where He met ten lepers. All of them asked Jesus for healing, and all of them experienced His grace and power. Ten were happy that they'd been healed, but only one returned to express his gratitude. He "came back, praising God in a loud voice. He threw himself at Jesus' feet and thanked him" (vv. 15–16).

Every day, we experience God's blessings in multiple ways. It could be as dramatic as an answered prayer to an extended time of suffering or receiving timely help from a stranger. Sometimes, His blessings come in ordinary ways too, such as good weather to accomplish an outdoor task. Like the Samaritan leper, let's remember to thank God for His kindness toward us. *Poh Fang Chia*

Practice Gratitude Today

Name one small kindness and one great kindness God has shown you recently. Thank Him for the big and little blessings in life.

God Uses Our Stories

PSALM 107:1–9

Let the redeemed of the Lord tell their story.
Psalm 107:2

I opened the memory box and pulled out a small silver lapel pin, the exact size and shape of a ten-week unborn baby's feet. Caressing the ten tiny toes, I remembered the loss of my first pregnancy and those who said I was "lucky" I wasn't "that far along." I grieved, knowing that my baby's feet were as real as the heart that once beat inside my womb. I thanked God for freeing me from depression and using my story to comfort others who were grieving after losing a child. More than two decades after my miscarriage, my husband and I named the child we lost Kai, which in some languages means "rejoice." Though I still ache from my loss, I thank God for healing my heart and using my story to help others.

The writer of Psalm 107 rejoiced in God's established character and sang: "Give thanks to the Lord, for he is good; his love endures forever" (v. 1). He urged "the redeemed of the Lord" to "tell their story" (v. 2), to "give thanks to the Lord for his unfailing love and his wonderful deeds for mankind" (v. 8). He offered hope with a promise that God alone "satisfies the thirsty and fills the hungry with good things" (v. 9).

No one can escape grief or affliction, even those who've been redeemed through Christ's sacrifice on the cross. We can, however, experience God's mercy as He uses our stories to point others to His redeeming love.

Xochitl Dixon

Practice Gratitude Today

Who might need to hear one of your stories of loss, grief, and hope in Christ today? As you share a story with them, end by rejoicing in God's goodness and mercy.

Running to Our Shelter

2 SAMUEL 22:1–7

The LORD is my rock. . . . He is my
stronghold, my refuge and my savior.
2 Samuel 22:2–3

The sixth-grade basketball game was well underway. Parents and grandparents were cheering on their players, while younger brothers and sisters of the boys on the teams entertained themselves out in the school hallway. Suddenly, sirens blared and lights flashed in the gym. A fire alarm had been tripped. Soon the siblings came streaming back into the gym in panic, looking for their parents.

There was no fire; the alarm had accidentally been activated. But as I watched, I was struck by the way the children—sensing a crisis—unashamedly ran to embrace their parents. What a picture of confidence in those who could provide a sense of safety and reassurance in a time of fear!

Scripture presents a time when David experienced great fear. Saul and numerous other enemies pursued him (2 Samuel 22:1). After God delivered David to safety, the grateful man sang an eloquent song of praise about His help. He called God "my rock, my fortress and my deliverer" (v. 2). When the "cords of the grave" and "the snares of death" (v. 6) hounded him, David "called out" to God and his "cry came to [God's] ears" (v. 7). In the end, David proclaimed He "rescued me" (vv. 18, 20, 49).

In times of fear and uncertainty, we can run to our "Rock" (v. 32). As we call on God's name, He alone provides the refuge and shelter we need (vv. 2–3). *Dave Branon*

Practice Gratitude Today

What are you afraid of today? Share your fears with God in prayer. Then thank Him that He is your Rock who always hears your cries.

Look Up!

PSALM 8:3–4; REVELATION 21:22–25

There will be no night there.
Revelation 21:25

When filmmaker Wylie Overstreet showed strangers a live picture of the moon as seen through his powerful telescope, they were stunned at the up-close view, reacting with whispers and awe. To see such a glorious sight, Overstreet explained, "fills us with a sense of wonder that there's something much bigger than ourselves."

The psalmist David also marveled at God's heavenly light. "When I consider your heavens, the work of your fingers, the moon and the stars, which you have set in place, what is mankind that you are mindful of them, human beings that you care for them?" (Psalm 8:3–4).

David's humbling question puts our awe in perspective when we learn that, after God creates His new heaven and earth, we'll no longer need the moon or the sun. Instead, said John the apostle, God's shimmering glory will provide all necessary light. "The city does not need the sun or the moon to shine on it, for the glory of God gives it light, and the Lamb is its lamp. . . . There will be no night there" (Revelation 21:23, 25).

What an amazing thought! Yet we can experience His heavenly light now—simply by seeking Christ, the Light of the world. In Overstreet's view, "We should look up more often." As we do, may we see God.

Patricia Raybon

Practice Gratitude Today

Find a video or photo online of the moon or sun as seen through a telescope. Worship God for His creative power, and thank Him that He is the Light of the World.

Extra Grace Required

EPHESIANS 2:1–10

For it is by grace you have been saved,
through faith . . . not by works.
Ephesians 2:8–9

While we decorated for a special event at church, the woman in charge griped about my inexperience. After she walked away, another woman approached me. "Don't worry about her. She's what we call an EGR—Extra Grace Required."

I laughed. Soon I started using that label every time I had a conflict with someone. Years later, I sat in that same church sanctuary listening to that EGR's obituary. The pastor shared how she had served God behind the scenes and given generously to others. I asked God to forgive me for judging and gossiping about her and anyone else I'd labeled as an EGR in the past. After all, I needed extra grace as much as any other believer in Jesus.

In Ephesians 2, the apostle Paul states that all believers were "by nature deserving of wrath" (v. 3). But God gave us the gift of salvation, a gift which we did nothing to deserve, a gift we'd never be able to earn "so that no one can boast" (v. 9). No one.

As we submit to God moment by moment during this lifelong journey, the Holy Spirit works to change our character so we can reflect the character of Christ. Every believer requires extra grace. But we can be grateful that God's grace is sufficient (2 Corinthians 12:9).

Xochitl Dixon

Practice Gratitude Today

In what ways do you feel that you require extra grace from those around you? Thank God that His grace can cover all sins, setbacks, and wounds.

I'm Rich!

PSALM 119:9–16

I rejoice in following your statutes as one rejoices in great riches.
Psalm 119:14

Perhaps you've seen the TV ads where a person answers the door and finds someone who hands over a check for an enormous amount of money. Then the amazed recipient begins shouting, dancing, jumping, and hugging everyone in sight. "I won! I'm rich! I can't believe it! My problems are solved!" Striking it rich evokes a great emotional response.

In Psalm 119, the longest chapter in the Bible, we find this remarkable statement: "I rejoice in following your statutes as one rejoices in great riches" (v. 14). What a comparison! Obeying God's instructions for living can be just as exhilarating as receiving a fortune. Verse 16 repeats this refrain as the psalmist expresses grateful gladness for the Lord's commands: "I delight in your decrees; I will not neglect your word."

But what if we don't feel that way? How can delighting in God's instructions for living be just as exhilarating as receiving a fortune? It all begins with gratitude, which is both an attitude and a choice. We pay attention to what we value, so we begin by expressing our gratitude for those gifts of God that nourish our souls. We ask Him to open our eyes to see the storehouse of wisdom, knowledge, and peace He has given us in His Word.

As our love for Jesus grows each day, we indeed strike it rich!

David McCasland

Practice Gratitude Today

How do you treat your prized possessions? Where are they in your house? How do you handle them? Treat your Bible the same way today, thanking God for giving you His Word and wisdom.

The Advocate

JOHN 16:7–15

When he, the Spirit of truth, comes, he
will guide you into all the truth.
John 16:13

As I boarded the airplane to study in a city a thousand miles from home, I felt nervous and alone. But during the flight, I remembered how Jesus promised His disciples the comforting presence of the Holy Spirit.

Jesus's friends must have felt bewildered when He told them, "It is for your good that I am going away" (John 16:7). How could they who witnessed His miracles and learned from His teaching be better off without Him? But Jesus told them that if He left, then the Advocate—the Holy Spirit—would come.

Jesus, nearing His last hours before the crucifixion, shared with His disciples to help them understand His death and ascension (John 14–17, today known as the "Farewell Discourse"). Central in this conversation was the coming Holy Spirit, an advocate (14:16–17) who would be with them (15:15), teaching (v. 26), testifying (v. 26), and guiding them (16:13).

We who have accepted God's offer of new life have been given this gift of His Spirit living within us. From Him we receive so much: He convicts us of our sins and helps us to repent. He brings us comfort when we ache, strength to bear hardships, wisdom to understand God's teaching, hope and faith to believe, love to share.

We can rejoice that Jesus sent us the Advocate. *Amy Boucher Pye*

Practice Gratitude Today

In what challenge, relationship, or area of your life do you need the Holy Spirit's guidance today? Thank Him that He already lives inside of you and is always advocating for you.

Living Well

ECCLESIASTES 7:1–4

Death is the destiny of everyone; the living should take this to heart.
Ecclesiastes 7:2

Free funerals for the living. That's the service offered by an establishment in South Korea. More than twenty-five thousand people—from teenagers to retirees—have participated in mass "living funeral" services, hoping to improve their lives by considering their deaths. Officials say that "the simulated death ceremonies are meant to give the participant a truthful sense of their lives, inspire gratitude, and aid in forgiveness and reconnection among family and friends."

These words echo the wisdom given by the teacher who wrote Ecclesiastes. "Death is the destiny of everyone; the living should take this to heart" (Ecclesiastes 7:2). Death reminds us of the brevity of life and that we only have a certain amount of time to live and love well. It loosens our grip on some of God's good gifts—such as money, relationships, and pleasure—and frees us to enjoy them in the here and now as we store up "treasures in heaven, where moths and vermin do not destroy, and where thieves do not break in and steal" (Matthew 6:20).

As we remember that death may come knocking anytime, perhaps it'll compel us to not postpone that visit with our parents, delay our decision to serve God in a particular way, or compromise our time with our children for our work. With God's help, we can learn to live wisely.

Poh Fang Chia

Practice Gratitude Today

If you were to die soon, what is one thing you would be disappointed you didn't say to or do with your loved ones? Try to get to it today, thanking God for the gift of your life.

A Matter of Trust

PSALM 5

Let all who take refuge in you be glad; let them ever sing for joy. Spread your protection over them.
Psalm 5:11

After eighteen years of being confined to a wheelchair, Pascale Honore, a paraplegic woman, has taken up surfing. How?

Ty Swan, a young surfer, straps her to his back with duct tape. After getting the balance perfect, Ty paddles out into the ocean so they can catch a wave and Pascale can experience the exhilaration of surfing. This requires a tremendous amount of trust; so many things could go wrong. Yet her confidence in Ty is enough to enable her to enjoy a dream come true in spite of the danger.

Life is like that for the follower of Christ. We live in a dangerous world, filled with unpredictable challenges and unseen perils. Yet we have joy because we know Someone who is strong enough to carry us through the churning waves of life that threaten to overwhelm us. The psalmist wrote, "Let all who take refuge in you be glad; let them ever sing for joy. Spread your protection over them, that those who love your name may rejoice in you" (Psalm 5:11).

In the face of life's great dangers and challenges, we can know a joy borne out of our trust in God. His strength is more than enough!

Bill Crowder

Practice Gratitude Today

When has God brought you through an unpredictable challenge or overwhelming danger? Thank God that you can continue to trust Him with joy and confidence today.

God's Good Heart

ROMANS 5:1–11

Consider it pure joy, my brothers and sisters,
whenever you face trials of many kinds.
James 1:2

Roger had been through a lot. He had open-heart surgery to repair a leaky valve. Then, within a couple of weeks, doctors had to perform the surgery again because of complications. He had just begun to heal with physical therapy when he had a biking accident and broke his collarbone. Added to this, Roger also experienced the heartbreak of losing his mother during this time. He became very discouraged. When a friend asked him if he had seen God at work in any small ways, he confessed that he really didn't feel he had.

I appreciate Roger's honesty. Feelings of discouragement or doubt are part of my life too. In Romans, the apostle Paul says, "We can rejoice . . . when we run into problems and trials, for we know that they help us develop endurance. And endurance develops strength of character, and character strengthens our confident hope of salvation" (5:3–4 NLT). But that doesn't mean we always feel the joy. We may just need someone to sit down and listen to us pour out our hearts to them, and to talk with God. Sometimes it takes looking back on the situation before we see how our faith has grown during trials and doubts.

Knowing that God wants to use our difficulties to strengthen our faith can help us to trust His good heart for us. *Anne Cetas*

Practice Gratitude Today

Ask a trusted friend to listen to you while you honestly share your discouragement or doubt. Talk in person if possible. End your time together by thanking God that He can use your struggles for good.

Greedy Birds

2 CORINTHIANS 9:6–15

God is able to bless you abundantly, so that . . .
you will abound in every good work.
2 Corinthians 9:8

Every year when I put out the hummingbird feeder, the busy little birds start battling for position. Even though there are four places at the "table," the birds fight for whatever place one of their neighbors is using. The source of food at each place is the same—a reservoir of syrup in the bottom of the feeder. Knowing that all the feeding stations are equal, I shake my head at their greediness.

But then I wonder, *Why is it so much easier to see the greed of the birds than it is to see my own?* I often want the place at God's table that someone else has, even though I know all good things come from the same source—God—and that His supply will never run out. Since God can prepare a table for us even in the presence of our enemies (Psalm 23:5), why be concerned that someone else might have the station in life that we want?

The Lord is able to give us "all things at all times" so that we will "abound in every good work" (2 Corinthians 9:8). When we recognize the importance of our work as ministers of the grace of God (1 Peter 4:10), we'll stop fighting to take over someone else's position and be grateful for the place God has given us to serve others on His behalf.

Julie Ackerman Link

Practice Gratitude Today

Whose position, role, status, or opportunity do you envy? Talk with God about it. Thank Him for inviting you to His table as His beloved child and giving you the good things you have.

Let Us Praise!

PSALM 67

May the nations be glad and sing for joy.
Psalm 67:4

When the alarm on Shelley's phone goes off every day at 3:16 in the afternoon, she takes a praise break. She thanks God and acknowledges His goodness. Although she communicates with God throughout the day, Shelley loves to take this break because it helps her celebrate her intimate relationship with Him.

Inspired by her joyful devotion, I decided to set a specific time each day to thank Christ for His sacrifice on the cross and to pray for those who have yet to be saved. I wonder what it would be like if all believers in Jesus stopped to praise Him in their own way and pray for others every day.

The image of a beautiful wave of worship rolling to the ends of the earth resounds in the words of Psalm 67. The psalmist pleads for God's grace, proclaiming his desire to make God's name great among all the nations (vv. 1–2). He sings, "May the peoples praise you, God; may all the peoples praise you" (v. 3). He celebrates God's sovereign rule and faithful guidance (v. 4). As a living testimony of God's great love and abundant blessings, the psalmist leads God's people into jubilant praise (vv. 5–6).

God's continued faithfulness toward His beloved children inspires us to acknowledge Him. As we do, others can join us in trusting Him, revering Him, following Him, and acclaiming Him as Lord.

Xochitl Dixon

Practice Gratitude Today

Set an alarm today for a time when you can take a praise break to thank God for who He is and what He's done.

Search and Rescue

GALATIANS 1:1–5

[Jesus] gave himself for our sins to rescue
us from the present evil age.
Galatians 1:4

Some friends went boating in the English Channel, hoping the forecast for stormy weather would change. But the winds rose, and the waves became choppy, threatening the safety of their vessel, so they radioed for help to the Royal National Lifeboat Institution (RNLI). After some tense moments, they spotted their rescuers in the distance and realized with relief they'd soon be safe. As my friend reflected gratefully afterward, "Whether or not people ignore the rules of the sea, the RNLI still comes to the rescue."

As he recounted the story, I thought about how Jesus lead God's search-and-rescue mission. He came to earth to become a man, living as one of us. Through His death and resurrection, He provided us with a rescue plan when our sin and disobedience separated us from God. This truth was emphasized by Paul when writing to the church at Galatia: "The Lord Jesus Christ . . . gave himself for our sins to rescue us from the present evil age" (Galatians 1:3–4). Paul reminded the Galatians of the gift of new life they received through Jesus's death so that they would honor God day by day.

Jesus, our rescuer, willingly died to save us from being lost. Because He did, we have life in the kingdom of God, and in gratitude we can share the life-saving news with those in our community.

Amy Boucher Pye

Practice Gratitude Today

Reflect on the sacrifices Jesus made in coming to earth as a baby, living sinlessly, keeping up a demanding public ministry, dying horrifically, and rising again to life. Thank Him for the high cost of His search-and-rescue mission.

Let's Celebrate

PSALM 150

Praise him with timbrel and dancing, praise
him with the strings and pipe.
Psalm 150:4

After Ghana's Asamoah Gyan scored a goal against Germany in the 2014 World Cup, he and his teammates did a coordinated dance step. When Germany's Miroslav Klose scored a few minutes later, he did a running front flip. "Soccer celebrations are so appealing because they reveal players' personalities, values, and passions," says Clint Mathis, who scored for the United States at the 2002 World Cup.

In Psalm 150, the psalmist invites "everything that has breath" (v. 6) to celebrate and praise the Lord in many different ways. He suggests that we use trumpets and harps, stringed instruments and pipes, cymbals and dancing. He encourages us to creatively and passionately celebrate, honor, and adore the Lord. Because the Lord is great and has performed mighty acts on behalf of His people, He is worthy of all praise. These outward expressions of praise will come from an inner wellspring overflowing with gratitude to God.

Though we may celebrate the Lord in different ways (I'm not encouraging backflips in our worship services!), our praise to God always needs to be expressive and meaningful. When we think about the Lord's character and His mighty acts toward us, we cannot help but celebrate Him through our praise and worship. *Marvin Williams*

Practice Gratitude Today

Make time today to worship God in a way that expresses your own personality, gifts, and unique experiences with God.

How Long?

PSALM 13

How long, Lord? Will you forget me forever?
How long will you hide your face from me?
Psalm 13:1

In Lewis Carroll's classic *Alice's Adventures in Wonderland*, Alice asks, "How long is forever?" The White Rabbit responds, "Sometimes, just one second."

That's how time felt when my brother David suddenly died. The days leading to his memorial dragged on, intensifying the sense of loss and grief we felt. Every second seemed to last forever.

Another David echoed this sentiment, singing, "How long, Lord? Will you forget me forever? How long will you hide your face from me? How long must I wrestle with my thoughts and day after day have sorrow in my heart? How long will my enemy triumph over me?" (Psalm 13:1–2). Four times in just two verses he asks God, "How long?" Sometimes the pains of life seem as though they will never end.

Into this heartache steps the presence and care of our heavenly Father. Like King David, we can honestly go to Him with our pain and loss, knowing that He will never leave us or forsake us (Hebrews 13:5). The psalmist discovered this as well, allowing his lament to move from a mournful minor key to a triumphant declaration: "But I trust in your unfailing love; my heart rejoices in your salvation" (Psalm 13:5).

Bill Crowder

Practice Gratitude Today

What grief, pain, or difficulty feels like it will never end? Honestly talk with God about it. When you are ready, thank Him that He never leaves you alone but is always with you in the pain.

Companions in Christ

PHILIPPIANS 1:3–8

I thank my God every time I remember you.
Philippians 1:3

The Harvard Study of Adult Development is a decades-long project that's resulted in a greater understanding of the importance of healthy relationships. The research began with a group of 268 sophomores at Harvard University in the 1930s and later expanded to, among others, 456 Boston city residents. Researchers have conducted interviews with the participants and pored over their medical records every few years. They discovered that close relationships are the biggest factor in predicting happiness and health. It turns out that if we surround ourselves with the right people, we'll likely experience a deeper sense of joy.

This appears to reflect what the apostle Paul is describing in Philippians 1. Writing from prison, Paul can't help but tell his friends that he thanks God for them every time he remembers them, praying "with joy" (v. 4). But these aren't just any friends; these are brothers and sisters in Jesus who "share in God's grace" (v. 7), partners in the gospel with Paul. Their relationship is one of sharing and mutuality—a true fellowship shaped by God's love and the gospel itself.

Yes, friends are important, but fellow companions in Christ are catalysts of a true and deep joy. The grace of God can bind us together like nothing else. And even through the darkest seasons of life, the joy that comes from that bond will last. *Glenn Packiam*

Practice Gratitude Today

Who is a fellow Christian who reflects God's joy, grace, and love to you? Thank that person today, whether in person, with a card or gift, or by text.

Thankful Despite Trials

PSALM 100

Enter his gates with thanksgiving and his courts with praise; give thanks to him and praise his name.
Psalm 100:4

I've been following and praying for a fellow writer who's been posting online about her cancer journey. She alternates between sharing updates about her physical pain and challenges and sharing prayer requests with Scripture and praises to God. It's beautiful to see her courageous smile whether she's in the hospital awaiting treatments or at home wearing a bandana because her hair is falling out. With each challenge, she never fails to encourage others to trust God during trials.

When we're going through difficulties, it may be hard to find reasons to be grateful and to praise God. However, Psalm 100 gives us reasons to rejoice and give God praise despite our circumstances. The psalmist says: "Know that the Lord is God. It is he who made us, and we are his; we are his people, the sheep of his pasture" (v. 3). He adds, "For the Lord is good and his love endures forever; his faithfulness continues through all generations" (v. 5).

Whatever our trial, we can take comfort knowing that God is near to our broken hearts (34:18). The more time we spend with God in prayer and reading the Bible, the more we'll be able to "enter his gates with thanksgiving and his courts with praise" and "give thanks to him and praise his name" (100:4). We can "shout for joy to the Lord" (v. 1) even and perhaps especially when we're in a difficult season because our God is faithful.

Nancy Gavilanes

Practice Gratitude Today

Thanks to Jesus, we can enter the "temple courts" of God's presence wherever we are (see Hebrews 10:19). Enjoy God's presence in prayer, and thank Him for a way He has been faithful to you in the past.

Acts of Gratitude

MICAH 6:1–8

What does the LORD require of you? To act justly and to love mercy and to walk humbly with your God.
Micah 6:8

Few people knew me better as a boy than Francis Allen, the pastor who led me to Jesus Christ. A fire-and-brimstone preacher in the pulpit, he was a near-perfect example of the gentleness of God's love outside of it.

Early on, Francis recognized a tendency in me to try to "buy" approval by working harder than expected and doing more than people asked. "These are good traits to give as gifts to others," he would tell me, "but you should never use them to buy acceptance and love from people—or from God."

To help me understand this, he told me to read Jesus's promise in Matthew 11:30 that His "yoke is easy"—a statement that sometimes seems too simple to be true. Then, pointing to Micah 6:6–8, he said, "Now read this and ask yourself if there are any gifts you can give God that He doesn't already have." The answer, of course, is no.

Then he went on to explain that God cannot be bought—the gift of grace is free. Since this is true, what should be our response? "To act justly and to love mercy and to walk humbly with your God" (v. 8). I learned that these were acts of gratitude—not of purchase.

Let Micah 6 be a reminder that grace is free and that faithful living is our grateful response.

Randy Kilgore

Practice Gratitude Today

How can you treat someone else with justice, mercy, or humility today? Thank God that He has already given you His grace, and that living in right relationship with others is a way for you to gratefully pass on His gift.

What God Owes Us

COLOSSIANS 1:9–14

Live a life worthy of the Lord and please him in every way.
Colossians 1:10

A story is told about a vendor who sold bagels for 50 cents each at a street corner food stand. A jogger ran past and threw a couple of quarters into the bucket but didn't take a bagel. He did the same thing every day for months. One day, as the jogger was passing by, the vendor stopped him. The jogger asked, "You probably want to know why I always put money in but never take a bagel, don't you?" "No," said the vendor. "I just wanted to tell you that the bagels have gone up to 60 cents."

Too often, as believers, we treat God with that same kind of attitude. Not only are we ungrateful for what He's given us—but we want more. Somehow we feel that God owes us good health, a comfortable life, material blessings. Of course, God doesn't owe us anything, yet He gives us everything.

G. K. Chesterton wrote, "Here dies another day during which I have had eyes, ears, hands and the great world round me; and with tomorrow begins another. Why am I allowed two?" The psalmist said, "This is the day the LORD has made. We will rejoice and be glad in it" (Psalm 118:24 NLT).

Each day, whether good or bad, is one more gift from our God. Our grateful response should be to live to please Him.

Cindy Hess Kasper

Practice Gratitude Today

Make a list of gifts God has given you today that you might otherwise take for granted. Thank Him for giving you everything that is yours.

A Fly's Reminder

ECCLESIASTES 9:4–12

Anyone who is among the living has hope.
Ecclesiastes 9:4

When I first began working in the small office I now rent, the only inhabitants were a few mopey flies. Several of them had gone the way of all flesh, and their bodies littered the floor and windowsills. I disposed of all but one, which I left in plain sight.

That fly carcass reminds me to live each day well. Death is an excellent reminder of life, and life is a gift. Solomon said, "Anyone who is among the living has hope" (Ecclesiastes 9:4). Life on earth gives us the chance to influence and enjoy the world around us. We can eat and drink happily and relish our relationships (vv. 7, 9).

We can also enjoy our work. Solomon advised, "Whatever your hand finds to do, do it with all your might" (v. 10). Whatever our vocation or job or role in life, we can still do things that matter and do them well. We can encourage people, pray, and express love with sincerity each day.

The writer of Ecclesiastes says, "Time and chance happen to them all. . . . No one knows when their hour will come" (vv. 11–12). It's impossible to know when our lives on earth will end, but gladness and purpose can be found in this day by relying on God's strength and depending on Jesus's promise of eternal life (John 6:47).

Jennifer Benson Schuldt

Practice Gratitude Today

What work lies before you today? Whether you find your work energizing or draining, pause to consider how you can do it for the glory of God. Thank Him for giving you life and work.

Join the Cry

PSALM 122:6–9

I urge . . . that petitions, prayers, intercession
and thanksgiving be made for all people.
1 Timothy 2:1

A women's prayer group in my country holds regular monthly prayer sessions for Ghana and other African countries. When asked why they pray so incessantly for the nations, their leader, Gifty Dadzie, remarked, "Look around, listen to and watch the news. Our nations are hurting: war, disaster, diseases, and violence threaten to overshadow God's love for humanity and His blessing upon us. We believe God intervenes in the affairs of nations, so we praise Him for His blessings and cry for His intervention."

The Bible reveals that God indeed intervenes in the affairs of nations (2 Chronicles 7:14). And when God intervenes, He uses ordinary people. We may not be assigned huge tasks, but we can play our part to help bring about peace and the righteousness that exalts a nation (Proverbs 14:34). We can do that through prayer. The apostle Paul wrote, "I urge, then, first of all, that petitions, prayers, intercession and thanksgiving be made for all people—for kings and all those in authority, that we may live peaceful and quiet lives in all godliness and holiness" (1 Timothy 2:1–2).

As the psalmist exhorted the ancient Israelites to "pray for the peace of Jerusalem" (Psalm 122:6), so may we pray for the peace and healing of our nations. When we pray in humility, turn from wickedness, and seek God, He hears us. *Lawrence Darmani*

Practice Gratitude Today

Pray for the peace and healing of your community, city, state or province, and nation. End by thanking God for hearing the prayers of His people.

Our Father's World

GENESIS 1:26–28

The earth is the LORD's, and everything in it, the world, and all who live in it.
Psalm 24:1

When Amanda Benavides was a sophomore at Point Loma Nazarene University in San Diego, California, she began to rethink her views on Christian stewardship of the earth. Amanda had grown up thinking that being conscious of the environment had nothing to do with her relationship with Jesus. All this changed when she was challenged to consider the Christian's role in caring for the planet—especially how that relates to reaching the most needy in the world.

Our stewardship of the beautiful world God gave us, and our care for the people in it, express our reverence for God and are grounded in two biblical principles.

First, the earth belongs to God (Psalm 24:1–2). The psalmist praised the Lord for His creation and His ownership of it. The heavens, the earth, and all that are in it are His. He created it, He is sovereign over it (93:1–2), and He cares for it (Matthew 6:26–30). Second, God delegated responsibility for the well-being of His earth to us (Genesis 1:26–28). This includes appreciation of and care for both nature (Leviticus 25:2–5, 11; Proverbs 12:10) and people (Romans 15:2).

This is our Father's world. Let's show Him how much we love Him by respecting it and caring for the people who populate it.

Marvin Williams

Practice Gratitude Today

What can you do today to care for God's creation around you and the people who live near you? Thank God for the gift of creation, and for trusting you to help Him steward His world.

Too Blessed

PSALM 107:1–8

Let them give thanks to the Lord for his unfailing love and his wonderful deeds for mankind.
Psalm 107:8

On my daily commute to and from the office, I have plenty of time for reading—bumper stickers on cars, that is. Some are surly, others clever, and still others downright distasteful. One bumper sticker I saw recently, however, gently challenged my heart about the way I often engage life. The sticker simply said, "Too blessed to complain."

I must confess that I felt convicted as I pondered those words. Too often I find myself lamenting moments in life that don't go my way rather than focusing on the wonderful gifts my heavenly Father has given me. Reading that simple message that day brought me a renewed commitment to be more actively and intentionally grateful because my God has been good to me in more ways than I could ever count.

Psalm 107 is a song that seeks to rectify thankless thinking. The psalmist (who many think was King David) makes a plea to hearts grown cold with ingratitude, repeating four times, "Let them give thanks to the Lord for his unfailing love and his wonderful deeds for mankind" (vv. 8, 15, 21, 31). Even in the worst of times, we have much to be thankful for. May we learn to thank God for His goodness to us!

Bill Crowder

Practice Gratitude Today

What do you feel like complaining about today? Talk with God about it. Then make a list of simple blessings that are yours to enjoy.

Sweet Sleep

PROVERBS 3:19–24

When you lie down, you will not be afraid;
. . . your sleep will be sweet.
Proverbs 3:24

When my friend Floss lies awake at night, she thinks about the lyrics of the hymn "My Jesus, I Love Thee." She calls it her "middle-of-the-night song" because it helps her to remember God's promises and the many reasons she loves Him.

Sleep is a necessary—but sometimes elusive—part of life. At times we may sense the voice of the Holy Spirit bringing unconfessed sin to our mind. Or we begin worrying about our job, our relationships, our finances, our health, or our children. Soon a full-scale dystopian future starts running on a loop in our brain. We think we nodded off for a bit, but when we look at the clock, it's been only moments since we last checked.

In Proverbs 3:19–24, King Solomon suggested that we can receive sleep benefits when we embrace God's wisdom, understanding, and knowledge. In fact, he claimed, "They will be life for you. . . . When you lie down, you will not be afraid; . . . your sleep will be sweet" (vv. 22, 24).

Maybe we all need a middle-of-the-night song, prayer, or Bible verse to softly whisper to shift our jumbled-up thoughts to a mind fully focused on God and His character. A clear conscience and a heart full of gratitude for God's faithfulness and love can help bring us sleep that's sweet.

Cindy Hess Kasper

Practice Gratitude Today

Before you go to bed tonight, choose a psalm, song, or prayer to read or listen to, to end your day on a note of gratitude to God for His love and faithfulness.

Hope in Grief

1 THESSALONIANS 4:13–18

Do not grieve like the rest of mankind, who have no hope.
1 Thessalonians 4:13

Louise was a lively, playful girl who brought smiles to all she met. At the age of five, she tragically succumbed to a rare disease. Her sudden passing was a shock to her parents, Day Day and Peter, and to all of us who worked with them. We grieved along with them.

Yet, Day Day and Peter have found the strength to keep going. When I asked Day Day how they were coping, she said they drew strength from focusing on where Louise was—in Jesus's loving arms. "We rejoice for our daughter whose time is up to go into eternal life," she said. "By God's grace and strength, we can navigate through the grief and continue to do what He has entrusted us to do."

Day Day's comfort is found in her confidence in the heart of God who revealed Himself in Jesus. Biblical hope is much more than mere optimism; it is an absolute certainty based on God's promise, which He will never break. In our sadness, we can cling to this powerful truth, as Paul encouraged those grieving over departed friends: "We believe that Jesus died and rose again, and so we believe that God will bring with Jesus those who have fallen asleep in him" (1 Thessalonians 4:14). May this certain hope give us strength and comfort today—even in our grief.

Leslie Koh

Practice Gratitude Today

Think of a believer in Christ who has died who you miss deeply. Thank God for the hope that you will see that person again in the life to come.

Grace-Filled Waiting

2 CORINTHIANS 4:7–18

We do not lose heart.
2 Corinthians 4:16

Roger lost his job due to his company being downsized. For months he searched, applied for jobs, prayed, asked others to pray, and trusted God. Roger's and his wife Jerrie's emotions fluctuated though. They saw God provide for them in unexpected ways and experienced His grace, but sometimes they worried that a job would never come. For fifteen long months, they waited.

Then Roger had three interviews with a company, and a week later the employment agency called and said, "Have you heard the saying, 'Sometimes clouds have a silver lining'? Well, you've got the job!" Jerrie told me later, "We wouldn't trade this hard experience for anything. It brought us closer together and closer to the Lord." Friends who had prayed rejoiced and gave thanks to God.

Paul wanted the Corinthian church to see the grace of God at work in his life, which could cause "thanksgiving to overflow to the glory of God" (2 Corinthians 4:15). His trials were so severe that he was "hard pressed on every side," "perplexed," "persecuted," and "struck down" (vv. 8–9). Yet he encouraged the people not to lose heart in troubles (v. 16) but to trust God. During our difficulties, we can be drawn nearer to God and others, as Roger and Jerrie experienced, and praise will go to the Lord for His grace. *Anne Cetas*

Practice Gratitude Today

What are you waiting for today? How can you choose to draw closer to God or loved ones, relying on and thanking them for their love and support during the wait?

Phone Zone

1 THESSALONIANS 5:16–24

Pray continually.
1 Thessalonians 5:17

One of the benefits of cell phones is that we have virtually unlimited access to others. As a result, many people talk on the phone or text even while driving—sometimes resulting in terrible car crashes. To avoid such disasters, many areas of the world have made distracted driving illegal. In the United States, highway signs have popped up to remind drivers of special cell phone zones where they can pull off the road to safely talk and text to their heart's delight.

While it is a good idea to restrict mobile phone communication for drivers, there is another kind of communication that has no restrictions: prayer. God invites us to call on Him whether we are coming, going, or sitting still. In the New Testament, Paul's words advise each person who wants to communicate with God to "pray continually" (1 Thessalonians 5:17). Paul brackets this divine open-door policy by encouraging us to "rejoice always" (v. 16) and to "give thanks in all circumstances" (v. 18). God calls us to joy and thanksgiving—expressions of faith in God through Christ that are anchored in continual prayer.

God is available for our quick cry or for a lengthy conversation. He welcomes us into a relationship with Him, a constant and endless sharing of our joys and gratitude, needs, questions, and concerns (Hebrews 4:15–16). We are always in the prayer zone. *Bill Crowder*

Practice Gratitude Today

Pray while you are in the middle of something else today—a commute, a house chore, a meeting you aren't leading. Thank God that He is always present and always listens.

Whatever Your Hand Finds to Do

ECCLESIASTES 9:4–12

Whatever your hand finds to do, do it with all your might.
Ecclesiastes 9:10

I've always wanted to learn how to play the cello. But I've never found the time to enroll in a class. Or, perhaps more accurately, I haven't made the time for it. I had thought that in heaven I could probably master that instrument. In the meantime, I wanted to focus on using my time in the particular ways God has called me to serve Him now.

Life is short, and we often feel the pressure to make the most of our time on earth before it slips away. But what does that really mean?

As King Solomon contemplated the meaning of life, he offered two recommendations. First, we're to live in the most meaningful way we can. This means fully enjoying the good things God allows us to experience in life, such as food and drink (Ecclesiastes 9:7), clothing and perfume (v. 8), marriage (v. 9), and all of God's good gifts—which might include learning how to play the cello!

His second recommendation was diligent work (v. 10). Life is full of opportunities, and there is always more work to be done. We're to take advantage of the opportunities God gives us, seeking His wisdom on how to prioritize work and play in a way that uses our abilities to serve Him.

Life is a wonderful gift from the Lord. We honor Him when we take pleasure both in His daily blessings and in meaningful service.

Poh Fang Chia

Practice Gratitude Today

Plan your day to include at least one thing you find pleasurable and one piece of work you find meaningful. While you're enjoying your play and work, thank God for the gift of life.

Sorrow and Joy

EZRA 3:8–13

No one could distinguish the sound of the shouts of joy from the sound of weeping.
Ezra 3:13

Angela's family reeled with sorrow as they experienced three bereavements in just four weeks. In one, after the sudden death of her nephew, Angela and her two sisters gathered around the kitchen table for three days, only leaving to buy an urn, get takeout, and attend the funeral. As they wept over the death of Mason, they also rejoiced over the ultrasound photos of the new life growing within their youngest sister.

In time, Angela found comfort and hope from the Old Testament book of Ezra. It describes God's people returning to Jerusalem after the Babylonians destroyed the temple and deported them from their beloved city (see Ezra 1). As they watched the temple being rebuilt, the people heard joyful praises being offered to God by the priests and Levites (3:10–11). But there was also the weeping of some of the older priests, Levites, and other leaders who remembered life before exile (v.12).

One verse especially consoled Angela: "No one could distinguish the sound of the shouts of joy from the sound of weeping, because the people made so much noise" (v. 13). She realized that even if she was drenched in deep sorrow, joy could still appear.

We too might grieve the death of a loved one or mourn a different loss. If so, we can express our cries of pain along with our moments of rejoicing to God, knowing that He hears us and gathers us in His arms.

Amy Boucher Pye

Practice Gratitude Today

Take inventory of your emotions. What has you feeling happy, sad, angry, relieved, disappointed, anxious, or excited? Thank God that He is at work amid the things you feel and experience today.

Inheritance Isn't Earned

EPHESIANS 1:3–14

He predestined us for adoption to sonship through Jesus Christ, in accordance with his pleasure and will.
Ephesians 1:5

"Thanks for dinner, Dad," I said as I set my napkin on the restaurant table. I was home on a break from college, and after being gone for a while, it felt strange to have my parents pay for me. "You're welcome, Julie," my dad replied, "but you don't have to thank me for everything all the time. I know you've been off on your own, but you're still my daughter and a part of the family." I smiled. "Thanks, Dad."

In my family, I haven't done anything to earn my parents' love or what they do for me. But my dad's comment reminds me that I haven't done anything to deserve to be a part of God's family either.

In the book of Ephesians, Paul tells his readers that God chose them "to be holy and blameless in his sight" (1:4), to stand without blemish before Him (5:25–27). But this is only possible through Jesus, in whom "we have redemption through his blood, the forgiveness of sins, in accordance with the riches of God's grace" (1:7). We don't have to earn God's grace, forgiveness, or entrance into His family. We simply accept His free gift.

When we turn our lives over to Jesus, we become children of God, which means we receive eternal life and have an inheritance waiting for us in heaven. Praise God for offering such a wonderful gift!

Julie Schwab

Practice Gratitude Today

As God's child, you are heir to everything that is God's—His Spirit, His life, His kingdom. Thank Him for something that is His that is now also yours in Christ.

Thirsty and Thankful

PSALM 42:1–5

As the deer pants for streams of water, so
my soul pants for you, my God.
Psalm 42:1

Two friends and I were checking off a bucket-list item—hiking the Grand Canyon. We wondered if we had enough water as we started our hike, and it ran out fast. We were completely out of water with still a ways to go to reach the rim. Panting, mixed with praying, set in. Then we rounded a corner and what we maintain as a miracle happened. We spotted three water bottles tucked in a cleft in the rock with a note: "Knew you'd need this. Enjoy!" We looked at each other in disbelief, whispered a thank-you to God, took a couple of much-needed sips, and then set out on the last stretch. I've never been so thirsty—and thankful—in my life.

The psalmist didn't have a Grand Canyon experience, but it's clear he knew how a deer acts when thirsty and possibly scared. The deer "pants" (Psalm 42:1), a word that brings to mind thirst and hunger, to the point where if something doesn't change, you're afraid you might die. The psalmist equates the deer's degree of thirst to his desire for God: "so my soul pants for you, my God" (v. 1).

Like much-needed water, God is our ever-present help. We pant for Him because He brings renewed strength and refreshment to our weary lives, equipping us for whatever the day's journey holds.

John Blase

Practice Gratitude Today

How can you leave a small, unexpected gift for someone else today? As you leave that gift, thank God that He has given you everything you need for today.

A Sincere Thank-You

PSALM 9:1–2, 7–10

I will give thanks to you, Lord, with all my heart;
I will tell of all your wonderful deeds.
Psalm 9:1

In preparation for Xavier's first job interview, my husband, Alan, handed our son a pack of thank-you cards for him to send out after he met with prospective employers. He then pretended to be a hiring interviewer, using his decades of experience as a manager to ask Xavier questions. After the role-playing, our son tucked several copies of his resume into a folder. He smiled when Alan reminded him about the cards. "I know," he said. "A sincere thank-you note will set me apart from all the other applicants."

When the manager called to hire Xavier, he expressed gratitude for the first handwritten thank-you card he'd received in years.

Saying thanks makes a lasting impact. The psalmists' heartfelt prayers and grateful worship were preserved in the book of Psalms. Among the 150 psalms, these two verses reflect a resounding message of thankfulness: "I will give thanks to you, Lord, with all my heart; I will tell of all your wonderful deeds. I will be glad and rejoice in you; I will sing the praises of your name, O Most High" (Psalm 9:1–2).

We will never be able to finish expressing our gratitude for all God's wonderful deeds. But we can start with a sincere thank-you through our prayers. We can nurture a lifestyle of grateful worship, praising God and acknowledging all He's done and all He promises to do.

Xochitl Dixon

Practice Gratitude Today

Write a thank-you card to God. Place it somewhere you normally display cards in your home—perhaps on your dresser, mantel, or fridge.

Attitude of Gratitude

COLOSSIANS 3:12–25

Let the peace of Christ rule in your hearts, since as members of one body you were called to peace. And be thankful.
Colossians 3:15

In my state in the United States, the winters can be brutal, with subzero temperatures and never-ending snow. One bitterly cold day, as I shoveled snow for what seemed like the thousandth time, our postman paused in his rounds to ask how I was doing. I told him that I disliked winter and was weary of all the heavy snow. I then commented that his job must be pretty rough during these extreme weather conditions. He responded, "Yeah, but at least I have a job. A lot of people don't. I'm thankful to be working."

I have to admit that I felt quite convicted by his attitude of gratitude. How easily we can lose sight of everything we have to be thankful for when the circumstances of life become unpleasant.

Paul told the followers of Christ at Colossae, "Let the peace of Christ rule in your hearts, since as members of one body you were called to peace. And be thankful" (Colossians 3:15). He wrote to the Thessalonians, "Give thanks in all circumstances; for this is God's will for you in Christ Jesus" (1 Thessalonians 5:18).

Even in our times of genuine struggle and pain, we can know God's peace and permit it to rule our hearts. And in that peace, we'll find reminders of all that we've been given in Christ. In that, we can truly be thankful.

Bill Crowder

Practice Gratitude Today

Throughout your day, look for reminders of what God has provided for you in Christ. At the end of the day, thank God for the provision you noticed.

Not Even a Nod

LUKE 17:11–19

One of them, when he saw he was healed, came back, praising God in a loud voice.
Luke 17:15

Traffic was bad and everyone was cranky on that hot afternoon. I noticed a car with two young men waiting to enter traffic from a fast-food restaurant driveway. I thought it was nice when the driver ahead of me let them in.

But when the "nice" driver ahead of me didn't get a nod or even a thank-you wave, he turned ugly. First he rolled down his window and shouted at the driver he had let in. Then he gunned his engine and raced forward as if to ram into his car, honking and yelling as he continued to vent his anger.

Who was more wrong? Did the young driver's ingratitude justify the other driver's angry response? Was he owed a thank-you?

Certainly the ten lepers Jesus healed owed gratitude to Him. How could only one return to say thank you? I'm struck by Jesus's response: "Has no one returned to give praise to God except this foreigner?" (Luke 17:18). If the King of Kings can get only a one in ten response of thanks, how can we expect more from others? Better to do our deeds to honor God and serve others than to do them to collect gratitude. May the grace of God be seen in us even when our kind acts go unappreciated.

Randy Kilgore

Practice Gratitude Today

What is something kind someone did for you that you never thanked them for? If possible, make time today to thank that person. Then thank God for His many kindnesses you are not even aware of.

Eyes in the Back of My Head

PSALM 33:6–19

From his dwelling place [God] watches all who live on earth.
Psalm 33:14

I was as mischievous as any other child in my early years and tried to hide my bad behavior to avoid getting into trouble. Yet my mother usually found out what I had done. I recall being amazed at how quickly and accurately she knew about my antics. When I marveled and asked how she knew, she always replied, "I have eyes in the back of my head." This, of course, led me to study her head whenever she'd turn her back. Were the eyes invisible or merely cloaked by her red hair? As I grew, I gave up looking for evidence of her extra pair of eyes and realized I just wasn't quite as sneaky as I had supposed. Her watchful gaze was evidence of her loving concern for her children.

As grateful as I am for my mother's attentive care (despite being occasionally disappointed I hadn't gotten away with something!), I'm even more grateful that God "sees all mankind" as He looks upon us from heaven (Psalm 33:13). He sees so much more than what we do; He sees our sadness, our delights, and our love for one another.

God sees our true character and always knows exactly what we need. With perfect vision, which even sees the inner workings of our hearts, He watches over those who love Him and put their hope in Him (v. 18). He's our attentive, loving Father. *Kirsten Holmberg*

Practice Gratitude Today

Where do you feel unseen, alone, or in need of guidance? Thank God that He always sees your heart because He is your attentive, loving Father.

God-Given Personality and Gifts

ROMANS 12:4–8

We have different gifts, according to the grace given to each of us.
Romans 12:6

Decades ago, I went to a college retreat where everyone was talking about a personality test. "I'm an ISTJ!" one said. "I'm an ENFP," another chirped. I was mystified. "I'm an ABCXYZ," I joked.

Since then, I've learned a lot about that test (the Myers-Briggs Type Indicator) and others such as DISC assessments. I find them fascinating because they can help us understand ourselves and others in helpful, revealing ways—shedding light on our preferences, strengths, and weaknesses. Provided we don't overuse them, they can be a useful tool God uses to help us grow.

Scripture doesn't offer us personality tests. But it does affirm each person's uniqueness in God's eyes (see Psalm 139:14–16; Jeremiah 1:5), and it shows us how God equips all of us with a unique personality and unique gifts to serve others in His kingdom. In Romans 12:6, Paul begins to unpack this idea when he says, "We have different gifts, according to the grace given to each of us."

Those gifts, Paul explains, are not for us alone but for the purpose of serving God's people, Christ's body (v. 5). They're an expression of His grace and goodness, working in and through all of us. They invite each of us to be a unique vessel in God's service. *Adam R. Holz*

Practice Gratitude Today

What gifts and strengths has God equipped you with, and how can you use them to serve someone else today? Thank God for the unique way He has created you.

Our Anchor of Hope

HEBREWS 6:16–20

We have this hope as an anchor for the soul, firm and secure.
Hebrews 6:19

I held up a picture of people sleeping under pieces of cardboard in a dim alley. "What do they need?" I asked my sixth-grade Sunday school class. "Food," someone said. "Money," said another. "A safe place," a boy said thoughtfully. Then one girl spoke up: "Hope."

"Hope is expecting good things to happen," she explained. I found it interesting that she talked about "expecting" good things when, due to challenges, it can be easy not to expect good things in life. The Bible nevertheless speaks of hope in a way that agrees with my student. If "faith is confidence in what we hope for" (Hebrews 11:1), we who have faith in Jesus can expect good things to happen.

What is this ultimate good that believers in Christ can hope for with confidence? "The promise of entering his rest" (4:1). For believers, God's rest includes His peace, confidence of salvation, reliance on His strength, and assurance of a future heavenly home. The guarantee of God and the salvation Jesus offers is why hope can be our anchor, holding us fast in times of need (6:18–20). The world needs hope, indeed: God's true and certain assurance that throughout good and bad times, He will have the final say and won't fail us. When we trust in Him, we know that He will make all things right for us in His time.

Karen Huang

Practice Gratitude Today

What situation in your life, in your community, or in the world seems hopeless? Thank God that He will make all things new, and ask Him how you can help build His kingdom of hope and peace today.

Whac-A-Mole

PHILIPPIANS 4:10–20

Godliness with contentment is great gain.
1 Timothy 6:6

You might know what it's like. The bills keep arriving after a medical procedure—from the anesthesiologist, the surgeon, the lab, the facility. Jason experienced this after an emergency surgery. He complained, "We owe thousands of dollars after insurance. If only we can get these bills paid, then life will be good and I'll be content! I feel like I'm playing the arcade game Whac-A-Mole"—where plastic moles pop up from their holes, and the player hits them wildly with a mallet.

Life comes at us like that at times. The apostle Paul certainly could relate. He said, "I know what it is to be in need," yet he'd "learned the secret of being content in any and every situation" (Philippians 4:12). His secret? "I can do all this through him who gives me strength" (v. 13). When I was going through a particularly discontented time, I read this on a greeting card: "If it isn't here, where is it?" That was a powerful reminder that if I'm not content here and now, what makes me think I'll be once I'm in another situation?

How do we learn to rest in Jesus? Maybe it's a matter of focus. Of enjoying and being thankful for the good. Of learning more about our faithful Father. Of growing in trust and patience. Of recognizing that life is about God and not me. Of asking Him to teach me contentment in Him.

Anne Cetas

Practice Gratitude Today

What do you feel like you need to be happy and content? Take it to God in prayer. Consider how you can intentionally enjoy a task, activity, or event you have to do today.

Who's Behind It

1 CHRONICLES 17:16–24

Every good and perfect gift is from above, coming down from the Father of the heavenly lights.
James 1:17

At a cultural show in Bandung, Indonesia, we enjoyed a wonderful orchestra performance. Before the finale, the two hundred people in the audience were each handed an angklung, a musical instrument made of bamboo. We were taught how to shake it in rhythm with the conductor's timing. Soon we thought we were performing like an orchestra; we felt so proud of how well we were doing! Then it dawned on me that we were not the ones who were good; it was the conductor who deserved the credit.

Similarly, when everything is going well in our lives, it's easy to feel proud. We're tempted to think that we are good and that it is by our abilities that we've achieved success. During such moments, we tend to forget that behind it all is our good God who prompts, prevents, provides, and protects.

David remembered that truth. "Then King David went in and sat before the Lord, and he said: 'Who am I, Lord God, and what is my family, that you have brought me this far?'" (1 Chronicles 17:16). David's heart swelled up in appreciation of God's goodness.

The next time we are tempted to take credit for the blessings we enjoy, let's pause and remember that it is the Lord who brings blessing.

Albert Lee

Practice Gratitude Today

Make a list of what is going well in your life. Where are you experiencing life-giving relationships, success, and growth? Thank God for the good gifts He has given you.

His Loving Presence

HEBREWS 13:1–6

Never will I leave you.
Hebrews 13:5

Our hearts sank when we learned that our good friend Cindy had been diagnosed with cancer. Cindy was a vibrant person whose life blessed all who crossed her path. My wife and I rejoiced when she went into remission, but a few months later her cancer returned with a vengeance. In our minds she was too young to die. Her husband told me about her last hours. When she was weak and hardly able to talk, Cindy whispered to him, "Just be with me." What she wanted more than anything in those dark moments was his loving presence.

The writer to the Hebrews comforted his readers by quoting Deuteronomy 31:6, where God told His people: "Never will I leave you; never will I forsake you" (Hebrews 13:5). In the darkest moments of life, the assurance of God's loving presence gives us confidence that we are not alone. He gives us the grace to endure, the wisdom to know He is working, and the assurance that Christ can "empathize with our weaknesses" (4:15).

Together let's embrace the blessing of His loving presence so we can confidently say, "The Lord is my helper; I will not be afraid" (13:6).

Joe Stowell

Practice Gratitude Today

Spend a few minutes enjoying God's loving presence. Consider if there is a place, music, candles, or other physical cues that will help you focus. At the end of your time, thank God for always being with you.

Thankful in All Things

1 THESSALONIANS 5:12–22

Give thanks in all circumstances.
1 Thessalonians 5:18

My daughter is allergic to peanuts. Her sensitivity is so acute that eating even the tiniest fragment of a peanut threatens her life. As a result, we scrutinize food package labels. We carry a prefilled syringe of medicine to treat allergic reactions wherever we go. And, when we eat out, we call ahead and quiz the waitstaff about the restaurant's menu items.

Despite these precautions, I still feel concerned—both for her current safety and for her future safety. This situation is not something I would naturally be thankful about. Yet, God's Word challenges: "Give thanks in all circumstances; for this is God's will for you in Christ Jesus" (1 Thessalonians 5:18). There's no getting around it. God wants us to pray with thanksgiving when the future is uncertain, when heartbreak hits, and when shortfalls come.

It's hard to be grateful in difficulties, but it's not impossible. Daniel "prayed, giving thanks" (Daniel 6:10), knowing that his life was in danger. Jonah called out "with shouts of grateful praise" (Jonah 2:9) while inside a fish! These examples, coupled with God's promise that He will work all things together for our good and His glory (Romans 8:28), can inspire us to be thankful in all things.

Jennifer Benson Schuldt

Practice Gratitude Today

What circumstance or challenge makes it hard to feel grateful today? Worship God for His goodness and love in the midst of your difficulties.

A Wise Builder

PROVERBS 14:1–3, 26–27, 33

The wise woman builds her house, but with her own hands the foolish one tears hers down.
Proverbs 14:1

Sojourner Truth, whose birth name was Isabella Baumfree, was born a slave in 1797 in Esopus, New York. Though nearly all her children were sold as slaves, she escaped to freedom in 1826 with one daughter and lived with a family who paid the money for her freedom. Instead of allowing an unjust system to keep her family apart, she took legal action to regain her small son Peter—an amazing feat for an African American woman in that day. Knowing she couldn't raise her children without God's help, she became a believer in Christ and later changed her name to Sojourner Truth to show that her life was built on the foundation of God's truth.

King Solomon, the writer of Proverbs 14, declares, "The wise woman builds her house" (v. 1). In contrast, one without wisdom "tears hers down." This building metaphor shows the wisdom God provides to those willing to listen. How does one build a house with wisdom? By saying "only what is helpful for building others up" (Ephesians 4:29; see also 1 Thessalonians 5:11). How does one tear down? Proverbs 14 gives the answer: "A fool's mouth lashes out with pride" (v. 3).

Sojourner had a "secure fortress" (v. 26) in a turbulent time, thanks to the wisdom of God. You may never have to rescue your children from an injustice. But you can build your house on the same foundation Sojourner did—the wisdom of God. *Linda Washington*

Practice Gratitude Today

Today, how can you speak constructively with God's wisdom and not destructively with pride? (Remember, truthful correction offered in love is constructive.) Thank God for the wisdom of His Word.

Wow!

ROMANS 11:33–36

Who among the gods is like you, LORD? Who is like you—majestic in holiness, awesome in glory, working wonders?
Exodus 15:11

One blustery day in June, our family, holidaying in the Canadian Rockies, went to a tourist site that was billed as a must-see. The cold wind made me reluctant to go on until I saw a group of people returning from the scenic spot. "Is it worth it?" I asked. "Definitely!" was their response. That gave us the incentive to go on. When we finally reached the spot, its beauty rendered us virtually speechless. "Wow!" was all we could manage.

Paul reached that point as he wrote about the work of God in saving Jew and Gentile in the book of Romans. Three things about God wowed him.

First, God is all-wise (11:33). His perfect plan of salvation shows that He has far better solutions to the problems of life than we are capable of devising.

Second, God is all-knowing. His knowledge is infinite. He needs no counselor (v. 34), and nothing surprises Him!

Third, God is all-sufficient (v. 35). No one can give to God what He has not first given to them. Nor can anyone ever repay Him for His goodness.

We can say with Moses, "Who is like you—majestic in holiness, awesome in glory, working wonders?" (Exodus 15:11). What a marvelous God we serve!

C. P. Hia

Practice Gratitude Today

What about who God is or what He has done wows you? Worship God for His majesty, awesome works, and everlasting love.

God Is Here

LUKE 4:16–21

He heals the brokenhearted and binds up their wounds.
Psalm 147:3

Leslie and her two daughters were about to be evicted from their home. Although Leslie believed that God could help, so far He hadn't given a clue as to how. She wondered, Where is God? As she drove to the courthouse, she prayed for God's intervention. Then she heard a song on the radio proclaiming, "God is here! Let the broken-hearted rejoice." Could this be the assurance from God that she was longing to hear?

Inside the courtroom, Leslie stood before the judge, heard his decision, and signed the legal documents, but still God had not given her an answer.

As Leslie was walking to her car, a truck pulled up beside her. "Ma'am," said the driver, "I heard your testimony inside the courtroom, and I believe God wants me to help you." And he did. Gary helped Leslie get in contact with a woman from a local church who was able to work with the parties involved to reverse the process so that she and her girls could stay in their home.

When people ask, "Where is God?" the answer is, "Right here." One way God is at work is through Christians like Gary who are continuing the work Jesus started—healing the brokenhearted and binding up their wounds (Psalm 147:3). *Julie Ackerman Link*

Practice Gratitude Today

How can you extend the love and generosity of Jesus to someone today? As you do, thank God that His Spirit works through His people—including you.

Johnny's Cap

PSALM 42

I will always have hope; I will praise you more and more.
Psalm 71:14

A story is told about a family that went on a picnic by a lake. At one point, their five-year-old son waded into the lake, stepped into deep water, and sank out of sight. None of the adults in the family knew how to swim, so they ran up and down the shore in panic while the child bobbed up and down and screamed for help. Just then, a man happened by who sized up the situation, leaped into the lake, and rescued the boy. He climbed out on the bank with the child, who was frightened but unharmed, only to hear the mother ask with irritation, "Where's Johnny's cap?"

So often we focus on small disappointments that cause us to grumble and complain rather than focusing on the wonderful things God has brought into our lives, not the least of which is His everlasting love and eternal salvation. When we complain about the small dissatisfactions of life, we're asking, in effect, "Where's Johnny's cap?"

Paul wrote, "Give thanks in all circumstances" (1 Thessalonians 5:18). We may not be thankful for everything that comes our way, but we can give thanks in everything. It may be difficult to be grateful when we lose our job or our health fails, but we can be thankful for the good that God has brought to us in this life and grateful for the life to come.

David Roper

Practice Gratitude Today

What minor loss, irritation, or setback occupies your mind today? Talk with God about it. Then put it into perspective by thanking Him for the many good things He has given you.

Sing Praise to God

1 CHRONICLES 15:29–16:11

Give praise to the Lord, proclaim his name; make known among the nations what he has done.
1 Chronicles 16:8

The heat and humidity of the Midwestern summer closed in on us all week at the discipleship conference, but on the last day we welcomed a front of cooler air. Giving thanks for the break in the weather and the amazing work God had done, hundreds joined voices to worship God. Many felt liberated to sing wholeheartedly before God, offering hearts, souls, bodies, and minds to Him. Decades later, as I think back to that day, I'm reminded of the pure wonder and joy of praising God.

King David knew how to wholeheartedly worship God. He rejoiced when the ark of the covenant, which signified God's presence, was placed in Jerusalem—by dancing, leaping, and celebrating (1 Chronicles 15:29). Even though his wife Michal observed his abandon and "despised him in her heart," David didn't let her criticism stop him from worshiping the one true God. Even if he appeared undignified, he wanted to give thanks to God for choosing him to lead the nation (see 2 Samuel 6:21–22).

David "appointed Asaph and his associates to give praise to the Lord in this manner: Give praise to the Lord, proclaim his name; make known among the nations what he has done. Sing to him, sing praise to him; tell of all his wonderful acts" (1 Chronicles 16:7–9). May we too give ourselves fully to worshiping God by pouring out our praise and adoration. *Amy Boucher Pye*

Practice Gratitude Today

Worship God wholeheartedly, with all that you are. For you this might mean music, singing, dancing, celebration, and community, or silence and solitude, time in nature, journaling, or painting.

Do I Belong?

ACTS 8:29–39

What can stand in the way of my being baptized?
Acts 8:36

Actress Sally Field finally felt what we all long for. When she won a second Academy Award in 1985, she exclaimed in her acceptance speech: "I've wanted more than anything to have your respect. The first time I didn't feel it. But this time I feel it. And I can't deny the fact that you like me—right now, you like me."

An Ethiopian eunuch was also amazed by his acceptance. As a Gentile and as a eunuch, he was denied entrance into the temple's inner courts (see Ephesians 2:11–12; Deuteronomy 23:1). Yet he yearned to be included. Philip found him returning from another unsatisfying pilgrimage to Jerusalem (Acts 8:27).

The Ethiopian man was reading Isaiah, which promised that eunuchs who "hold fast to my covenant" would receive "within my temple and its walls a memorial and . . . an everlasting name" (Isaiah 56:4–5). How could this be? Then Philip "told him the good news about Jesus," and the man responded, "Look, here is water. What can stand in the way of my being baptized?" (Acts 8:35–36).

He was asking, Am I really allowed in? Do I belong? Philip baptized him as a sign that Jesus had bulldozed every barrier (Ephesians 2:14). Jesus embraces—and unites—everyone who turns from sin and puts their trust in Him. The man "went on his way rejoicing" (Acts 8:39). He finally and fully belonged. *Mike Wittmer*

Practice Gratitude Today

Where in your life do you feel like you don't belong or aren't accepted? Thank God that, in Christ, you belong in His presence and in His family.

Heavenly Abundance

1 TIMOTHY 1:12–17

The grace of our Lord was poured out on me abundantly, along with the faith and love that are in Christ Jesus.
1 Timothy 1:14

I expected eight bananas. Instead, when I opened the grocery bags delivered to my home, I discovered twenty bananas! I quickly realized that my move to England meant I also moved from ordering groceries in pounds to requesting them in kilograms. Instead of three pounds, I had ordered three kilograms (nearly seven pounds!) of bananas.

With such an abundance, I made several batches of a favorite banana bread recipe to share the blessing with others. As I mashed up the fruit, I began thinking about the other areas of my life where I have experienced unexpected abundance—and each path led back to God.

Paul appears to have had a similar experience of reflecting on God's abundance in his life. In his first letter to Timothy, Paul paused to describe his life before Jesus, describing himself as "a persecutor and a violent man, . . . the worst of sinners" (1 Timothy 1:13, 16). Into Paul's brokenness, God lavishly poured out grace, faith, and love (v. 14). After recounting all the abundance in his life, the apostle couldn't help but express praise to God, declaring Him worthy of all "honor and glory for ever and ever" (v. 17).

Like Paul, we all received an overwhelming abundance of grace when we accepted Jesus's offer of rescue from sin (v. 15). As we pause to reflect on all the resulting blessings, we'll find ourselves joining Paul in grateful praise to our generous God. *Lisa M. Samra*

Practice Gratitude Today

Where are you experiencing God's abundance today? How can you share some of that abundance with someone else?

Better than Life

PSALM 63

Because your love is better than life, my lips will glorify you.
Psalm 63:3

After another unexpected health setback, I joined my husband and others during a retreat in the mountains. I trudged up the wooden staircase that led to the tiny church on the top of a hill. Alone in the dark, I stopped to rest on a splintered step. "Help me, Lord," I whispered as the music began. I walked slowly until I stepped into the small room. I breathed through the lingering pain, grateful that God hears us in the wilderness!

Some of the most intimate moments of worshiping God recorded in Scripture took place in the wilderness. While hiding in the Desert of Judah and most likely on the run from his son Absalom, King David sang: "You, God, are my God, earnestly I seek you; I thirst for you, my whole being longs for you" (Psalm 63:1). Having experienced God's power and glory, David deemed God's love as "better than life" (v. 3), and it was the reason he committed to a lifetime of worship—even while in the wilderness (vv. 2–6). David said, "Because you are my help, I sing in the shadow of your wings. I cling to you; your right hand upholds me" (vv. 7–8).

Like David, regardless of our circumstances or the fierceness of those standing against us, we can demonstrate confidence in God by praising Him (v. 11). Though we'll suffer, sometimes by no fault of our own, we can trust that God's love is always better than life.

Xochitl Dixon

Practice Gratitude Today

In what way are you in the wilderness today? Pause to thank God that His love is always with you, and that His love is better than life.

A Cultivated Life in Christ

GENESIS 2:4–9

There was no one to work the ground.
Genesis 2:5

When we built our home, it stood on little more than a muddy, empty lot at the end of a gravel road. We needed grass, trees, and shrubs to match the surrounding Oregon foothills. As I got out my lawn tools and set to work, I thought of the first garden waiting for humans: "No shrub had yet appeared on the earth and no plant had yet sprung up, . . . and there was no one to work the ground" (Genesis 2:5).

The creation account in Genesis 1 repeats God's assessment of creation: it was "good" or "very good" (vv. 4, 10, 12, 18, 21, 25, 31). However, it wasn't complete. Adam and Eve needed to cultivate the ground—to exercise stewardship of God's creation (v. 28). They weren't meant to live in an unchanging paradise but one that needed care and development.

Since the beginning, God has been inviting humans to partner with Him in His creation. He did it in the garden of Eden, and He does it with "the new creation" He makes of us when we put our faith in Christ (2 Corinthians 5:17). Upon salvation, we're not made perfect. As the apostle Paul says, "Do not conform to the pattern of this world" (Romans 12:2). God works in us as we pursue a life pleasing to Him, "conformed to the image of his Son" (8:29).

Whether it's caring for the earth or caring for our new life in Christ, we need to cultivate the gift God has given us. *Matt Lucas*

Practice Gratitude Today

Today, how can you care for God's creation, or the new creation that you are in Christ? Praise God that He invites you to cocreate His world with Him.

My God Is Near

PHILIPPIANS 4:4–7

The Lord is near. Do not be anxious about anything,
but . . . present your requests to God.
Philippians 4:5–6

For more than thirty years, Lourdes, a voice teacher in Manila, had taught students face-to-face. When she was asked to conduct classes online, she was anxious. "I'm not good with computers," she recounted. "My laptop is old, and I'm not familiar with videoconferencing platforms."

While it may seem a small thing to some, it was a real stressor for her. "I live alone, so there is no one to help," she said. "I'm concerned that my students will quit, and I need the income."

Before each class, Lourdes would pray for her laptop to work properly. "Philippians 4:5–6 was the wallpaper on my screen," she said. "How I clung to those words."

Paul exhorts us to not be anxious about anything because "the Lord is near" (Philippians 4:5). God's promise of His presence is ours to hold on to. As we rest in His nearness and commit everything—both big and small—to Him in prayer, His peace guards our "hearts and . . . minds in Christ Jesus" (v. 7).

"God led me to websites about fixing computer glitches," Lourdes said. "He also gave me patient students who understood my technological limitations." God's presence, help, and peace are ours to enjoy as we seek to follow Him all the days of our life. We can say with confidence: "Rejoice in the Lord always. I will say it again: Rejoice!" (v. 4).

Karen Huang

Practice Gratitude Today

What is an upcoming event or situation today or this week that you find stressful? Thank God that He will be present with you during that time.

Forest Darkroom

2 SAMUEL 22:1–7, 29–30

The Lord turns my darkness into light.
2 Samuel 22:29

The army wouldn't give Tony Vaccaro a chance as a photographer, but that didn't stop him. Between terrifying moments of dodging artillery shells and shrapnel that seemed to rain from the trees, he took pictures anyway. Then, as his friends slept, he used their helmets to mix the chemicals to develop his film. The nighttime forest became the darkroom in which Vaccaro created a timeless record of World War II's Battle of Hürtgen Forest.

King David lived through his share of battles and dark times. Second Samuel 22 says, "The Lord delivered him from the hand of all his enemies and from the hand of Saul" (v. 1). David used those experiences to produce a record of God's faithfulness. He said, "Waves of death swirled about me; the torrents of destruction overwhelmed me" (v. 5).

David soon pivoted from desperation to hope: "In my distress I called to the Lord," he recalled. "From his temple he heard my voice" (v. 7). David made certain to praise God for His unfailing help. "The Lord turns my darkness into light," he said. "With your help I can advance against a troop; with my God I can scale a wall" (vv. 29–30).

David turned his difficulties into an opportunity to tell the world about his faithful God. We can do the same. After all, we rely on the one who turns darkness into light. *Tim Gustafson*

Practice Gratitude Today

When was a time God turned your darkness into light? Find an opportunity to share that story with someone today, thanking God for His faithfulness to you.

You Can Beat It!

MATTHEW 28:1–10

Where, O death, is your sting?
1 Corinthians 15:55

The radio ad for an upcoming seminar sounded intriguing. The announcer said, "You can beat death—for good! Attend my seminar and I'll show you how." I wondered for a few moments what the speaker would claim could beat death and what his suggestions might be. Perhaps something about diet or exercise or freezing our bodies? After listening a little longer, though, I realized he had said, "You can beat debt—for good."

The most wonderful news is that we can beat death because Jesus paid our debt (1 Corinthians 15:55–57)! Our debt of sin meant separation from God, but Jesus willingly gave up His life and was crucified on a cross to pay what we owed. As Mary Magdalene and another Mary went to the tomb on the third day to anoint His body, an angel told them: "He is not here; he has risen, just as he said" (Matthew 28:6). With great joy they ran to bring the word to His other disciples. On their way, Jesus met them Himself. He had risen, and His followers had reason for rejoicing.

Jesus has removed the sting of death (1 Corinthians 15:55). Now we too have victory by believing in the Son of God's death and resurrection for us. Through Jesus's perfect work, we can beat death—for good!

Anne Cetas

Practice Gratitude Today

Honestly consider how you feel about death. Are you scared of the pain? Do you fear the temporary separation from loved ones? Talk with Jesus about it—and thank Him for defeating death.

The Power of Affirmation

1 CORINTHIANS 1:4–9

I always thank my God for you because of
his grace given you in Christ Jesus.
1 Corinthians 1:4

During a recent study, two hundred thousand employees were interviewed to discover the missing ingredient in their productivity. The study concluded that appreciation and affirmation topped the list of what they wanted most from their superiors. This research implies that receiving affirmation is a basic human need.

The apostle Paul seemed to realize this basic need in the Corinthian believers, so before he peppered them with firm words of discipline, he showered them with affirmation. As their spiritual leader, Paul began his letter with thanksgiving to God for the grace displayed in their lives.

Once far from God, these believers were now participating in His grace through the death and resurrection of Christ. United with Jesus, they were drawing their spiritual life from Him, and the fruit of this union was their spiritual growth in godliness (1 Corinthians 1:4–7). Paul deliberately and continually thanked God for His work in the Corinthian believers' lives. I imagine that they were better able to bear firm criticism from Paul because of his tender affirmation.

When we see people who are obeying God, let's take time to affirm them and to thank God for what He's doing through them.

Marvin Williams

Practice Gratitude Today

Who can you affirm today for how they are reflecting God's love and peace to others? In person or digitally, thank that person for pointing others to Christ.

Mighty Waters

REVELATION 1:9–17

His feet were like bronze glowing in a furnace, and
his voice was like the sound of rushing waters.
Revelation 1:15

While in Brazil, I went to see Iguazú Falls, one of the greatest waterfalls in the world. The massive falls are breathtaking, but what impressed me most at Iguazú was not the sight of the falls or the spray of the water. It was the sound. The sound was beyond deafening—I felt as if I was actually inside the sound itself. It was an overwhelming experience that reminded me how small I am by comparison.

Later, with this scene in mind, I couldn't help but think about John in Revelation 1:15. While on the island of Patmos, he saw a vision of the risen Christ. The apostle described Jesus in the glory of His resurrection, noting both His clothing and His physical qualities. Then John described Christ's voice "like the sound of rushing waters."

I'm not sure I fully appreciated what that meant until I visited Iguazú and was overwhelmed by the thundering sound of the falls. As those mighty waters reminded me of my own smallness, I better understood why John fell at the feet of Christ as though dead (v. 17).

Perhaps that description will help you grasp the awesomeness of Jesus's presence and prompt you to follow John's example of worshiping the Savior.

Bill Crowder

Practice Gratitude Today

Reflect on an awe-inspiring or overwhelming natural wonder you've experienced. Praise God that He is infinitely more powerful and awesome than His creation.

The True Owner

PSALM 95:1–7

All things have been created through him and for him.
Colossians 1:16

Did you hear about the church that didn't have enough room for parking? Fortunately, it was located right next to a store that was closed on Sundays, so a church member asked the store owner if they could overflow into his parking lot. "No problem," he said. "You can use it fifty-one weeks out of the year. On the fifty-second week, though, it will be chained off." The man was grateful, but asked curiously, "What happens that week?" The store owner smiled. "Nothing. I just want you to remember that it's not your parking lot."

It's easy to take for granted all the material and spiritual blessings that God has given us. That's why we need to stop and remember that Scripture says the true owner of all we possess is God: "Everything in heaven and earth is yours. Yours, Lord, is the kingdom; you are exalted as head over all" (1 Chronicles 29:11). Even our bodies do not belong to us: "Do you not know that your bodies are temples of the Holy Spirit . . . ? You are not your own; you were bought at a price" (1 Corinthians 6:19–20).

As 1 Timothy 6:17 reminds us: "God . . . richly provides us with everything for our enjoyment." We are so abundantly blessed with good things! Let's never take our Father for granted but use wisely and gratefully all that He has given us. *Cindy Hess Kasper*

Practice Gratitude Today

How can you use God's gifts—your abilities, material possessions, and body—to honor God today, and to remind yourself that everything you enjoy is from His hand?

Unchanging God

JAMES 1:2–18

Blessed is the one who perseveres under trial.
James 1:12

An iconic photo shows the tread of a boot against a gray background. It's astronaut Buzz Aldrin's footprint, which he left on the moon in 1969. Scientists say that footprint is likely still there, unchanged after all these years. In fact, it may be there as long as the moon itself lasts. On the moon there is no wind or water to change the landscape. Nothing gets eroded. What happens on the lunar landscape stays on the lunar landscape.

It's even more awesome to reflect on the constant presence of God Himself. James writes, "[God] does not change like shifting shadows" (James 1:17). The apostle puts this in the context of our own struggles: "When troubles of any kind come your way, consider it an opportunity for great joy" (v. 2 NLT). Why? Because we're loved by a great and unchanging God: "Every good and perfect gift is from above, coming down from the Father of the heavenly lights, who does not change like shifting shadows" (v. 17).

In times of trouble, we need to remember God's constant provision. Perhaps we might recall the words of the great hymn "Great Is Thy Faithfulness": "There is no shadow of turning with thee; thou changest not, thy compassions, they fail not; as thou hast been, thou forever wilt be." Yes, our God has left his permanent footprint on our world. He will always be there for us. Great is His faithfulness.

Kenneth Petersen

Practice Gratitude Today

Make a list of the constants in your life that you have come to rely on or even take for granted. Thank God that He is more unchanging and faithful than anything else you depend on.

Running from God

JONAH 2:1–10

From deep in the realm of the dead I called
for help, and you listened to my cry.
Jonah 2:2

Julie and Liz kayaked off the coast of California, scouting for humpback whales. Humpbacks are known for being active near the surface, making them easy to spot. The two women got the surprise of their lives when one surfaced directly underneath them. An onlooker caught footage of their encounter that showed the large mouth of the whale dwarfing the women and their kayaks. After briefly being dragged underwater, the women escaped unharmed.

Their experience offers perspective on the biblical account of the prophet Jonah being swallowed by a "huge fish" (Jonah 1:17). God had instructed him to preach to the Ninevites, but because they'd rejected God, Jonah didn't feel they were worthy of His forgiveness. Instead of obeying, he ran away and took passage on a ship headed in the opposite direction. God sent a dangerous storm, and Jonah was thrown overboard.

God provided a way to preserve Jonah from certain death on the high seas, sparing him the far-worse consequences of his actions. Jonah "called to the Lord" and God listened (2:2). After Jonah admitted his wrongdoing and expressed his praise and acknowledgment of God's goodness, he was—at God's command—expelled from the fish "onto dry land" (v. 10).

By God's grace, when we acknowledge our wrongdoings and express faith in Jesus's sacrifice, we're spared the spiritual death we deserve and experience new life through Him. *Kirsten Holmberg*

Practice Gratitude Today

Who do you tend to feel is not worthy of God's love and forgiveness? Thank God that while no one deserves His forgiveness, He has offered it to you because of His kindness and mercy.

Breathtaking

ECCLESIASTES 2:1–11

There is nothing better for a person under the sun than to eat and drink and be glad. Then joy will accompany them in their toil all the days of the life God has given them under the sun.
Ecclesiastes 8:15

A popular slogan says, "Life is not measured by the number of breaths we take, but by the moments that take our breath away." I see the phrase everywhere, on everything from T-shirts to pieces of art. It's a catchy phrase, but I think it's misleading.

If we measure life by breathtaking moments, we miss the wonder of ordinary moments. Eating, sleeping, and breathing seem ordinary in that we do them every day, usually without much thought. But they are not ordinary at all. Every bite and every breath are miracles. In fact, having breath is more miraculous than anything that takes our breath away.

King Solomon may have had more breathtaking moments than anyone. He said, "I refused my heart no pleasure" (Ecclesiastes 2:10). But he expressed cynicism about it by saying, "All of it is meaningless" (v. 17).

Solomon's life reminds us that it's important to find joy in ordinary things, for they are indeed wonderful. Bigger is not always better. More is not always an improvement. Busier doesn't make us more important.

Rather than look for meaning in breathtaking moments, we should find meaning in every breath we take, and make every breath meaningful.

Julie Ackerman Link

Practice Gratitude Today

Pay attention to the ordinary things today: breathing, eating, seeing, hearing, speaking, moving, laughing, singing, smelling, feeling. Thank God for the everyday miracles of life.

Asking God

PSALM 6:4–9

The Lord has heard my cry for mercy;
the Lord accepts my prayer.
Psalm 6:9

When my husband, Dan, was diagnosed with cancer, I couldn't find the "right" way to ask God to heal him. In my limited view, other people in the world had such serious problems—war, famine, poverty, natural disasters. Then one day, during our morning prayer time, I heard my husband humbly ask, "Dear Lord, please heal my disease."

It was such a simple but heartfelt plea that it reminded me to stop complicating every prayer request, because God perfectly hears our righteous cries for help. As David simply asked, "Turn, Lord, and deliver me; save me because of your unfailing love" (Psalm 6:4).

That's what David declared during a time of spiritual confusion and despair. His exact situation isn't explained in this psalm. His honest pleas, however, show deep desire for godly help and restoration. "I am worn out from my groaning," he wrote (v. 6).

Yet David didn't let his own limits, including sin, stop him from going to God with his need. Thus, even before God answered, David was able to rejoice, "The Lord has heard my weeping. The Lord has heard my cry for mercy; the Lord accepts my prayer" (vv. 8–9).

Despite our own confusion and uncertainty, God hears and accepts the honest pleas of His children. He's ready to hear us, especially when we need Him most.

Patricia Raybon

Practice Gratitude Today

What has felt too unimportant, too complicated, or too self-focused to bring to God in prayer? Talk with God about it, thanking Him that He always hears you.

Seeing Masterpieces

PSALM 139:11–18

You knit me together in my mother's womb.
Psalm 139:13

My father creates custom quivers designed for archers to carry their arrows. He carves elaborate wildlife pictures into pieces of genuine leather, before stitching the material together.

During a visit, I watched him construct one of his works of art. His careful hands applied just the right pressure as he pressed a sharp blade into the supple leather, creating various textures. Then he dipped a rag into crimson dye and covered the leather with even strokes, magnifying the beauty of his creation.

As I admired my dad's confident craftsmanship, I realized how often I fail to acknowledge and appreciate my heavenly Father's creativity manifested in others and even in myself. Reflecting on the Lord's magnificent workmanship, I recalled King David's affirmation that God creates our "inmost being" and that we're "fearfully and wonderfully made" (Psalm 139:13–14).

We can praise our Creator in confidence because we know His "works are wonderful" (v. 14). And we can be encouraged to respect ourselves and others more, especially when we remember that the Maker of the universe knew us inside and out and planned our days "before one of them came to be" (v. 16).

Like the pliable leather carved by my father's skilled hands, we are each beautiful and valuable simply because we are God's one-of-a-kind creations. Each one of us, intentionally designed to be unique and purposed as God's beloved masterpieces, contributes to reflect God's magnificence.

Xochitl Dixon

Practice Gratitude Today

Spend a few minutes looking at yourself in a mirror. Thank God that you are a one-of-a-kind creation made in His image.

Gates of Worship

PSALM 100

Enter his gates with thanksgiving and his courts with praise; give thanks to him and praise his name.
Psalm 100:4

When you enter some of the greatest cities in the world, you can encounter famous gates such as the Brandenburg Gate in Berlin, the Jaffa Gate in Jerusalem, and the gates at Downing Street in London. Whether the gates were built for defensive or ceremonial purposes, they all represent the difference between being outside or inside certain areas of the city. Some are open; some are closed to all but a few.

The gates into the presence of God are always open. The familiar song of Psalm 100 is an invitation for the Israelites to enter into the presence of God through the temple gates. They were told to "shout for joy" and "come before him with joyful songs" (vv. 1–2). Shouting for joy was an appropriate expression when greeting a monarch in the ancient world. All the earth was to sing joyfully about God! The reason for this joyful noise was that God had given them their identity (v. 3). They entered the gates with praise and thanksgiving because of God's goodness and His steadfast and enduring love that continues through all generations (vv. 4–5). Even when they forgot their identity and wandered away from Him, God remained faithful and still invited them to enter His presence.

The gates into God's presence are still open, inviting us to come and worship.

Marvin Williams

Practice Gratitude Today

Where in life do you feel shut out, unwelcome, or uninvited? Share your disappointments with God, then thank Him that the gate to His presence and love is always open to you through Jesus.

Crazy Horse

1 SAMUEL 7:3–12

Samuel took a stone and . . . named it Ebenezer,
saying, "Thus far the Lord has helped us."
1 Samuel 7:12

In 1876, the Oglala Lakota leader Crazy Horse joined forces with Sitting Bull to defeat General Custer and his army at the Battle of the Little Bighorn. Not much later, though, starvation caused Crazy Horse to surrender to US troops. He was killed while trying to escape. Despite this sad conclusion to his life, he became a symbol of heroic leadership of a threatened people.

Today in the Black Hills of South Dakota, he is commemorated with a monument being carved into a mountain—the Crazy Horse Memorial. If completed, it will be 641 feet long and 563 feet high. It will show Crazy Horse riding a galloping horse, pointing the way to his people.

Thousands of years ago, the prophet Samuel used a much smaller memorial stone in a significant way. In the midst of a crucial battle with the Philistines, Samuel called out to God on Israel's behalf. The Lord answered his prayer (1 Samuel 7:10). In gratitude, Samuel set up a stone and "named it Ebenezer, saying, 'Thus far the Lord has helped us'" (v. 12).

Samuel has set an example for our spiritual journey. We too can use tangible reminders of God's faithfulness to help us worship and serve Him. It's good to remember "thus far the Lord has helped us."

Dennis Fisher

Practice Gratitude Today

Find a stone you can use as a reminder of a specific time God met your needs. You may choose to paint, carve, or customize the stone. Place it where you will see it often.

Godly Sorrow

2 CORINTHIANS 7:5–10

I am happy, not because you were made sorry, but because your sorrow led you to repentance. For you became sorrowful as God intended.
2 Corinthians 7:9

Thieves stole nearly $5,000 in sound and office equipment from a church in West Virginia, only to break in the following night to return the items they had taken. Apparently the guilt of stealing from a church weighed so heavily on their consciences that they felt the need to correct their criminal behavior of breaking the commandment "You shall not steal" (Exodus 20:15). Their actions make me think about the differences between worldly sorrow and godly sorrow.

Paul praised the Corinthians for understanding this difference. His first letter to them was biting, as he addressed issues of sin. His words caused sorrow among them, and because of this Paul rejoiced. Why? Their sorrow did not stop at just feeling sad about getting caught or suffering the unpleasant consequences of their sins. Their sorrow was godly sorrow, a genuine remorse for their sins. This led them to repentance—a change in their thinking that led to a renouncing of their sin and turning to God. Their repentance ultimately led to deliverance from their sinful habits.

Repentance is not something we can do unless we have the prompting of the Holy Spirit; it's a gift from God. Pray for repentance today (2 Timothy 2:24–26).

Marvin Williams

Practice Gratitude Today

Where are you hurting God, others, yourself, or God's creation? Confess your sin to God, and thank Him for giving you the wisdom and conviction to know where you are in the wrong.

Secret Delivery

MATTHEW 6:1–4

When you give to the needy, do not let your left hand know what your right hand is doing.
Matthew 6:3

A clear glass vase with bell-shaped lilies of the valley, pink tulips, and yellow daffodils greeted Kim at her front door. For seven months, an anonymous believer in Jesus sent Kim beautiful bouquets from a local flower shop. Each monthly gift arrived with a note filled with scriptural encouragement and signed with these words: "Love, Jesus."

Kim shared photos of these secret deliveries on Facebook. The flowers gave her opportunity to celebrate an individual's kindness and to acknowledge the way God expressed His love to her through His people. Month after month, each secret delivery caused her friends to be grateful for the priceless gift of time the Lord gave Kim. As she trusted Him through her battle with a terminal disease, every colorful blossom and handwritten note affirmed God's loving compassion for her.

The sender's anonymity reflects the heart motive Jesus encourages His people to adopt when giving. The Lord warns against practicing righteous acts "to be seen" by others (Matthew 6:1). Good deeds are intended to be expressions of worship overflowing from hearts grateful for all God has done for us. Highlighting our own generosity with the hope or expectation of being honored can take the focus off the Giver of all good things—Jesus.

God knows when we give with good intentions (v. 4). He simply wants our generosity motivated by love as we give Him the glory, the honor, and the praise.

Xochitl Dixon

Practice Gratitude Today

How can you give anonymously to someone today? Thank God that out of His love, He has given you so many gifts that you are not even aware of.

Full, Abundant Life

JOHN 10:7–11

I have come that they may have life, and have
it to the full. I am the good shepherd.
John 10:10–11

Seventeenth-century philosopher Thomas Hobbes famously wrote that human life in its natural state is "solitary, poor, nasty, brutish, and short." Hobbes argued that our instincts tend toward war in a bid to attain dominance over others; thus, the establishment of government is necessary to maintain law and order.

This bleak view of humanity sounds like the state of affairs that Jesus described when He said, "All who have come before me are thieves and robbers" (John 10:8). But Jesus offers hope in the midst of despair. "The thief comes only to steal and kill and destroy," but then the good news: "I have come that they may have life, and have it to the full" (v. 10).

Psalm 23 paints a refreshing portrait of the life our Shepherd gives us. In Him, we "lack nothing" (v. 1) and are refreshed (v. 3). He leads us down the right paths of His perfect will, so that even when we face dark times, we need not be afraid, for He is present to comfort us (vv. 3–4). He causes us to triumph in the face of adversity and overwhelms us with blessings (v. 5). His goodness and love follow us every day, and we have the privilege of His presence forever (v. 6).

May we answer the Shepherd's call and experience the full, abundant life He came to give us. *Remi Oyedele*

Practice Gratitude Today

Honestly reflect on your idea of a full, abundant life. Compare this with Psalm 23. Thank God that while He doesn't promise you luxuries or achievement, He promises you Himself.

Finding Joy in Praise

HABAKKUK 3:6, 16–19

Yet I will rejoice in the LORD.
Habakkuk 3:18

When the famous British writer C. S. Lewis first gave his life to Jesus, he initially resisted praising God. In fact, he called it "a stumbling block." His struggle was "in the suggestion that God Himself demanded it." Yet Lewis finally realized "it is in the process of being worshipped that God communicates His presence" to His people. Then we, "in perfect love with God," find joy in Him no more separable "than the brightness a mirror receives" from the "brightness it sheds."

The prophet Habakkuk arrived at this conclusion centuries earlier. After complaining to God about evils aimed at the people of Judah, Habakkuk came to see that praising Him leads to joy—not in what God does, but in who He is. Thus, even in a national or world crisis, God is still great. As the prophet declared: "Though the fig tree does not bud and there are no grapes on the vines, though the olive crop fails and the fields produce no food, though there are no sheep in the pen and no cattle in the stalls, yet I will rejoice in the LORD" (Habakkuk 3:17–18). "I will be joyful in God my Savior," he added.

As C. S. Lewis realized, "The whole world rings with praise." Habakkuk, likewise, surrendered to praising God always, finding rich joy in the One who "marches on forever" (v. 6). *Patricia Raybon*

Practice Gratitude Today

When have you found it hard to praise God? Even if it feels difficult, worship God today through music or prayer. Thank God that in worship, you can focus on His presence with you.

Learning to Lament

LAMENTATIONS 3:19–27

This I call to my mind and therefore I have hope.
Lamentations 3:21

On February 14, 1884, Theodore Roosevelt's wife, Alice, died giving birth to their daughter, also named Alice. Roosevelt was so distraught with the loss of his wife that he never spoke of her again. But reminders of her absence haunted the family. Because the newborn had the same name as her mother, she was called "Sister"—never Alice. On Valentine's Day, the holiday for sweethearts, few in the Roosevelt household felt inclined to celebrate it or Sister's birthday. Broken hearts made moods strained and stoic.

Burying our feelings doesn't help, but prayerful grieving can. Jeremiah's heart was broken by Israel's disobedience and the Babylonian captivity that followed. Memories of Jerusalem's destruction haunted him (Lamentations 1–2). Yet he had learned how to lament. He identified what caused him grief, began to pray, and let his tears flow. Soon his focus shifted from his loss to the steadfast grace of the Lord's provision. "Because of the LORD's great love we are not consumed, for his compassions never fail. They are new every morning; great is your faithfulness" (3:22–23). Grief gave way to thankfulness.

Learning to lament can give us a fresh vision of hope and begin the process of healing and restoration. *Dennis Fisher*

Practice Gratitude Today

What loss, wound, or difficulty have you not let yourself grieve? Talk openly with God about it. End by thanking Him for giving you your emotions, and that He too knows what it is to grieve.

Forever Flowers

ISAIAH 40:1–8

The grass withers and the flowers fall, but the word of our God endures forever.
Isaiah 40:8

As a toddler, my son Xavier enjoyed giving me flowers. I appreciated every freshly picked weed or store-bought blossom he purchased with his dad. I treasured each gift until it wilted and had to be thrown away.

One day, Xavier gave me a beautiful bouquet of artificial silk flowers. He grinned as he arranged the white calla lily, yellow sunflower, and purple hydrangea in a glass vase. "Look, Mommy," he said. "They'll last forever. That's how much I love you."

Since then, my boy has grown into a young man. Those silk petals have frayed. The colors have faded. Still, the forever flowers remind me of his adoration. And there is something else they bring to mind, one thing that truly stands forever: the limitless and lasting love of God, as revealed in His infallible and enduring Word (Isaiah 40:8).

As the Israelites faced continual trials, Isaiah comforted them with confidence in God's enduring words (40:1). He proclaimed that God paid the debt caused by the Israelites' sin (v. 2), securing their hope in the coming Messiah (vv. 3–5). They trusted the prophet because his focus remained on God rather than their circumstances.

In a world filled with uncertainties and affliction, human opinions and even our own feelings are ever-shifting and as limited as our mortality (vv. 6–7). Still, we can trust God's unchanging love and character as revealed through His constant and eternally true Word.

Xochitl Dixon

Practice Gratitude Today

What gift from a loved one reminds you of God's forever love for you? Put it on your nightstand or bathroom counter—somewhere you will see it when you get up in the morning.

When Beauty Never Ends

PSALM 27:1–4

Because your love is better than life, my lips will glorify you.
Psalm 63:3

I love looking at the Grand Canyon. Whenever I stand at the canyon rim, I see new brushstrokes of God's handiwork that take my breath away.

Even though it's a (very large) hole in the ground, the Grand Canyon causes me to reflect on heaven. A very honest twelve-year-old asked me once, "Won't heaven be boring? Don't you think we'll get tired of praising God all the time?" But if a "hole in the ground" can be so overwhelmingly beautiful we can't stop looking at it, we can only imagine the joy of one day seeing the very Source of beauty—our loving Creator—in all of the pristine wonder of the new creation.

David expressed this longing when he wrote, "One thing I ask from the Lord, this only do I seek: that I may dwell in the house of the Lord all the days of my life, to gaze on the beauty of the Lord" (Psalm 27:4). There's nothing more beautiful than the presence of God, which draws near to us on this earth as we seek Him by faith and look forward to seeing Him face-to-face.

On that day we'll never tire of praising our amazing Lord, because we will never come to an end of fresh, new discoveries of His exquisite goodness and the wonders of the works of His hands. Every moment in His presence will bring a breathtaking revelation of His beauty and His love.

James Banks

Practice Gratitude Today

What is something about God that you recently learned, experienced, or rediscovered? Thank God that you will never come to an end of God revealing His infinite beauty and love to you.

Choosing Celebration

1 PETER 2:1–3, 9–10

A heart at peace gives life to the body, but envy rots the bones.
Proverbs 14:30

Writer Marilyn McEntyre shares the story of learning from a friend that "the opposite of envy is celebration." Despite this friend's physical disability and chronic pain, which limited her ability to develop her talents in the ways she'd hoped, she was somehow able to uniquely embody joy and to celebrate with others, bringing "appreciation into every encounter" before she passed away.

That insight—"the opposite of envy is celebration"—lingers with me, reminding me of friends in my own life who seem to live out this kind of comparison-free, deep, and genuine joy for others.

Envy is an easy trap to fall into. It feeds on our deepest vulnerabilities, wounds, and fears, whispering that if we were only more like so-and-so, we wouldn't be struggling, and we wouldn't be feeling bad.

As Peter reminded new believers in 1 Peter 2, the only way to "rid" ourselves of the lies that envy tells us is to be deeply rooted in the truth, to "have tasted that the Lord is good" (vv. 1–3). We can "love one another deeply, from the heart" (1:22) when we know the true source of our joy—"the living and enduring word of God" (v. 23).

We can surrender comparison when we remember who we really are—beloved members of "a chosen people, . . . God's special possession." We're called "out of darkness into his wonderful light" (2:9).

Monica La Rose

Practice Gratitude Today

Plan some small way to celebrate God's goodness to you today. You may choose to include family or friends in your celebration, or to celebrate alone with God.

Right beside You

DEUTERONOMY 4:5–8

The LORD our God is near us whenever we pray to him.
Deuteronomy 4:7

Each day at a post office in Jerusalem, workers sort through piles of undeliverable letters in an attempt to guide each to its recipient. Many end up in a specially marked box labeled "Letters to God."

About a thousand such letters reach Jerusalem each year, addressed simply to God or Jesus. Puzzled by what to do with them, one worker began taking the letters to Jerusalem's Western Wall to have them placed between its stone blocks with other written prayers. Most of the letters ask for a job, a spouse, or good health. Some request forgiveness, others just offer thanks. One man asked God if his deceased wife could appear in his dreams because he longed to see her again. Each sender believed God would listen, if only He could be reached.

The Israelites learned much as they journeyed through the wilderness. One lesson was that their God wasn't like the other gods known at the time—distant, deaf, geographically bound, reached only by lengthy pilgrimage or international mail. No, "the LORD our God is near us whenever we pray to him" (Deuteronomy 4:7). What other people could claim that? This was revolutionary news!

God doesn't live in Jerusalem. He's close by us, wherever we are. Some still need to discover this radical truth. If only each of those letters could be sent the reply: God is right beside you. Just talk to Him.

Sheridan Voysey

Practice Gratitude Today

Write a handwritten letter to God, telling Him about your concerns and desires. Don't mail it. Thank Him for always being right beside you, even as you wrote your letter.

The Spirit of Fika

LUKE 24:28–35

When he was at the table with them, he took bread, gave thanks, broke it and began to give it to them.
Luke 24:30

The coffeehouse in the town near my house is named Fika. It's a Swedish word meaning to take a break with coffee and a pastry, always with family, coworkers, or friends. I'm not Swedish, yet the spirit of fika describes one thing I love most about Jesus—His practice of taking a break to eat and relax with others.

Scholars say Jesus's meals weren't random. Theologian Mark Glanville calls them "the delightful 'second course'" of Israel's feasts and celebrations in the Old Testament. At the table, Jesus lived what God had intended Israel to be: "a center of joy, celebration and justice for the whole world."

From the feeding of the five thousand to the Last Supper—even to the meal with two believers after His resurrection (Luke 24:30)—the table ministry of Jesus invites us to stop our constant striving and abide in Him. Indeed, not until eating with Jesus did the two believers recognize Him as the risen Lord. "He took bread, gave thanks, broke it and began to give it to them. Then their eyes were opened" (vv. 30–31) to the living Christ.

Sitting with a friend recently at Fika, enjoying hot chocolate and rolls, we found ourselves also talking of Jesus. He is the Bread of Life. May we linger at His table and find more of Him. *Patricia Raybon*

Practice Gratitude Today

Pause to enjoy a meal, coffee time, or a snack with a loved one. Use videoconferencing if necessary. Thank Jesus that He is your example for a life of joy and celebration.

Amazing Skill

PSALM 139:7–16

I praise you because I am fearfully and wonderfully made;
your works are wonderful, I know that full well.
Psalm 139:14

The leader of our college singing group directed the group and accompanied us on the piano at the same time, skillfully balancing those responsibilities. At the close of one concert, he looked particularly weary, so I asked him if he was okay. He responded, "I've never had to do that before." Then he explained. "The piano was so out of tune that I had to play the whole concert in two different keys—my left hand playing in one key and my right hand in another!" I was blown away by the startling skill he displayed, and I was amazed at the One who creates humans to be capable of such things.

King David expressed an even greater sense of wonder when he wrote, "Thank you for making me so wonderfully complex! Your workmanship is marvelous—how well I know it" (Psalm 139:14 NLT). Whether in people's abilities or nature's marvels, the wonders of creation point us to the majesty of our Creator.

One day, when we're in God's presence, people from every generation will worship Him with the words, "You are worthy, our Lord and God, to receive glory and honor and power, for you created all things, and by your will they were created and have their being" (Revelation 4:11). The amazing skills God gives us and the great beauty God has created are ample reason to worship Him. *Bill Crowder*

Practice Gratitude Today

What skills have others recognized in you, or what skills have you recognized in your loved ones? Thank God that He has made us wonderfully complex.

Grateful for Everything

DEUTERONOMY 8:6–18

When you have eaten and are satisfied, praise the LORD your God for the good land he has given you.
Deuteronomy 8:10

In Australia, it can take hours to drive between towns, and fatigue can lead to accidents. So at busy holiday times rest stops are set up on major highways with volunteers offering free coffee. My wife, Merryn, and I grew to enjoy these stops during our long drives there.

On one trip, we pulled in and walked over to order our coffee. An attendant handed over the two cups, and then asked me for two dollars. I asked why. She pointed to the small print on the sign. At this stop, only the driver got free coffee; you had to pay for passengers. Annoyed, I told her this was false advertising, paid the two dollars, and walked off. Back at the car, Merryn pointed out my error: I had turned a gift into an entitlement and become ungrateful for what I received. She was right.

When the Israelites were about to enter the promised land, Moses urged them to be a grateful people (Deuteronomy 8:10). Thanks to the blessings of God, the land was abundant, but they could easily treat this prosperity as something they deserved (vv. 17–18). From this, the Jews developed a practice of giving thanks for every meal, no matter how small. For them, it was all a gift.

I went back to the woman and apologized. A free cup of coffee was a gift I didn't deserve—and something to be thankful for.

Sheridan Voysey

Practice Gratitude Today

What is something you tend to feel God owes you? Perhaps it is your health, a more interesting job, or a family. In prayer, thank God for the things He has given you.

Giving Back to God

1 CHRONICLES 29:10–16

Everything comes from you, and we have given
you only what comes from your hand.
1 Chronicles 29:14

One year, the leaders of our congregation invited us to give, in addition to our regular weekly offerings, gifts to build a new gymnasium—a space we could use to minister to the families in our community. After prayerfully considering the medical expenses caused by living with a disability, I asked my husband, "Are you sure we can do this?" He nodded. "We're not giving God anything that's not already His," he said. "He'll provide all we need." And He did! Over a decade later, our church family still has the privilege of serving Jesus by serving people in that facility.

In 1 Chronicles 29, King David showed the leaders of Israel his commitment to support his son Solomon as his God-chosen successor and the builder of the temple (vv. 1–5). Everyone followed suit, "gave willingly," and "rejoiced" (vv. 6, 9). David praised God and declared that "everything in heaven and earth" belonged to Him (v. 11). He prayed: "Lord our God, all this abundance that we have provided for building you a temple for your Holy Name comes from your hand, and all of it belongs to you" (v. 16).

As we consider all God has done and given to us, specifically the gift of a personal relationship with Jesus, we can express our worship and show our gratitude and love by simply giving back to God, the Giver of all good things.

Xochitl Dixon

Practice Gratitude Today

Everything you have is from God. What is one thing God has given you that you can give to someone else today?

Only Trust

1 KINGS 17:8–16

So there was food every day for Elijah and
for the woman and her family.
1 Kings 17:15

Three hundred children were dressed and seated for breakfast, and a prayer of thanks was offered for the food. But there was no food! Situations like this were not unusual for orphanage director and missionary George Müller (1805–1898). Here was yet another opportunity to see how God would provide. Within minutes of Müller's prayer, a baker who couldn't sleep the night before showed up at the door. Sensing that the orphanage could use the bread, he had made three batches. Not long afterward, the town milkman appeared. His cart had broken down in front of the orphanage. Not wanting the milk to spoil, he offered it to Müller.

It's normal to experience bouts of worry, anxiety, and self-pity when we lack resources essential to our well-being—food, shelter, health, finances, friendships. First Kings 17:8–16 reminds us that God's help can come through unexpected sources like a needy widow. "I don't have any bread," the widow told the prophet Elijah, "only a handful of flour in a jar and a little olive oil in a jug" (v. 12). Earlier it was a raven that provided for Elijah (vv. 4–6). Concerns for our needs to be met can send us searching in many directions. A clear vision of God as the Provider who has promised to supply our needs can be liberating. Before we seek solutions, may we be careful to seek Him first. Doing so can save us time, energy, and frustration. *Arthur Jackson*

Practice Gratitude Today

When have you experienced provision from an unexpected source? Bring today's needs to God in prayer, thanking Him that He is your Provider.

Treasure the Moments

ECCLESIASTES 3:1–14

[God] has made everything beautiful in its time.
Ecclesiastes 3:11

Su Dongpo (also known as Su Shi) was one of China's greatest poets and essayists. While in exile and gazing upon a full moon, he wrote a poem to describe how much he missed his brother. "We rejoice and grieve, gather and leave, while the moon waxes and wanes. Since times of old, nothing remains perfect," he writes. "May our loved ones live long, beholding this beautiful scene together though thousands of miles apart."

His poem carries themes found in the book of Ecclesiastes. The author, known as the Teacher (1:1), observed that there is "a time to weep and a time to laugh, . . . a time to embrace and a time to refrain from embracing" (3:4–5). By pairing two contrasting activities, the Teacher, like Su Dongpo, seems to suggest that all good things must inevitably come to an end.

As Su Dongpo saw the waxing and waning of the moon as another sign that nothing remains perfect, the Teacher also saw in creation God's providential ordering of the world He'd made. God oversees the course of events, and "he has made everything beautiful in its time" (v. 11).

Life may be unpredictable and sometimes filled with painful separations, but we can take heart that everything takes place under God's gaze. We can enjoy life and treasure the moments—the good and the bad—because our loving God is with us. *Poh Fang Chia*

Practice Gratitude Today

How is the world around you changing? This may be a big change, like the seasons passing, or a small change, like a rainstorm. Thank God that everything takes place under His loving gaze.

From Wailing to Worship

PSALM 30

You turned my wailing into dancing;
you . . . clothed me with joy.
Psalm 30:11

Four days after Kim's treatment for breast cancer ended, doctors diagnosed her with a progressive lung disease and gave her three to five years to live. She grieved, sobbing prayers as she processed her emotions before God for the first year. By the time I met Kim a year later, she had surrendered her situation to Him and radiated contagious joy and peace. Though some days are still hard, God continues to transform her heart-wrenching suffering into a beautiful testimony of hope-filled praise as she encourages others.

Even when we're in dire circumstances, God can turn our wailing into dancing. Though His healing won't always look or feel like we'd hoped or expected, we can be confident in God's ways (Psalm 30:1–3). No matter how tear-stained our path may be, we have countless reasons to praise Him (v. 4). We can rejoice in God as He secures our confident faith (vv. 5–7). We can cry out for His mercy (vv. 8–10), celebrating the hope He's brought to many weeping worshipers. Only God can transform wails of despair into vibrant joy that doesn't depend on circumstances (vv. 11–12).

As our merciful God comforts us in our sorrow, He envelops us in peace and empowers us to extend compassion toward others and ourselves. Our loving and faithful Lord can and does turn our wailing into worship that can lead to heart-deep trust, praise, and maybe even joyful dancing.

Xochitl Dixon

Practice Gratitude Today

What are you mourning today? Tell God about it. Then thank Him that one day—in this life or the next—He will turn your wailing into worship.

In Abundance or Affliction

JOB 1:13–22

The LORD gave and the LORD has taken away;
may the name of the LORD be praised.
Job 1:21

Ann Voskamp's book *One Thousand Gifts* encourages readers to search their lives each day for what the Lord has done for them. In it, she daily notes God's abundant generosity to her in gifts both large and small, ranging from the simple beauty of iridescent bubbles in the dish sink to the incomparable salvation of sinners like herself (and the rest of us!). Ann contends that gratitude is the key to seeing God in even the most troubling of life's moments.

Job is famous for a life of such troubling moments. Indeed, his losses were deep and many. Just moments after losing all his livestock, he learns of the simultaneous death of all his ten children. Job's profound grief was evidenced in his response: he "tore his robe and shaved his head" (1:20). His words in that painful hour make me think Job knew the practice of gratitude, for he acknowledges that God had given him everything he'd lost (v. 21). How else could he worship in the midst of such incapacitating grief?

The practice of daily gratitude can't erase the magnitude of pain we feel in seasons of loss. Job questioned and grappled through his grief as the rest of the book describes. But recognizing God's goodness to us—in even the smallest of ways—can prepare us to kneel in worship before our all-powerful God in the darkest hours of our earthly lives.

Kirsten Holmberg

Practice Gratitude Today

What are God's small gifts to you today? List as many as you can think of. Thank God that even amid painful difficulties, He shows His small kindnesses to you.

Best Friend—Forever

JAMES 2:18–26

"Abraham believed God . . . ," and he was called God's friend.
James 2:23

One of the pieces of wisdom I have come to appreciate is my dad's often-repeated statement, "Joe, good friends are one of life's greatest treasures." How true! With good friends, you are never alone. They're attentive to your needs and gladly share life's joys and burdens.

Before Jesus came to earth, only two individuals were called friends of God. The Lord spoke to Moses "as one speaks to a friend" (Exodus 33:11), and Abraham "was called God's friend" (James 2:23; see 2 Chronicles 20:7; Isaiah 41:8).

I am amazed that Jesus calls those of us who belong to Him friends: "I have called you friends, for everything that I learned from my Father I have made known to you" (John 15:15). And His friendship is so deep that He laid down His life for us. As Jesus Himself said, "Greater love has no one than this: to lay down one's life for one's friends" (v. 13).

What a privilege and blessing to have Jesus as our friend! He is a friend who will never leave us or forsake us. He intercedes for us before the Father and supplies all our needs. He forgives all our sins, understands all our sorrows, and gives us sufficient grace in times of trouble. He is indeed our best friend. *Joe Stowell*

Practice Gratitude Today

Think about your best friends and what you appreciate about them. Then thank God that He is a friend who never leaves you and always loves you.

Priceless Lives in Christ

LUKE 15:8–10

There is rejoicing in the presence of the angels
of God over one sinner who repents.
Luke 15:10

Tears streamed down my cheeks during a frantic search for my lost wedding and anniversary rings. After an hour of lifting couch cushions and scouring every nook and cranny of our home, Alan said, "I'm sorry. We'll replace them."

"Thanks," I responded. "But their sentimental value surpasses their material worth. They're irreplaceable." Praying, I continued hunting for the jewelry. "Please, God. Help me find them."

Later, while reaching into the pocket of a sweater worn earlier in the week, I found the priceless jewels. "Thank you, Jesus!" I exclaimed. As my husband and I rejoiced, I slipped on the rings and recalled the parable of the woman who lost a coin (Luke 15:8–10). Like the woman who searched for her lost silver coin, I knew the worth of what had been lost. Neither of us was wrong for wanting to find our valuables. Jesus simply used that story to emphasize His desire to save every person He created. One sinner repenting results in a celebration in heaven.

What a gift it would be to become a person who prays as passionately for others as we pray for lost treasures to be found. What a privilege it is to celebrate when people repent and surrender their lives to Christ. If we've placed our trust in Jesus, we can be thankful we've experienced the joy of being loved by Someone who never gave up because He thought we were worth finding. *Xochitl Dixon*

Practice Gratitude Today

Spend time today enjoying a favorite possession. What makes it so valuable to you? Thank God that you are His prized possession, and He rejoices over you.

An Unexpected Guest

LUKE 19:1–10

Jesus . . . said to him, "Zacchaeus, come down immediately. I must stay at your house today."
Luke 19:5

Zach was a lonely guy. When he walked down the city streets, he could feel the hostile glares. But then his life took a turn. Clement of Alexandria, one of the church fathers, says that Zach became a very prominent Christian leader and a pastor of the church in Caesarea. Yes, we're talking about Zacchaeus, the chief tax collector who climbed a sycamore tree to see Jesus (Luke 19:1–10).

What prompted him to climb the tree? Tax collectors were perceived as traitors because they heavily taxed their own people to serve the Roman Empire. Yet Jesus had a reputation for accepting them. Zacchaeus might have wondered if Jesus would accept him too. Being short in stature, however, he couldn't see over the crowd (v. 3). Perhaps he climbed a tree to seek Him out.

And Jesus was seeking Zacchaeus too. When Christ reached the tree where he was perched, He looked up and said, "Zacchaeus, come down immediately. I must stay at your house today" (v. 5). Jesus considered it absolutely necessary that He be a guest in this outcast's home. Imagine that! The Savior of the world wanting to spend time with a social reject.

Whether it's our hearts, relationships, or lives that need mending, like Zacchaeus we can have hope. Jesus will never reject us when we turn to Him. He can restore what's been lost and broken and give our lives new meaning and purpose. *Poh Fang Chia*

Practice Gratitude Today

What in your life feels lost or broken today? Thank Jesus that you are never out of His sight, because He came to restore you and be with you.

True Happiness

ECCLESIASTES 3:9–14

I know that there is nothing better for people than
to be happy and to do good while they live.
Ecclesiastes 3:12

In the tenth century, Abd al-Rahman III was the ruler of Córdoba, Spain. After fifty years of reigning successfully ("beloved by my subjects, dreaded by my enemies, and respected by my allies"), al-Rahman took a deeper look at his life. "Riches and honors, power and pleasure, have waited on my call," he said of his privileges. But when he counted how many days of genuine happiness he'd had during that time, they amounted to just fourteen. How sobering.

The writer of Ecclesiastes was also a man of riches and honor (2:7–9), power and pleasure (1:12; 2:1–3). And his own life evaluation was equally sobering. Riches, he realized, just led to a desire for more (5:10–11), while pleasures accomplished little (2:1–2), and success could be due to chance as much as ability (9:11). But his assessment didn't end as bleakly as al-Rahman's. Believing God was his ultimate source of happiness, the Teacher saw that eating, working, and doing good could all be enjoyed when done with Him (2:25; 3:12–13).

"O man!" al-Rahman concluded his reflections, "place not thy confidence in this present world!" The writer of Ecclesiastes would agree. Since we've been made for eternity (3:11), earthly pleasures and achievements won't satisfy by themselves. But with Him in our lives, genuine happiness is possible in our eating, working, and living.

Sheridan Voysey

Practice Gratitude Today

When have you looked for fulfillment in an experience, success, or relationship that disappointed you? Today, slow down to enjoy God's common gifts: food, work, family, and friends.

Jesus Removes the Stain

JEREMIAH 2:1–5, 21–22

"Although you wash yourself . . . , the stain of your guilt is still before me," declares the Sovereign LORD.
Jeremiah 2:22

"Are. You. Kidding?" I yelled. Digging through our dryer looking for my shirt, I'd found it . . . and something else.

My white shirt had an ink spot on it. In fact, it looked like a jaguar pelt: ink splotches coated everything. I clearly hadn't checked my pockets, and a leaky pen had stained the entire load.

Scripture often uses the word *stain* to describe sin. A stain permeates the fabric of something, ruining it. And that's how God, speaking through the prophet Jeremiah, described sin, reminding His people that its stain was beyond their ability to cleanse. "Although you wash yourself with soap and use an abundance of cleansing powder, the stain of your guilt is still before me" (Jeremiah 2:22).

Thankfully, sin doesn't get the last word. In Isaiah 1:18, we hear God's promise that He can cleanse us from sin's stain: "Though your sins are like scarlet, they shall be as white as snow; though they are red as crimson, they shall be like wool."

I couldn't get the ink stain out of my shirt. Neither can I undo the stain of my sin. Thankfully, God cleanses us in Christ, just as 1 John 1:9 promises: "If we confess our sins, he is faithful and just and will forgive us our sins and purify us from all unrighteousness."

Adam R. Holz

Practice Gratitude Today

What sin, past or present, feels like it's stained your life, relationships, or reputation? Talk with God about it. Thank Him that when you confess your sins, He forgives you, washing you clean.

Generous God

EPHESIANS 3:14–21

[God] is able to do immeasurably more
than all we ask or imagine.
Ephesians 3:20

When our family lived in Chicago several years ago, we enjoyed many benefits. Near the top of my list were the amazing restaurants that seemed to try to outdo each other, not only in great cuisine but also in portion sizes. At one Italian eatery, my wife and I would order a half portion of our favorite pasta dish and still have enough to bring home for dinner the next night! The generous portions made us feel like we were at Grandma's house when she poured on the love through her cooking.

I also feel an outpouring of love when I read that my heavenly Father has lavished on us the riches of His grace (Ephesians 1:7–8) and that He is able to do "immeasurably more than all we ask or imagine" (3:20). I'm so grateful that our God is not a stingy God who begrudgingly dishes out His blessings in small portions. Rather, He is the God who pours out forgiveness for the prodigal (Luke 15) and daily crowns us "with love and compassion" (Psalm 103:4).

At times we think God hasn't provided for us as we would like. But if He never did anything more than forgive our sins and guarantee eternal life for us, He has already been abundantly generous! So today, let's rejoice in our generous God.

Joe Stowell

Practice Gratitude Today

Count ten good things God has given you today. Thank God that He is immeasurably more generous than you can imagine.

Reasons to Rejoice

PSALM 64

The righteous will rejoice in the LORD and take refuge in him; all the upright in heart will glory in him!
Psalm 64:10

When Ms. Glenda walked into the church commons area, her infectious joy filled the room. She had just recovered from a difficult medical procedure. As she approached me for our usual after-church greeting, I thanked God for all the times over the years that she's wept with me, gently corrected me, and offered encouragement. She's even asked for forgiveness when she thought she'd hurt my feelings. Whatever the situation, she always invites me to share my struggles honestly and reminds me that we have many reasons to praise God.

Mama Glenda, as she lets me call her, wrapped me in a gentle hug. "Hi, baby," she said. We enjoyed a short conversation and prayed together. Then she left—humming and singing as always, looking for someone else to bless.

In Psalm 64, David boldly approached God with his complaints and concerns (v. 1). He voiced his frustrations about the wickedness he saw around him (vv. 2–6). But he didn't lose confidence in God's power or the reliability of His promises (vv. 7–9). He knew that one day "the righteous will rejoice in the LORD and take refuge in him; all the upright in heart will glory in him!" (v. 10).

As we wait for Jesus's return, we'll face tough times. But we'll always have reasons to rejoice in every day God has made. *Xochitl Dixon*

Practice Gratitude Today

In prayer, openly share your frustrations, challenges, and complaints with God. End by thanking God for His power, reliability, and love, some of the many reasons we have to praise God.

Jesus's Ultimate Victory

2 CHRONICLES 20:15–22

As they began to sing and praise, the LORD set ambushes . . . and they were defeated.
2 Chronicles 20:22

At some military camps across Europe during World War II, an unusual supply was air-dropped for homesick soldiers—upright pianos. They were specially manufactured to contain only 10 percent of the normal amount of metal, and they received special water-resistant glue and anti-insect treatments. The pianos were rugged and simple but provided hours of spirit-lifting entertainment for soldiers who gathered around to sing familiar songs of home.

Singing—especially songs of praise—is one way that believers in Jesus can find peace in the battle too. King Jehoshaphat found this to be true when he faced vast invading armies (2 Chronicles 20). Terrified, the king called all the people together for prayer and fasting (vv. 3–4). In response, God told him to lead out soldiers to meet the enemy, promising that they'd "not have to fight this battle" (v. 17). Jehoshaphat believed God and acted in faith. He appointed singers to go ahead of the soldiers and sing praise to God for the victory they believed they would see (v. 21). And as their music began, God miraculously defeated their enemies and saved His people (v. 22).

Victory doesn't always come when and how we want it to. But we can always proclaim Jesus's ultimate victory over sin and death that's already been won for us. We can choose to rest in a spirit of worship even in the middle of a war zone. *Karen Pimpo*

Practice Gratitude Today

Listen to or sing along with a song that celebrates Jesus's victory over sin and death. Pray the lyrics as you worship God amid the challenges and anxieties of your day.

Thanks for Who God Is

PSALM 95:1–7

Let us come before him with thanksgiving
. . . for the Lord is the great God.
Psalm 95:2–3

Among the thousands of sentiments printed on greeting cards, perhaps one of the most touching is this simple statement: "Thanks for being you." If you receive that card, you know that someone cares for you not because you did something spectacular for that person but because you're appreciated for your essence.

I wonder if this sentiment indicates for us one of the best ways to say thank you to God. Sure, there are times when God intervenes in our lives in a tangible way, and we say something like, "Thank You, Lord, for allowing me to get that job." But most often, we can simply say, "Thank You, God, for being who You are."

That's what's behind verses like 1 Chronicles 16:34: "Give thanks to the Lord, for he is good; his love endures forever." Thank You, God, for who You are—good and loving. And Psalm 7:17: "I will give thanks to the Lord because of his righteousness." Thank You, God, for who You are—the Holy One. And "Let us come before him with thanksgiving . . . for the Lord is the great God" (Psalm 95:2–3). Thank You, God, for who You are—the almighty God of the universe.

Who God is. That's reason enough for us to stop what we're doing and praise and thank Him. Thank You, God, for just being You!

Dave Branon

Practice Gratitude Today

Spend a few minutes thinking about who God is—His character, His relationships, His actions, His words. Then thank Him for being Himself.

When God Says No

ISAIAH 25:1–5

In perfect faithfulness you have done wonderful things, things planned long ago.
Isaiah 25:1

When I was conscripted into the military at age eighteen, as all young Singaporean men are, I prayed desperately for an easy posting. A clerk or driver, perhaps. Not being particularly strong, I hoped to be spared the rigors of combat training. But one evening as I read my Bible, one verse leaped off the page: "My grace is sufficient for you" (2 Corinthians 12:9).

My heart dropped—but it shouldn't have. God had answered my prayers. Even if I received a difficult assignment, He would provide for me.

So I ended up as an armored infantryman, doing things I didn't always enjoy. Looking back now, I'm grateful God didn't give me what I wanted. The training and experience toughened me physically and mentally and gave me confidence to enter adulthood.

In Isaiah 25:1–5, after prophesying Israel's punishment and subsequent deliverance from her enemies, the prophet praises God for His plans. All these "wonderful things," Isaiah notes, had been "planned long ago" (v. 1), yet they included some arduous times.

It can be hard to hear God saying no, and even harder to understand when we're praying for something good—like someone's deliverance from a crisis. That's when we need to hold on to the truth of God's good plans. We may not understand why, but we can keep trusting in His love, goodness, and faithfulness. *Leslie Koh*

Practice Gratitude Today

Where is God saying no to you? Write yourself a letter about it; end by thanking God that you can trust His love and goodness. Put the letter where you will lose track of it but find it again in a year or two.

No Comparison

JOHN 21:17–25

A heart at peace gives life to the body, but envy rots the bones.
Proverbs 14:30

"One of these days I'm going to put it all on Facebook—not just the good stuff!"

My friend Sue's comment—made casually over lunch with her husband—caused me to laugh out loud and also to think. Social media can be a good thing, helping us stay in touch with and pray for friends across the years and miles. But if we're not careful, it can also create an unrealistic outlook on life. When much of what we see posted is a highlight reel of the good stuff, we can be misled into thinking others' lives are without trouble and wonder where our own went wrong.

Comparing ourselves with others is a sure recipe for unhappiness. When the disciples compared themselves to each other (see Luke 9:46; 22:24), Jesus quickly discouraged it. Soon after His resurrection, Jesus told Peter how he would suffer for his faith. Peter then turned to John and asked, "Lord, what about him?" Jesus answered, "If I want him to remain alive until I return, what is that to you? You must follow me" (John 21:21–22).

Jesus pointed Peter to the best remedy for unhealthy comparisons. When our minds are focused on God and all He's done for us, self-focused thoughts fall gently away and we long to follow Him. In place of the world's competitive strain and stress, He gives us His loving presence and peace. Nothing can compare with Him. *James Banks*

Practice Gratitude Today

Who do you compare yourself to, concluding that your life isn't good enough? In prayer, thank God for the relationships, opportunities, and resources He has given you.

Open Invitation

EPHESIANS 2:14–22

Let us then approach God's throne of grace with confidence, so that we may receive mercy and find grace to help us in our time of need.
Hebrews 4:16

Versailles was made the capital of France by King Louis XIV in 1682 and remained the capital (except for a short time) until 1789, when it was moved back to Paris. The beautiful Palace of Versailles includes an opulent 241-foot-long Hall of Mirrors. When a visitor approached the king, he had to curtsy every five steps as he walked the entire distance to meet the king sitting on his dazzling silver throne.

Foreign emissaries to France submitted to that humiliating ritual to court the French monarch's favor toward their country. By contrast, our God, the King of Kings, invites His people to come to His throne freely. We can come to Him anytime—no advance appointments and no bowing required!

How grateful we should be that our heavenly Father is so much more inviting. "Through him [Christ] we . . . have access to the Father by one Spirit" (Ephesians 2:18). Because of this, the writer of Hebrews urges us to "approach God's throne of grace with confidence, so that we may receive mercy and find grace to help us in our time of need" (Hebrews 4:16).

Have you responded to God's open invitation? Come in awe and gratitude, for the God of this universe is willing to hear your petitions anytime.

C. P. Hia

Practice Gratitude Today

What part of your day feels mundane, messy, or unremarkable? Pause in the middle of that circumstance to pray, thanking God that He, the infinite Creator of everything, invites you to bring everything to Him—no matter how small it seems.

Lost and Found

LUKE 15:4–24

This son of mine was dead and is alive
again; he was lost and is found.
Luke 15:24

A newspaper article by Jennifer Saranow chronicled the extraordinary efforts of middle-aged American men who are trying to find the favorite car they once owned and loved but lost. They are scouring online car ads, phoning junkyards, and even hiring specialists who charge $400 an hour to help them search for an automobile that once symbolized their youth. These men want the actual car they owned, not one just like it.

Some would call their efforts frivolous—a waste of time and money. But the value of a car, like many things, is in the eye of the beholder.

In Luke 15, people who were despised by their society came to hear Jesus. But some religious leaders complained, "This man welcomes sinners and eats with them" (v. 2). To affirm how valuable these "sinners" are to God, Jesus told three memorable stories about a lost sheep (vv. 4–7), a lost coin (vv. 8–10), and a lost son (vv. 11–32). Each parable records the anguish of losing, the effort of searching for, and the joy of finding something of great worth. In every story, we see a picture of God, the loving Father, who rejoices over every lost soul who is found.

Even if you feel far from God today, you are highly valued by Him. He's searching for you. *David McCasland*

Practice Gratitude Today

What is something precious you've lost—perhaps a possession, friendship, or season of life? Thank God that you are so precious to Him that He never stops pursuing you.

The Mood Mender

PSALM 94:2, 16–23

When anxiety was great within me, your consolation brought me joy.
Psalm 94:19

As I waited at the train station for my weekly commute, negative thoughts crowded my mind like commuters lining up to board a train—stress over debt, unkind remarks said to me, helplessness in the face of a recent injustice done to a family member. By the time the train arrived, I was in a terrible mood.

On the train, another thought came to mind: write a note to God, giving Him my lament. Soon after I finished pouring out my complaints in my journal, I pulled out my phone and listened to the praise songs in my library. Before I knew it, my bad mood had completely changed.

Little did I know that I was following a pattern set by the writer of Psalm 94. The psalmist first poured out his complaints: "Rise up, Judge of the earth; pay back to the proud what they deserve. . . . Who will rise up for me against the wicked? Who will take a stand for me against evildoers?" (Psalm 94:2, 16.) He didn't hold anything back as he talked to God about injustice done to widows and orphans. Once he'd made his lament to God, the psalmist transitioned into praise: "But the LORD has become my fortress, and my God the rock in whom I take refuge" (v. 22).

God invites us to take our laments to Him. He can turn our fear, sadness, and helplessness into praise. *Linda Washington*

Practice Gratitude Today

Write a note to God in your journal or on your phone. Honestly pour out your complaints, lamenting what is difficult in your life. End by praising God for who He is and what He's done.

When God Intervenes

NUMBERS 23:13–23

Do not touch my anointed ones; do my prophets no harm.
Psalm 105:15

In a poem titled "This Child Is Beloved," Omawumi Efueye, known affectionately as Pastor O, writes about his parents' attempts to end the pregnancy that would result in his birth. After several unusual events that prevented them from aborting him, they decided to welcome their child instead. The knowledge of God's preservation of his life motivated Omawumi to give up a lucrative career in favor of full-time ministry. Today, he faithfully pastors a London church.

Like Pastor O, the Israelites experienced God's intervention at a vulnerable time in their history. While traveling through the wilderness, they came within sight of King Balak of Moab. Terrified of their conquests and their vast population, Balak engaged a seer named Balaam to place a curse on the unsuspecting travelers (Numbers 22:2–6).

But something amazing happened. Whenever Balaam opened his mouth to curse, a blessing issued instead. "I have received a command to bless; he has blessed, and I cannot change it," he declared. "No misfortune is seen in Jacob, no misery observed in Israel. The Lord their God is with them. . . . God brought them out of Egypt" (23:20–22). God preserved the Israelites from a battle they didn't even know was raging!

Whether we see it or not, God still watches over His people today. May we worship in gratitude and awe the One who calls us blessed.

Remi Oyedele

Practice Gratitude Today

When has God brought you through a time of vulnerability, weakness, or scarcity? Pause to thank Him for watching over you.

Camping Psalms

PSALM 8:1–9

LORD, our Lord, how majestic is your name in all the earth!
Psalm 8:1

When my husband and I go for nature walks, we bring our cameras and take close-ups of the plants at our feet, which are like microcosms of the world. What amazing variety and beauty we see, even in the fungi that spring up overnight and dot the woods with splashes of bright orange, red, and yellow.

The snapshots of life that surround us inspire me to lift my eyes to the Maker who created not only mushrooms but also the stars in the heavens. He designed a world of infinite scope and variety. And He made you and me and placed us in the very middle of this beauty to enjoy and to rule over it (Genesis 1:27–28; Psalm 8:6–8).

My thoughts turn to one of our family's "camping psalms"—psalms we read as we sit around the fire. "LORD, our Lord, how majestic is your name in all the earth! You have set your glory in the heavens. . . . When I consider your heavens, the work of your fingers, the moon and the stars, which you have set in place, what is mankind that you are mindful of them, human beings that you care for them?" (Psalm 8:1, 3–4).

How amazing that the great God who created the world in all its splendor cares for you and me! *Alyson Kieda*

Practice Gratitude Today

Find a tiny bit of God's creation that reveals His glory: an ant, a snowflake, a blade of grass. Thank God that He cares for all His creation—including you.

Answering Anxiety

PHILIPPIANS 4:1–9

Do not be anxious about anything, but in every situation, by prayer and petition, with thanksgiving, present your requests to God.
Philippians 4:6

We were excited about moving for my husband's job. But the unknowns and challenges left me feeling anxious. Thoughts of sorting and packing up belongings. Looking for a place to live. My finding a new job too. Making my way around a new city and getting settled. It was all . . . unsettling. As I thought about my to-do list, words written by the apostle Paul echoed in my mind: don't worry, but pray (Philippians 4:6–7).

If anyone could have been anxious about unknowns and challenges, it was Paul. He was shipwrecked. He was beaten. He was jailed. In his letter to the Philippian church, he encouraged his friends who also were facing unknowns, telling them, "Do not be anxious about anything, but in every situation, by prayer and petition, with thanksgiving, present your requests to God" (v. 6).

Paul's words encourage me. Life is not without uncertainties—whether they come in the form of a major life transition, family issues, health scares, or financial trouble. What I continue to learn is that God cares. He invites us to let go of our fears of the unknown by giving them to Him. When we do, He, who knows all things, promises that His peace, "which transcends all understanding, will guard" our hearts and minds in Christ Jesus (v. 7). *Karen Wolfe*

Practice Gratitude Today

What are you anxious about today? Bring your worries and uncertainties to God in prayer, thanking Him that He can provide a peace that doesn't make sense amid your circumstances.

Praising God's Goodness

PSALM 136:1–15

Give thanks to the LORD, for he is good. His love endures forever.
Psalm 136:1

Someone in our Bible study group suggested, "Let's write our own psalms!" Initially, some protested that they didn't have the flair for writing, but after some encouragement everyone wrote a moving poetic song narrating how God had been working in their lives. Out of trials, protection, provision, and even pain and tears came enduring messages that gave our psalms fascinating themes. Like Psalm 136, each psalm revealed the truth that God's love endures forever.

We all have a story to tell about God's love—whether we write or sing or tell it. For some, our experiences may be dramatic or intense—like the writer of Psalm 136 who recounted how God delivered His people from captivity and conquered His enemies (vv. 10–15). Others may simply describe God's marvelous creation: "who by his understanding made the heavens, . . . who spread out the earth upon the waters, . . . who made the great lights— . . . the sun to govern the day . . . the moon and stars to govern the night" (vv. 5–9).

Remembering who God is and what He has done brings out praise and thanksgiving that glorifies Him. We can then speak "to one another with psalms, hymns, and songs from the Spirit" (Ephesians 5:19) about the goodness of the Lord whose love endures forever. Turn your experience of God's love into a praise song of your own and enjoy an overflow of His never-ending goodness. *Lawrence Darmani*

Practice Gratitude Today

Write a psalm. Don't overthink it! Simply write about who God is and what He has done, and praise Him for His love and goodness.

I Can Only Imagine

2 CORINTHIANS 5:1–10

The dust returns to the ground it came from,
and the spirit returns to God who gave it.
Ecclesiastes 12:7

I settled into the church pew behind a woman wearing a colorful scarf as the music team began playing "I Can Only Imagine." Raising my hands, I praised God as the woman's sweet soprano voice harmonized with mine. After service, we introduced ourselves. Louise told me about her health struggles, and we decided to read Scripture and pray together during her cancer treatment appointments.

A few months later, Louise told me she feared dying. Leaning onto her hospital bed, I rested my head next to hers, whispered a prayer, and quietly sang our song. I can only imagine what it was like for Louise when she worshiped Jesus face-to-face just a few days later.

The apostle Paul offered comforting assurance for his readers who were facing death (2 Corinthians 5:1). The suffering experienced on this side of eternity may cause groaning, but our hope remains anchored to our heavenly dwelling—our eternal existence with Jesus (vv. 2–4). Though God designed us to yearn for everlasting life with Him (vv. 5–6), His promises are meant to impact the way we live for Him now (vv. 7–10).

As we live to please Jesus while waiting for Him to return or call us home, we can rejoice in the peace of His constant presence. What will we experience that moment we leave our earthly bodies and join Jesus in eternity? We can only imagine! *Xochitl Dixon*

Practice Gratitude Today

What struggle, pain, or sin are you most grateful will be no more in the life to come? Thank God for the hope of eternal life in Christ, and for His presence amid the difficulties of this life.

Warts and All

COLOSSIANS 3:12–15

Forgive as the Lord forgave you.
Colossians 3:13

Oliver Cromwell, who ruled as Lord Protector of England, was a military commander in the seventeenth century. It was common practice during those days for people of importance to have their portraits painted. And it wasn't unusual for an artist to avoid depicting the less attractive aspects of a person's face. Cromwell, however, wanted nothing to do with a likeness that would flatter him. He cautioned the artist, "You must paint me just as I am—warts and all—or I won't pay you."

Apparently the artist complied. The finished portrait of Cromwell displays a couple of prominent facial warts that nowadays would surely be filtered out before being posted on social media.

The expression "warts and all" has come to mean that people should be accepted just as they are—with all their annoying faults, attitudes, and issues. In some cases, we feel that's too difficult a task. Yet when we take a hard inward look, we might find some pretty unattractive aspects of our own character.

We're grateful that God forgives our "warts." And in Colossians 3, we're taught to extend grace to others. The apostle Paul encourages us to be more patient, kind, and compassionate—even to those who aren't easy to love. He urges us to have a forgiving spirit because of the way God forgives us (vv. 12–13). By His example, we're taught to love others the way God loves us—warts and all. *Cindy Hess Kasper*

Practice Gratitude Today

What is one foible, habit, or flaw of someone you will interact with today that annoys you? Intentionally extend grace to that person, remembering that God forgives your flaws and sins.

Choose Joy

PHILIPPIANS 1:12–21

Rejoice in the Lord always. I will say it again: Rejoice!
Philippians 4:4

Keith was feeling down as he trudged through the produce aisle. His hands trembled from the first signs of Parkinson's disease. How long before his quality of life began to slide? What would this mean for his wife and children? Keith's gloom was shattered by laughter. Over by the potatoes, a man pushed a giggling boy in a wheelchair. The man leaned over and whispered to his son, who couldn't stop grinning. He was noticeably worse off than Keith, yet he and his dad were finding joy where they could.

Writing from prison or under house arrest as he awaited the outcome of his trial, the apostle Paul seemingly had no right to be joyful (Philippians 1:12–13). The emperor was Nero, a wicked man who had a growing reputation for violence and cruelty, so Paul had reason to be concerned. He also knew there were preachers who were taking advantage of his absence to gain glory for themselves. They thought they could "stir up trouble" for the apostle while he was imprisoned (v. 17).

Yet Paul chose to rejoice (vv. 18–21), and he told the Philippians to follow his example: "Rejoice in the Lord always. I will say it again: Rejoice!" (4:4). Our situation might seem bleak, yet Jesus is with us now, and He's guaranteed our glorious future. Christ, who walked out of His tomb, will return to raise His followers to live with Him. Whatever situation we face, may we rejoice! *Mike Wittmer*

Practice Gratitude Today

What difficulty or struggle makes it feel like joy isn't an option today? Thank God that His love, joy, and salvation don't depend on your circumstances.

Beauty in the Church

EXODUS 36:1–7

All who are skilled among you are to come and make everything the LORD has commanded.
Exodus 35:10

When my husband, Jay, and I decided to build a new house, we didn't recruit friends and family who enjoy working with power tools; instead, we hired a skilled builder to create something both functional and beautiful.

Beauty in church buildings, however, is not always a high priority. Some associate it with impracticality, so anything ornate or decorative is considered wasteful. But that wasn't God's attitude when He established a place of worship for the ancient Israelites. He didn't recruit just anybody to set up an ordinary tent. He appointed skilled artisans, Bezalel and Oholiab (Exodus 36:1), to decorate the tabernacle with finely woven tapestries and intricately designed ornaments (37:17–20).

I think the beauty was important then because it reminded the people of the worth of God in their worship. During the dry and dusty days of desert wanderings, they needed a reminder of God's majesty.

The beauty created by God's people in worship settings today can serve the same purpose. We offer God our best talents because He is worthy. Beauty also gives us a glimpse of heaven and whets our appetites for what God is preparing for our future. *Julie Ackerman Link*

Practice Gratitude Today

How can you create a little beauty today? As you do so, thank God that you can bring a little heaven to earth, whether in a friendship, in your home, in your work, or in some other area.

Reflecting the Light of the Son

MATTHEW 5:14–16

You are the light of the world.
Matthew 5:14

After I had a conflict with my mother, she finally agreed to meet with me more than an hour away from my home. But upon arriving, I discovered she'd left before I got there. In my anger, I wrote her a note. But I revised it after I felt God nudging me to respond in love. After my mother read my revised message, she called me. "You've changed," she said. God used my note to lead my mom to ask about Jesus and, eventually, receive Him as her personal Savior.

In Matthew 5, Jesus affirms that His disciples are the light of the world (v. 14). He said, "Let your light shine before others, that they may see your good deeds and glorify your Father in heaven" (v. 16). As soon as we receive Christ as our Savior, we receive the power of the Holy Spirit. He transforms us so we can be radiant testimonies of God's truth and love wherever we go.

Through the power of the Holy Spirit, we can be joyful lights of hope and peace who look more and more like Jesus every day. Every good thing we do then becomes an act of grateful worship, which looks attractive to others and can be perceived as vibrant faith. Surrendered to the Holy Spirit, we can give honor to the Father by reflecting the light of the Son—Jesus.

Xochitl Dixon

Practice Gratitude Today

Thank God that His Spirit lives inside you, guiding you and transforming you into the image of His Son. Ask the Holy Spirit to show you opportunities to share Christ's love with others today.

A Second Chance

LAMENTATIONS 3:22–33

His compassions never fail. They are new every morning; great is your faithfulness.
Lamentations 3:22–23

One hundred and fifty-five people on US Airways Flight 1549 thought they were going to die. During takeoff from New York City, their plane struck a flock of geese, disabling both engines. In a powerless glide, the captain maneuvered over the densely populated area, then announced: "Brace for impact." Less than ninety seconds later, the crippled plane made a water landing in the frigid Hudson River, where boats and ferries quickly arrived to rescue the passengers and crew, all of whom survived. People called it the "miracle on the Hudson" and praised the pilot and crew. One grateful passenger said simply, "We have a second chance in life."

In times of crisis, we grasp the importance of every hour. During our ordinary routine, however, we often forget that each day is a second chance. "Because of the LORD's great love we are not consumed, for his compassions never fail. They are new every morning; great is your faithfulness. I say to myself, 'The LORD is my portion; therefore I will wait for him'" (Lamentations 3:22–24).

We can choose to live with thankfulness for God's mercy and grace, with confidence in His faithful care, and with hope because He is with us forever. Today, God offers us a second chance in life. Let's make the most of it!

David McCasland

Practice Gratitude Today

As often as you can given your schedule, set an alarm or reminder to go off every hour or so today. Pause each time the alarm goes off to thank God for another hour to love and live for Him.

Step-by-Step

1 PETER 4:7–11

How good and pleasant it is when God's
people live together in unity!
Psalm 133:1

A dozen teams, each including three people standing shoulder to shoulder, prepared for the four-legged race. Bound to the person in the middle by colorful rags at their ankles and knees, each trio locked their eyes on the finish line. When the whistle blew, the teams lunged forward. Most of them fell and struggled to regain their footing. A few groups chose to hop instead of walk. Some gave up. But one team delayed their start, confirmed their plan, and communicated as they moved forward. They stumbled along the way but pressed on and soon passed all the teams. Their willingness to cooperate, step-by-step, enabled them to cross the finish line together.

Living for God within the community of believers in Jesus often feels as frustrating as trying to move forward during a four-legged race. We often stumble when interacting with people who hold opinions different from us. Frequently, we push forward when others aren't with us on the same page.

Peter speaks of prayer, hospitality, and using our gifts to align ourselves in unity for life ahead. He urges believers in Jesus to "love each other deeply" (1 Peter 4:8), to be hospitable without complaining, and to "serve others, as faithful stewards of God's grace in its various forms" (v. 10). When we ask God to help us communicate and cooperate, we can lead the race in showing the world how to celebrate differences and live together in unity.

Xochitl Dixon

Practice Gratitude Today

Where do you feel out of step with others in your church community? Talk to God about it. End by thanking Him for including and celebrating all different kinds of people in His family.

God's Sure Pursuit

PSALM 23

Surely your goodness and love will follow
me all the days of my life.
Psalm 23:6

A man was walking about a block ahead of me. I could clearly see his arms were full of packages. All of a sudden, he tripped, dropping everything. A couple of people helped him to his feet, assisting him in collecting what he'd dropped. But they missed something—his wallet. I picked it up and took off in hot pursuit of the stranger, hoping to return that important item. I yelled, "Sir, sir!" and finally got his attention. He turned just as I reached him. As I held out the wallet, I'll never forget his look of surprised relief and immense gratitude.

What began as following along after that man turned into something quite different. Most English translations use the word "follow" in the final verse of the familiar Psalm 23—"Surely your goodness and love will follow me" (v. 6). While "follow" fits, the actual Hebrew word used is more forceful, aggressive even. The word literally means "to pursue or chase," much like a predator pursues its prey (think of a wolf pursuing sheep).

God's goodness and love don't merely follow along after us at a casual pace, in no real hurry. No, "surely" we are being pursued—chased even—with intention. Much like pursuing a man to return his wallet, we're pursued by the Good Shepherd who loves us with an everlasting love (v. 1).

John Blase

Practice Gratitude Today

Find a video of a predator, such as a lion or wolf, pursuing prey. Thank God that His goodness and love will pursue you all the days of your life.

Strong and Good

PSALM 118:13–14, 22–29

The stone the builders rejected has become the cornerstone.
Psalm 118:22

The young campus minister was troubled. But he looked conflicted when I dared to ask if he prays for God's direction—for His help. To pray, as Paul urged, without ceasing. In reply, the young man confessed, "I'm not sure I believe anymore in prayer." He frowned. "Or believe that God is listening. Just look at the world." That young leader was trying to build a ministry in his own strength, and, sadly, he was failing. Why? He was rejecting God.

Jesus, as the cornerstone of the church, has always been rejected—starting, in fact, with His own people (John 1:11). Many still reject Him today, struggling to build their lives, work, even churches on lesser foundations—their own schemes, dreams, and other unreliable ground. Yet, our good Savior alone is our strength and defense (Psalm 118:14). Indeed, "the stone the builders rejected has become the cornerstone" (v. 22).

Set at the vital cornerstone of our lives, He provides the only right alignment for anything His believers seek to accomplish for Him. To Him, therefore, we pray, "Lord, save us! Lord, grant us success!" (v. 25). The result? "Blessed is he who comes in the name of the Lord" (v. 26). May we give thanks to Him because He's strong and good.

Patricia Raybon

Practice Gratitude Today

Where are you experiencing doubt about God's attention and intentions? Talk with Him about it. Ask Him to be the foundation of your plans, and thank Him for being strong and good.

Don't Miss the Chance

PSALM 19:1–4

The heavens declare the glory of God; the skies proclaim the work of his hands.
Psalm 19:1

"Don't ever miss the chance to show your babies the moon!" she said. Before our midweek prayer service began, a group of us talked about the previous night's harvest moon. The full moon was striking, as it seemed to sit on the horizon. Mrs. Webb was the elder voice in our conversation, a gray-haired lover of God's grand creation. She knew my wife and I had two children in our home at the time, and she wanted to help me train them in a way worth going. Don't ever miss the chance to show your babies the moon!

Mrs. Webb would've made a good psalmist. Her brand of attentiveness is reflected in David's description of the heavenly bodies that "have no speech. . . . Yet their voice goes out into all the earth, their words to the ends of the world" (Psalm 19:3–4). Neither the psalmist nor Mrs. Webb had any intention of worshiping the moon or the stars, but rather the creative hands behind them. The heavens and skies reveal nothing less than the glory of God (v. 1).

We too can encourage those around us—from babies and teenagers to spouses and neighbors—to stop, look, and listen for declarations and proclamations of God's glory that are all around us. Drawing attention to the work of His hands in turn leads to worshiping the awesome God behind the whole show. Don't ever miss the chance.

John Blase

Practice Gratitude Today

Today, draw someone's attention to an aspect of God's creation that you find wonderful. Thank God that all His works reflect His power, creativity, and love.

Drop by Drop

1 JOHN 4:9–19

We love because he first loved us.
1 John 4:19

"In everything we look for pleasant ways of serving God," writes sixteenth-century believer Teresa of Ávila. She poignantly reflects on the many ways we seek to stay in control through easier, more "pleasant" methods than total surrender to God. We tend to slowly, tentatively, and even reluctantly grow to trust Him with all of ourselves. And so, Teresa confesses, "even as we measure out our lives to you a bit at a time, we must be content to receive your gifts drop by drop, until we have surrendered our lives wholly to you."

As human beings, trust doesn't come naturally to many of us. So if experiencing God's grace and love were dependent on our ability to trust and receive it, we'd be in trouble!

But, as we read in 1 John 4, God's love for us comes first (v. 19). He loved us long before we could love Him, so much that He was willing to sacrifice His Son for us. "This is love," John writes in wonder and gratitude (v. 10).

Gradually, gently, little by little, God heals our hearts to receive His love. Drop by drop, His grace helps us surrender our fears (v. 18). Drop by drop, His grace reaches our hearts until we find ourselves experiencing showers of His abundant beauty and love.

Monica La Rose

Practice Gratitude Today

What wounds or fears make it difficult for you to trust God's love? Thank God that He first loved you—and will always love you.

Five Good Things

PSALM 107:1–9

Give thanks to the Lord, for he is good; his love endures forever.
Psalm 107:1

According to research, people who are intentionally grateful for what they have report better sleep, fewer symptoms of illness, and more happiness. Those are impressive benefits. Psychologists even suggest keeping a gratitude journal to improve our well-being, writing down five things we're grateful for each week.

Scripture has long promoted the practice of gratitude. From meals and marriage (1 Timothy 4:3–5) to the beauties of creation (Psalm 104), the Bible calls us to see such things as gifts and to thank the Giver for them. Psalm 107 lists five things Israel could be especially grateful for: their rescue from the desert (vv. 4–9), their release from captivity (vv. 10–16), healing from disease (vv. 18–22), safety at sea (vv. 23–32), and their flourishing in a barren land (vv. 33–42). "Give thanks to the Lord," the psalm repeats, for these are all signs of God's "unfailing love" (vv. 8, 15, 21, 31).

Do you have a notepad handy? Why not write down five good things you're grateful for now? It might be the meal you just enjoyed, your marriage, or, as for Israel, God's times of rescue in your life to date. Give thanks for the birds singing outside, the smells from your kitchen, the comfort of your chair, the murmurs of loved ones. Each is a gift and a sign of God's unfailing love. *Sheridan Voysey*

Practice Gratitude Today

List five things you've experienced in the past twenty-four hours that you're grateful for. Be specific. Thank God for His goodness and love for you.

Perfect Peace

JOHN 14:25–31

Peace I leave with you; my peace I give you.
John 14:27

A friend shared with me that for years she searched for peace and contentment. She and her husband built up a successful business, so she was able to buy a big house, fancy clothes, and expensive jewelry. But these possessions didn't satisfy her inner longings for peace, nor did her friendships with influential people. Then one day, when she was feeling low and desperate, a friend told her about the good news of Jesus. There she found the Prince of Peace, and her understanding of true peace and contentment was forever changed.

Jesus spoke words of such peace to His friends after the Last Supper (John 14), when He prepared them for the events that would soon follow: His death, resurrection, and the coming of the Holy Spirit. Describing a peace—unlike anything the world can give—He wanted them to learn how to find a sense of well-being even in the midst of hardship.

Later, when the resurrected Jesus appeared to the frightened disciples after His death, He greeted them, saying, "Peace be with you!" (20:19). Now He could give them, and us, a new understanding of resting in what He has done for us. As we do, we can find the awareness of a confidence far deeper than our ever-changing feelings.

Amy Boucher Pye

Practice Gratitude Today

Spend a few minutes sitting quietly with the Prince of Peace. Thank Him for the peace He's made possible with God, with others, with your circumstances, and with yourself.

Ring the Bell

PSALM 47

Shout to God with cries of joy.
Psalm 47:1

After an astounding thirty rounds of radiation treatments, Darla was finally pronounced cancer-free. As part of hospital tradition, she was eager to ring the "cancer-free bell" that marked the end of her treatment and celebrated her clean bill of health. Darla was so enthusiastic and vigorous in her celebratory ringing that the rope actually detached from the bell! Peals of joyous laughter ensued.

Darla's story brings a smile to my face and gives me a sense of what the psalmist might have envisioned when he invited the Israelites to celebrate God's work in their lives. The writer encouraged them to "clap [their] hands," "shout to God," and "sing praises" because God had routed their enemies and chosen the Israelites as His beloved people (Psalm 47:1, 6).

God doesn't always grant us victory over our struggles in this life, whether health-related or financial or relational. He's worthy of our worship and praise in even those circumstances because we can trust that He's still "seated on his holy throne" (v. 8). When He does bring us to a place of healing—at least in a way we recognize in this earthly life—it's cause for great celebration. We may not have a physical bell to ring, but we can joyfully celebrate His goodness to us with the same kind of exuberance Darla showed. *Kirsten Holmberg*

Practice Gratitude Today

How have you recently experienced God's healing, or where are you longing for God's healing? Today, how can you celebrate God's goodness amid that circumstance?

Praise in the Dark

MATTHEW 26:17–30

Through Jesus, therefore, let us continually offer to God a sacrifice of praise—the fruit of lips that openly profess his name.
Hebrews 13:15

Even though my friend Mickey was losing his eyesight, he told me, "I'm going to keep praising God every day, because He's done so much for me."

Jesus gave Mickey, and us, the ultimate reason for such never-ending praise. Matthew 26 tells us about how Jesus shared the Passover meal with His disciples the night before He went to the cross. Verse 30 shows us how they concluded the meal: "When they had sung a hymn, they went out to the Mount of Olives."

It wasn't just any hymn they sang that night—it was a hymn of praise. For millennia, Jews have sung a group of Psalms called the Hallel at Passover (*hallel* is the Hebrew word for "praise"). The last of these prayers and songs of praise, found in Psalms 113–118, honors the God who has become our salvation (118:21). It refers to a rejected stone that became a cornerstone (v. 22) and one who comes in the name of the Lord (v. 26). They may very well have sung, "The Lord has done it this very day; let us rejoice today and be glad" (v. 24).

As Jesus sang with His disciples on this Passover night, He was giving us the ultimate reason to lift our eyes above our immediate circumstances. He was leading us in praise of the never-ending love and faithfulness of our God. *James Banks*

Practice Gratitude Today

Where does your life feel dim, unknown, or in decline? Pray the words of Psalm 113, 116, or 118 to God as you choose to remember His love and faithfulness.

Spare Beds

HEBREWS 13:1–6

Do not forget to show hospitality to strangers,
for by so doing some people have shown
hospitality to angels without knowing it.
Hebrews 13:2

When Casey Fenton cofounded Couchsurfing, it began as a nonprofit service to help travelers find a "friendlier alternative" to unfriendly hotels. The organization finds homeowners who are willing to offer their spare beds and couches to others.

The group boasts hundreds of thousands of friendships that have been formed from their service. "The more we network," said Fenton, "the better chance we have of this world being a better place."

The heart of that service sounds a lot like biblical hospitality. In the final pages of his letter to the Hebrews, the writer instructed believers to practice their faith in Jesus Christ through hospitality (13:2). That was defined by early Christ followers as acts of generosity toward strangers.

In the first century, hospitality often included housing a guest. This was hardest to do during a time of persecution. These believers would not know whether the person was a spy or a fellow believer being pursued. But by entertaining strangers, the writer said, they could indeed be inviting a blessing into their homes.

As God's people, we are called to be hospitable to others as part of our gratitude for the salvation we have received from God.

Marvin Williams

Practice Gratitude Today

What is a small way you can show hospitality to someone today? As you show generosity to another, thank God that He generously invited you into His family and to share eternity with Him.

Details, Details

PHILEMON 1:4–16

Give thanks in all circumstances.
1 Thessalonians 5:18

Details make a difference. Ask the man from Germany who planned to visit his fiancée for Christmas but ended up in snowy Sidney, Montana, instead of sunny Sydney, Australia.

Prepositions in our language seem like insignificant details, but they can make a big difference. The words "in" and "for" are an example.

The apostle Paul wrote, "Give thanks in all circumstances" (1 Thessalonians 5:18). That doesn't mean we have to be thankful *for* everything. We need not be thankful for the bad choices someone makes, but we can be thankful in the circumstances because the Lord can use the resulting difficulties for good.

The letter to Philemon illustrates this idea. Paul was imprisoned with Onesimus, a runaway slave. He certainly didn't have to give thanks for his bad situation. Yet his letter is full of gratitude because he knew that God was using it for good. Onesimus had become something more than a slave; he was a beloved brother in the Lord (v. 16).

Knowing that God can use all things for good is more than enough reason to give thanks in everything. Giving thanks in difficult circumstances is a small detail that makes a big difference.

Julie Ackerman Link

Practice Gratitude Today

What difficult circumstances are you experiencing today? Bring them to God in prayer, thanking Him for His faithfulness and presence amid the difficulty.

I Hear You, God!

JOHN 10:1–11, 16

The gatekeeper opens the gate for him,
and the sheep listen to his voice.
John 10:3

Baby Graham fussed and wiggled as his mother held him in her lap while the doctors inserted his first hearing aid. Moments after the doctor turned on the device, Graham stopped crying. His eyes widened. He grinned. He could hear his mother's voice comforting him, encouraging him, and calling his name.

Baby Graham heard his mother speaking, but he needed help learning how to recognize her voice and understand the meaning of her words. Jesus invites people into a similar learning process. Once we accept Christ as our Savior, we become the sheep He knows intimately and guides personally (John 10:3). We can grow to trust and obey Him as we practice hearing and heeding His voice (v. 4).

In the Old Testament, God spoke through the prophets. In the New Testament, Jesus—God in the flesh—spoke directly to people. Today, believers in Jesus have access to the power of the Holy Spirit, who helps us understand and obey God's words which He inspired and preserved in the Bible. We can communicate directly with Jesus through our prayers as He speaks to us through Scripture and through His people. As we come to recognize God's voice, which is always in alignment with His words in the Bible, we can cry out with grateful praise, "I hear You, God!"

Xochitl Dixon

Practice Gratitude Today

Read a favorite passage or chapter of the Bible. Thank God for speaking to you, and for living inside of you and guiding you by His Spirit.

Disposable Culture

PSALM 136:1–9, 23–26

Give thanks to the LORD, for he is good. His love endures forever.
Psalm 136:1

More than ever, we live in a disposable culture. Think for a minute about some of the things that are made to be thrown away—razors, water bottles, lighters, paper plates, plastic eating utensils. Products are used, tossed, and then replaced.

This disposable culture is also reflected in more significant ways. Many times true commitment in relationships is seen as optional. Marriages struggle to survive. Long-term employees are discharged just before retirement for cheaper options. A highly revered athlete leaves to join another team. It seems as if nothing lasts.

Our unchanging God, however, has promised that His loving mercy endures forever. In Psalm 136, the singer celebrates this wonderful promise by making statements about God's wonder, work, and character. He then punctuates each statement about God with the phrase "his love endures forever." Whether it is the wonder of His creation (vv. 4–9), the rescue of His people (vv. 10–22), or His tender care for His own (vv. 23–26), we can trust God because His love will never fail. In a temporary world, the permanence of God's love gives us hope. We can sing with the psalmist, "Give thanks to the LORD, for he is good. His love endures forever" (v. 1). *Bill Crowder*

Practice Gratitude Today

What was something you counted on lasting that didn't? Perhaps it was a job, relationship, or church community. Turn to God in prayer, and thank Him that His love will never fail.

Food That Says I Love You

LUKE 22:14–20

He took bread, gave thanks and broke it, and gave it to them.
Luke 22:19

I attended a family birthday gathering where the hostess wove the theme of "favorite things" into the decor, the gifts, and—best of all—the food. Because the birthday girl loved steak and salad and white chocolate raspberry Bundt cake, the hostess grilled steak, spun spinach, and ordered that favorite cake. Favorite foods say "I love you."

The Bible contains many references to banquets, feasts, and festivals, pairing the physical act of eating with celebrations of God's faithfulness. Feasting was a part of the sacrificial system of worship practiced by the Israelites, including Passover, the Festival of Weeks, and new moon feasts held every month (Numbers 28:11–31). And in Psalm 23:5, God prepares a table with an abundant meal and cups overflow with mercy and love. Perhaps the most lavish pairing of food and wine ever expressed was when Jesus broke a piece of bread and took a cup of wine, illustrating the gift of His death on a cross for our salvation. He then challenged us to "do this in remembrance of me" (Luke 22:19).

As you partake of food today, take a moment to consider the God who made both mouth and stomach and offers food to you as a language of His love in celebration of His faithfulness. Ours is a God who feasts with the faithful, pairing His perfect provision with our great need, saying, "I love you." *Elisa Morgan*

Practice Gratitude Today

If possible, prepare or order a favorite food today. Whatever you eat today, slow down to intentionally enjoy this gift from God, and thank Him for it.

Accepted and Approved

ISAIAH 43:1–4

You are precious and honored in my sight, and . . . I love you.
Isaiah 43:4

As a child, Tenny felt insecure. He sought approval from his father, but he never received it. It seemed that whatever he did, whether in school or at home, it was never good enough. Even when he entered adulthood, the insecurity remained. He continually wondered, *Am I good enough?*

Only when Tenny received Jesus as his Savior did he find the security and approval he'd long yearned for. He learned that God—having created him—loved and cherished him as His son. Tenny finally could live with the confidence that he was truly valued and appreciated.

In Isaiah 43:1–4, God told His chosen people that, having formed them, He would use His power and love to redeem them. "You are precious and honored in my sight," He proclaimed (v. 4). He would act on their behalf because He loved them.

The value God places on those He loves doesn't come from anything we do but from the simple and powerful truth that He's chosen us to be His own.

These words in Isaiah 43 not only gave Tenny great security but also empowered him with the confidence to do his best for God in whatever task he was called to do. Today he's a pastor who does all he can to encourage others with this life-giving truth: we're accepted and approved in Jesus. May we confidently live out this truth today.

Leslie Koh

Practice Gratitude Today

What experiences have made you feel inadequate, unapproved, or not good enough? Talk with God about it. Thank Him that you are chosen and approved by the God of all creation.

A Slower Pace

EXODUS 20:8–11

Six days you shall labor and do all your work, but the seventh day is a sabbath to the Lord your God. On it you shall not do any work.
Exodus 20:9–10

When writer Bruce Feiler was diagnosed with bone cancer in his thigh, he couldn't walk without some help for over a year. Learning to get around on crutches caused him to appreciate a slower pace of life. Feiler said, "The idea of slowing down became the number one lesson I learned from my experience."

After God's people were liberated from Egypt, He gave them a commandment that would cause them to slow down and view Him and the world "in pause." The fourth commandment introduced a dramatic contrast to the Israelites' slavery under Pharaoh when they had no break in their daily work routine.

The commandment insisted that God's people set aside one day a week to remember several important things: God's work in creation (Genesis 2:2), their liberation from Egyptian bondage (Deuteronomy 5:12–15), their relationship with God (6:4–6), and their need for personal refreshment (Exodus 31:12–18). This was not to be a day of laziness but one where God's people acknowledged, worshiped, and rested in Him.

We too are called to slow down; to be refreshed physically, mentally, and emotionally; and to behold God in His good creation.

Marvin Williams

Practice Gratitude Today

Make space in your schedule today to enjoy an intentional pause. As you slow down, thank God that He intended you to experience times of personal refreshment.

As Advertised

JOHN 16:25–33

In this world you will have trouble. But take heart! I have overcome the world.
John 16:33

During a vacation, my husband and I signed up for a leisurely rafting tour down Georgia's Chattahoochee River. Dressed in sandals, a sundress, and a wide-brimmed hat, I groaned when we discovered—contrary to the advertisement—that the trip included light rapids. Thankfully, we rode with a couple experienced in white water rafting. They taught my husband the basics of paddling and promised to navigate us safely to our destination. Grateful for my life jacket, I screamed and gripped the raft's handle until we reached the muddy bank downriver. I stepped ashore and dumped water from my purse as my husband helped wring out the hem of my soaked dress. We enjoyed a good laugh, even though the trip had not turned out as advertised.

Unlike the tour brochure, which clearly left out a key detail about the trip, Jesus explicitly warned His disciples that rough waters were ahead. He told them that they'd be persecuted and martyred and that He would die and be resurrected. He also guaranteed His trustworthiness, affirming that He would guide them toward undeniable triumph and everlasting hope (John 16:16–33).

Although it would be nice if life were easier when we follow Jesus, He made it clear that His disciples would have troubles. But He promised to be with us. Trials won't define, limit, or destroy God's plan for us, because Jesus's resurrection has already propelled us to eternal victory.

Xochitl Dixon

Practice Gratitude Today

What difficulty, struggle, or sin do you feel like following Jesus should remove from your life? Thank Jesus for His honesty—and His promised presence.

He Changed My Life

PSALM 107:1–16

Let the redeemed of the Lord tell their story—
those he redeemed from the hand of the foe.
Psalm 107:2

Following the death of computer pioneer Steve Jobs, more than one million people from around the world posted tributes to him online. The common theme was how Jobs had changed their lives. They said they lived differently because of his creative innovations, and they wanted to express their appreciation and their sorrow. The screen of one tablet computer said in large letters: iSad.

Gratitude fuels expression, which is exactly what Psalm 107 describes: "Let the redeemed of the Lord tell their story—those he redeemed from the hand of the foe" (v. 2). The theme of this psalm is people in great trouble who were delivered by the Lord. Some were homeless and in need (vv. 4–5); some had rebelled against God's Word (vv. 10–11); others were at their wits' end when they cried out to God (vv. 26–27). All were rescued by God. "Let them give thanks to the Lord for his unfailing love and his wonderful deeds for mankind" (vv. 8, 15, 21, 31).

When we consider the greatness of God's love, His grace in sending Jesus Christ to die for us and rise again, and what He has delivered us from, we cannot keep from praising Him and wanting to tell others how He changed our lives!

David McCasland

Practice Gratitude Today

How has Jesus changed your life? Today, tell someone how grateful you are for Jesus's rescue and presence in your life.

Waving the White Flag

DEUTERONOMY 6:1–9

Hear, O Israel: The LORD our God, the LORD
is one. Love the LORD your God.
Deuteronomy 6:4–5

While watching a video of a church service held in South America, I noticed something I had never seen before in church. As the pastor passionately called his flock to yield their lives to Jesus, one of the parishioners took a white handkerchief out of his pocket and started waving it in the air. Then another, and another. With tears running down their cheeks, they were expressing full surrender to Christ.

But I wonder if there was more to the moment than the flags of surrender. I think they were waving flags of love to God. When God told His people to "love the LORD your God" (Deuteronomy 6:5), it was in the context of His urging them to surrender their lives to Him.

From God's point of view, life with Him is far more than just trying to be good. It is always about relationship—relationship in which surrender is the way we express our grateful love to Him. Jesus, in amazing love for us, surrendered Himself on the cross to rescue us from our helpless bondage to sin and set us on a journey to all that is good and glorious.

We don't have enough words to tell God how much we love Him! So let's show Him our love by surrendering our hearts and lives to follow Him.

Joe Stowell

Practice Gratitude Today

Where do you need to surrender your pride, circumstances, or desires to God? Thank Jesus that He surrendered Himself on the cross, so you can surrender yourself to Him.

Saying Grace

COLOSSIANS 3:12–17

Whatever you do, whether in word or deed, do it all in the name of the Lord Jesus, giving thanks to God the Father through him.
Colossians 3:17

For many years, I've enjoyed the writings of British author G. K. Chesterton. His humor and insight often cause me to chuckle and then pause for more serious contemplation. For example, he wrote, "You say grace before meals. All right. But I say grace before the play and the opera, and grace before the concert and pantomime, and grace before I open a book, and grace before sketching, painting, swimming, fencing, boxing, walking, playing, dancing; and grace before I dip the pen in the ink."

It's good for us to thank the Lord before every meal, but it shouldn't stop there. The apostle Paul saw every activity, every endeavor, as something for which we should thank God and that we should do for His glory. "Whatever you do, whether in word or deed, do it all in the name of the Lord Jesus, giving thanks to God the Father through him" (Colossians 3:17). Recreation, occupation, and education are all avenues through which we can honor the Lord and express our gratefulness to Him.

Paul also encouraged the believers in Colossae to "let the peace of Christ rule in your hearts, since as members of one body you were called to peace. And be thankful" (v. 15).

The best place to "say grace" is anywhere and anytime we want to give thanks to the Lord and honor Him. *David C. McCasland*

Practice Gratitude Today

As you go about your responsibilities, activities, and recreation today, pause to thank God for each endeavor.

Much More than Words

ROMANS 8:22–30

In the same way, the Spirit helps us in our weakness.
Romans 8:26

At a dedication ceremony for a Bible translation into a local African language, the area chief was presented with his own copy. In appreciation, he lifted the Bible to the skies and exclaimed, "Now we know God understands our language! We can read the Bible in our own native mother tongue."

No matter our language, our heavenly Father understands it. But often we feel unable to express our deepest longings to Him. The apostle Paul encourages us to pray regardless of how we feel. Paul speaks of our suffering world and our own pain: "The whole creation has been groaning as in the pains of childbirth" (Romans 8:22). But he compares that to the Holy Spirit's work on our behalf. "The Spirit helps us in our weakness," he writes. "We do not know what we ought to pray for, but the Spirit himself intercedes for us through wordless groans" (v. 26).

God's Holy Spirit knows us intimately. He knows our longings, our heart language, and our unspoken words, and He helps us in our communication with God. His Spirit draws us to be transformed into the image of God the Son (v. 29).

Our heavenly Father understands our language and speaks to us through His Word. When we think our prayers are weak or too short, His Holy Spirit helps us by speaking through us to the Father. He yearns for us to talk with Him in prayer. *Lawrence Darmani*

Practice Gratitude Today

Spend a few minutes in prayer. Begin by speaking your worship and requests to God. Then simply sit in silence with Him. End by thanking the Holy Spirit for interceding for you.

Imperfect Gifts

JAMES 1:2–18

Every good and perfect gift is from above, coming
down from the Father of the heavenly lights.
James 1:17

When I was a child, I wondered why I had to thank God for food I didn't want to eat. In my immature mind, gratitude was a response to receiving something I wanted—like a hamburger and french fries, not asparagus. So why did I have to be thankful for something I didn't want?

In the human realm, my thinking was logical. Not everything people give us is for our good. And of course not everything we want is good.

But the situation with God is different. As Christ reminded us, loving parents do not give their children a stone rather than bread, a snake instead of a fish. And God is far more loving than our earthly parents (Matthew 7:9–11).

This doesn't mean that God's children can expect a pain-free, stress-free life. James tells us not only that every good gift comes from our heavenly Father (1:17) but also that we are to "consider it pure joy" when we "face trials of many kinds" (v. 2). The testing of our "faith produces perseverance," and the work of perseverance makes us "mature and complete, not lacking anything" (vv. 3–4).

Even when we receive something that doesn't seem good, we can be grateful because we know there is more to it than we can see. What seems like an imperfect gift may be the means by which God perfects us.

Julie Ackerman Link

Practice Gratitude Today

How can you choose perseverance today when experiencing less than perfect circumstances? Amid that difficult circumstance, pause to thank God for using challenges to mature you.

The Gift and the Giver

LUKE 1:67–79

Because of God's tender mercy, the morning light
from heaven is about to break upon us.
Luke 1:78 NLT

It's only a key chain. Five little blocks held together by a shoelace. My daughter gave it to me years ago when she was seven. Today the lace is frayed and the blocks are chipped, but they spell a message that never grows old: "I ♥ DAD."

The most precious gifts are determined not by what went into them but by who they are from. Ask any parent who ever received a bouquet of dandelions from a chubby hand. The best gifts are valued not in money but in love.

Zechariah understood that. We hear it in his prophetic song as he praised God for giving him and his wife, Elizabeth, their son, John, when they were well past their childbearing years (Luke 1:67–79). Zechariah rejoiced because John was to be a prophet who would proclaim God's greatest gift to all people—the coming Messiah: "Because of God's tender mercy, the morning light from heaven is about to break upon us" (Luke 1:78 NLT). Those words point to a gift given with so much love that it will even "shine on those living in darkness and in the shadow of death" (1:79).

The sweetest gift we can receive is God's tender mercy—the forgiveness of our sins through Jesus. That gift cost Him dearly at the cross, but He offers it freely out of His deep love for us. *James Banks*

Practice Gratitude Today

What are some of your favorite gifts you've received? Who did you receive them from? Thank God for the sweetest gift of mercy and forgiveness given at the cross of Jesus.

Marvelous Maker

PSALM 104:24–34

How many are your works, LORD! In wisdom you made them all; the earth is full of your creatures.
Psalm 104:24

As an amateur photographer, I enjoy capturing glimpses of God's creativity with my camera. I see His fingerprints on each delicate flower petal, each vibrant sunrise and sunset, and each cloud-painted and star-speckled sky canvas.

My camera's powerful zoom allows me to take photos of the Lord's creatures too. I've snapped shots of a chattering squirrel in a cherry blossom tree, a colorful butterfly flitting from bloom to bloom, and sea turtles sunning on a rocky black beach. Each one-of-a-kind image prompted me to worship my marvelous Maker.

I'm not the first of God's people to praise Him while admiring His unique creations. The writer of Psalm 104 sings of the Lord's many works of art in nature (v. 24). He regards "the sea, vast and spacious, teeming with creatures beyond number" (v. 25), and rejoices in God for providing constant and complete care for His masterpieces (vv. 27–31). Considering the majesty of the God-given life around him, the psalmist bursts with worshipful gratitude: "I will sing to the LORD all my life; I will sing praise to my God as long as I live" (v. 33).

While reflecting on the Lord's magnificent and immense creation, we can look closely at His intentional creativity and attention to detail. And like the psalmist, we can sing to our Creator with thankful praise for how powerful, majestic, and loving He is and always will be. Hallelujah!

Xochitl Dixon

Practice Gratitude Today

Take a photo of God's creation. If you can't get outside, this could be a view out a window or a selfie. Spend a minute enjoying the photo and thanking God for His power, majesty, creativity, and love.

We Thank the Lord

PROVERBS 3:1–12

Trust in the LORD with all your heart and
lean not on your own understanding.
Proverbs 3:5

Anna Anderson's husband died early in their marriage, leaving her with three young daughters and a difficult future. Although trained in Virginia as a teacher, she lacked full credentials to work in the Philadelphia schools, so she took in laundry, did ironing, and later scrubbed floors at a large department store. As African Americans, Anna and her daughters often experienced racial prejudice and discrimination. When doors of opportunity closed, Anna believed that if they would trust the Lord with all their heart and acknowledge Him in all their ways, He would direct their paths (Proverbs 3:5–6). She taught her daughters to depend on God, follow Him, and always be thankful.

When her firstborn, Marian, rose to become an internationally acclaimed classical singer, Anna continued to pray for her and always gave God credit for her success. Reporters, who asked Anna how she felt after attending Marian's concerts at Carnegie Hall and her 1955 debut with the Metropolitan Opera, heard her say, "We thank the Lord." Her reply was not a cliché but sincere gratefulness to God.

Rather than lament what she lacked, Anna Anderson expressed gratitude for what she had and used it for God's glory. Today, we can follow her example with faith, confidence, and a heartfelt "We thank the Lord."

David McCasland

Practice Gratitude Today

Are you experiencing scarcity and opposition, or success and recognition? Trust God and acknowledge Him in all your ways. Thank Him for what you do have today.

In Small Ways

1 JOHN 4:7–12, 19–21

We love because he first loved us.
1 John 4:19

When she was struck by cancer, Elsie was prepared to go home to heaven to be with Jesus. But she recovered, though the disease left her immobile. It also left her wondering why God had spared her life. "What good can I do?" she asked Him. "I don't have much money or skills, and I can't walk. How can I be useful to You?"

Then she found small, simple ways to serve others, especially her home cleaners who were migrants. She bought them food or gave them a few dollars whenever she saw them. These cash gifts were small, yet they went a long way toward helping the workers make ends meet. As she did so, she found God providing for her: friends and relatives gave her gifts and money, enabling her to bless others in return.

As she shared her story, I couldn't help but think of how Elsie was truly putting into practice the call to love one another in 1 John 4:19: "We love because he first loved us." She lived the truth of Acts 20:35, which reminds us that "it is more blessed to give than to receive."

Elsie gave because she received and was in turn encouraged as she gave. Yet it took little more from her than a loving, grateful heart and a readiness to offer what she had—which God multiplied in a virtuous circle of giving and receiving. Let's ask Him to give us a thankful and generous heart to give as He leads us! *Leslie Koh*

Practice Gratitude Today

What is a small, simple way you can give to someone today? Thank God for the resources He has given you, and ask Him to give you a generous heart like His heart.

Never Overlooked by God

NUMBERS 6:22–27

The LORD make his face shine on you.
Numbers 6:25

"Sometimes I just feel so . . . invisible." The word hung in the air as Joanie talked to her friend. Her husband had left her for another woman, leaving Joanie with young children still at home. "I gave him my best years," she confided. "And now I don't know if anyone would really see me or take the time to actually know me."

"I'm so sorry," her friend responded. "My dad walked out when I was six, and it was hard for us, especially Mom. But she said this thing when she tucked me in at night that I never forgot: 'God never closes His eyes.' When I was older, she explained she was trying to teach me that God loved me and watched over me always, even while I slept."

The Bible records words that God gave Moses to share with His people during a challenging time, when they were wandering in Sinai's desert: "The LORD bless you and keep you; the LORD make his face shine on you and be gracious to you; the LORD turn his face toward you and give you peace" (Numbers 6:24–26). The blessing was to be spoken by the priests over the people.

Even in life's wildernesses—those places where we wonder if anyone sees us or truly understands—God is faithful. God's favor—His shining face and enduring love—is always turned toward those who love Him, even when we can't feel Him because of our pain. No one is invisible to God.

James Banks

Practice Gratitude Today

Ask someone to read Numbers 6:24–26 over you today. If that isn't possible, read this blessing aloud to yourself. Thank God for turning His face toward you and always seeing you.

Our Reason for Joy

PSALM 149:1–5

Let Israel rejoice in their Maker; let the people of Zion be glad in their King.
Psalm 149:2

When the school year began, fourteen-year-old CJ would hop off the bus every afternoon and dance down his driveway. His mom recorded and shared videos of CJ's after-school boogie time. He danced because he enjoyed life and "making people happy" with every move. One day, two garbage collectors took time out of their busy work schedule to stomp, spin, and sway with the young boy who inspires others to dance with him. This trio demonstrates the power of sincere and infectious joy.

The writer of Psalm 149 describes the original source of enduring and unconditional joy—God. The psalmist encourages God's people to join together and "sing to the Lord a new song" (v. 1). He invites Israel to "rejoice in their Maker" and "be glad in their King" (v. 2). He calls us to worship God with dancing and music (vv. 1–3). Why? Because "the Lord takes delight in his people; he crowns the humble with victory" (v. 4).

Our adoring Father created us and sustains the universe. He delights in us just because we're His beloved children. He designed us, knows us, and invites us into a personal relationship with Him. What an honor! Our loving and living God is our reason for everlasting joy. We can rejoice in the gift of His constant presence and be grateful for every day our Maker has given us. *Xochitl Dixon*

Practice Gratitude Today

Today, how can you express the joy you feel because of God's constant love and presence? If possible, share your joy with others.

Three-Lettered Faith

HABAKKUK 3:17–19

Yet I will rejoice in the LORD; I will be joyful in God my Savior.
Habakkuk 3:18

With a tendency toward pessimism, I quickly jump to negative conclusions about how situations in my life will play out. If I'm thwarted in my efforts on a work project, I'm easily convinced none of my other projects will be successful either, and—even though utterly unrelated—I will probably never be able to touch my toes comfortably. And, woe is me, I'm an awful mother who can't do anything right. Defeat in one area unnecessarily affects my feelings in many.

It's easy for me to imagine how the prophet Habakkuk might have reacted to what God showed him. He had great cause for despair after having seen the coming troubles for God's people; long and arduous years lay ahead. Things really did look dismal: no fruit, no meat, and no creature comforts. His words lure me into a pessimistic bed of hopelessness until he jars me awake again with a small three-letter word: *yet*. "Yet I will rejoice in the LORD" (Habakkuk 3:18). Despite all the hardships he anticipated, Habakkuk found cause for rejoicing simply because of who God is.

While we might be prone to exaggerating our problems, Habakkuk truly faced some extreme hardships. If he could summon praise for God in those moments, perhaps we can too. When we're bogged down in the depths of despair, we can look to God who lifts us up.

Kirsten Holmberg

Practice Gratitude Today

Where or when in your life do you tend to think the worst about how things will turn out? Talk with God about your fears. Then thank Him that, yet, you can rejoice in His faithfulness.

Breathtaking Glory

1 CHRONICLES 29:10–15

Yours, LORD, is the greatness and the power and
the glory and the majesty and the splendor.
1 Chronicles 29:11

One of the pleasures of a trip to Europe is visiting the grand cathedrals that dot the landscape. They are breathtakingly beautiful as they soar toward the heavens. The architecture, art, and symbolism found in these amazing buildings present a spellbinding experience of wonder and magnificence.

As I thought about the fact that these structures were built to reflect God's magnificence and His all-surpassing splendor, I wondered how we could possibly recapture in our hearts and minds a similar feeling of God's grandeur and be reminded again of His greatness.

One way we can do that is to look beyond humanity's grand, regal structures and contemplate the greatness of what God Himself has created. Take one look at a starry night sky and think of God's power as He spoke the universe into existence. Hold a newborn baby in your arms and thank God for the miracle of life itself. Look at the snow-covered mountains of Alaska or the majestic Atlantic Ocean teeming with millions of God-designed creatures and imagine the power that makes that ecosystem work.

Humankind is not wrong to reach for the sky with structures that are intended to point us to God. But our truest admiration should be reserved for God Himself as we say to Him, "Yours, LORD, is the greatness and the power and the glory and the majesty and the splendor" (1 Chronicles 29:11).

Dave Branon

Practice Gratitude Today

Slow down to marvel at God's creation today, whether that's a stunning mountain range, an ocean, or simply a tree or the sky. Thank Him for His majesty, creativity, and power.

The Small Things

PSALM 116:1–9

Every good and perfect gift is from above.
James 1:17

My friend Gloria called with excitement in her voice. She had not been able to leave her home except for doctors' appointments. So I understood why she was so happy to tell me, "My son just attached new speakers to my computer, so now I can go to my church!" Now she could hear the live broadcast of her church's worship service. She raved about God's goodness and the "best gift my son could have given me!"

Gloria teaches me about having a thankful heart. Despite her many limitations, she's thankful for the smallest of things—sunsets, helpful family and neighbors, quiet moments with God, the ability to remain in her own apartment. She's had a lifetime of seeing God provide for her, and she talks about Him to anyone who visits or calls.

We don't know what difficulties the author of Psalm 116 was encountering. Some Bible commentaries say it was probably sickness because he said, "The cords of death entangled me" (v. 3). But he gave thanks to the Lord for being gracious and full of compassion when he was "brought low" (v. 6).

When we're low, it can be hard to look up. Yet if we do, we see that God is the giver of all good gifts in our life—great and small—and we learn to give Him thanks. *Anne Cetas*

Practice Gratitude Today

Keep a list of small gifts today on a piece of paper or on your phone. At the end of the day, tell someone else about one of God's small gifts. Thank Him for being the giver of all good things.

Impossible Forgiveness

LUKE 23:32–43

Father, forgive them.
Luke 23:34

Liberators found the following prayer crumpled among the remains of the Ravensbrück concentration camp where Nazis exterminated nearly fifty thousand women: "O Lord, remember not only the men and women of goodwill, but also those of ill will. But do not remember the suffering they have inflicted upon us. Remember the fruits we brought thanks to this suffering—our comradeship, our loyalty, our humility, the courage, the generosity, the greatness of heart which has grown out of this. And when they come to judgment, let all the fruits that we have borne be their forgiveness."

I can't imagine the fear and pain inflicted on the terrorized woman who wrote this prayer. I can't imagine what kind of inexplicable grace these words required of her. She did the unthinkable: she sought God's forgiveness for her oppressors.

This prayer echoes Christ's prayer. After being wrongly accused, mocked, beaten, and humiliated before the people of Jerusalem, Jesus was "crucified . . . along with [two] criminals" (Luke 23:33). As He hung from a rough-hewn cross, with mutilated body and gasping for breath, I would expect Jesus to pronounce judgment on His tormentors, to seek retribution or divine justice. However, Jesus uttered a prayer contradicting every human impulse: "Father, forgive them, for they do not know what they are doing" (v. 34).

The forgiveness Jesus offers seems impossible, but He offers it to us. In His divine grace, impossible forgiveness spills free. *Winn Collier*

Practice Gratitude Today

What sin, against you or against others, feels unforgivable? Talk with God about it. Thank Him that when anyone turns to God in repentance, His grace is ready to restore and make new.

Someone to Touch

LUKE 5:12–16

Jesus reached out his hand and touched the man.
Luke 5:13

Commuters on a Canadian metro train witnessed a heart-moving conclusion to a tense moment. They watched as a seventy-year old woman gently reached out and offered her hand to a young man whose loud voice and disturbing words were scaring other passengers. The lady's kindness calmed the man, who sank to the floor of the train with tears in his eyes. He said, "Thanks, Grandma," stood up, and walked away. The woman later admitted to being afraid. But, she said, "I'm a mother, and he needed someone to touch." While better judgment might have given her reason to keep her distance, she took a risk of love.

Jesus understands such compassion. He didn't side with the fears of unnerved onlookers when a desperate man, covered with leprosy, showed up begging to be healed. Neither was He helpless like the other religious leaders, who could only have condemned the man for bringing his leprosy into the village (Leviticus 13:45–46). Instead, Jesus reached out to someone who probably hadn't been touched by anyone for years and healed him.

Thankfully, for that man and for us, Jesus came to offer what no law could ever offer—the touch of His hand and heart.

Mart DeHaan

Practice Gratitude Today

Who in your life could use a touch of compassion and kindness today? As you reach out to another, thank Jesus that He reaches out to you whenever you are hurting, confused, or angry.

Divine Diversions

ACTS 16:6–10

They tried to enter Bithynia, but the Spirit of Jesus would not allow them to.
Acts 16:7

It can be difficult when we're told "no" or "not now," especially when we sense God has opened a door for us to serve others. Early in my ministry, two opportunities came my way where I thought my gifts and skills matched the churches' needs, but both doors eventually closed. After these two disappointments, another position came along, and I was selected. With that ministry call came thirteen years of life-touching pastoral labors.

Twice in Acts 16, Paul and company were redirected by God. First, they were "kept by the Holy Spirit from preaching the word in the province of Asia" (v. 6). Then, "When they came to the border of Mysia, they tried to enter Bithynia, but the Spirit of Jesus would not allow them to" (v. 7). Unknown to them, God had other plans that would be right for His work and workers. His no to the previous plans put them in a position to listen to and be confidently led by Him (vv. 9–10).

Who among us hasn't grieved what we initially thought to be a painful loss? We've felt wounded when we didn't get a certain job, when a service opportunity didn't materialize, when a relocation got derailed. Though such things can momentarily be weighty, time often reveals that such detours are actually divine diversions that God graciously uses to get us where He wants us, and we are grateful. *Arthur Jackson*

Practice Gratitude Today

Where does it feel like God is saying no in your life? Bring your confusion to Him in prayer. End by thanking Him for using all things for His glory and your good—to make you more like Christ.

In His Presence

PSALM 89:1–17

Blessed are those who have learned to acclaim you,
who walk in the light of your presence, LORD.
Psalm 89:15

The seventeenth-century monk Brother Lawrence, before a day's work as cook in his community, would pray, "O my God . . . grant me your grace to stay in your presence. Help me in my labors. Possess all my affections." As he worked, he kept talking to God, listening for His leading and dedicating his work to Him. Even when he was busiest, he would use intervals of relative calm to ask for His grace. No matter what was happening, he sought for and found a sense of his Maker's love.

As Psalm 89 confesses, the fitting response to the Creator of all who rules the oceans and is worshiped by hosts of angels is to lift up our lives—our whole lives to Him. When we understand the beauty of who God is, we "hear the joyful call to worship"—whenever and wherever we are, "all day long" (vv. 15–16 NLT).

Whether it's standing in store or airport lines, or waiting on hold minute after minute, our lives are full of moments like these, times when we could get annoyed. Or these can be times when we catch our breath and see each of these pauses as an opportunity to learn to "walk in the light of [God's] presence" (v. 15).

The "wasted" moments of our lives, when we wait or lie ill or wonder what to do next, are all possible pauses to consider our lives in the light of His presence.

Harold Myra

Practice Gratitude Today

Keep an eye open for "wasted" moments today—at a stoplight, while your computer turns on, as you're washing dishes. Use these moments to thank God for and savor His presence with you.

The End?

1 CORINTHIANS 15:50–58

But thanks be to God! He gives us the victory
through our Lord Jesus Christ.
1 Corinthians 15:57

Everything in this world eventually comes to an end, which at times can be disheartening. It's the feeling you get when you read a book that's so good you don't want it to end. Or when you watch a movie that you wish would go on a little while longer.

But all things—good and bad—do come to "The End." In fact, life ultimately comes to an end—sometimes sooner than we expect. All of us who have stood by the casket of a loved one know the painful emptiness of a heart that wishes it wasn't over yet.

Thankfully, Jesus steps into the fray of terminal disappointments and, through His death and resurrection, interjects hope for us. In Him, "the end" is a prelude to a death-free eternity, and words like "it's over" are replaced by a joy-filled "forever." Since our earthly bodies are not an eternal reality, Paul assures us that "we will all be changed" (1 Corinthians 15:51) and reminds us that because of Christ's conquering work, we can confidently say, "Where, O death, is your victory?" (v. 55).

So let not your heart be troubled. Our sorrow is real, but we can be filled with gratitude because God "gives us the victory through our Lord Jesus Christ" (v. 57). *Joe Stowell*

Practice Gratitude Today

When have you mourned the end of something good in your life? In prayer, thank God that your ultimate end is eternity with Christ.

God's Life-Changing Gift

PSALM 119:9–20

I delight in your decrees; I will not neglect your word.
Psalm 119:16

I greeted our youth group as my husband and I handed out Bibles. "God will use these priceless gifts to change your life," I said. That night, a few students committed to reading the gospel of John together. We continued inviting the group to read Scripture at home while we taught them during our weekly meetings. More than a decade later, I saw one of our students. "I still use the Bible you gave me," she said. I saw the evidence in her faith-filled life.

God empowers His people to go beyond reading, reciting, and remembering where to find Bible verses. He enables us to "stay on the path of purity" by living "according to" the Scriptures (Psalm 119:9). God wants us to seek and obey Him as He uses His unchanging truth to free us from sin and change us (vv. 10–11). We can ask God daily to help us know Him and understand what He says in the Bible (vv. 12–13).

When we recognize the priceless value of living God's way, we can "rejoice" in His instruction "as one rejoices in great riches" (v. 14). Like the psalmist, we can sing, "I delight in your decrees; I will not neglect your word" (v. 16). As we invite the Holy Spirit to empower us, we can savor each moment spent prayerfully reading the Bible—God's life-changing gift to us. *Xochitl Dixon*

Practice Gratitude Today

Set aside time today to read a short book of the Bible, such as Ruth, Ecclesiastes, a minor prophet, or a New Testament epistle. At the end, thank God for His life-changing Word.

Chameleon Crawl

ACTS 2:42–47

Every day they continued to meet together.
Acts 2:46

When we think of the chameleon, we probably think of its ability to change color according to its surroundings. But this lizard has another interesting characteristic. On several occasions I've watched a chameleon walk along a pathway and wondered how it ever reached its destination. Reluctantly, the chameleon stretches out one leg, seems to change its mind, attempts again, and then carefully plants a hesitant foot, as if afraid the ground will collapse under it. That was why I couldn't help laughing when I heard someone say, "Do not be a chameleon church member who says, 'Let me go to church today; no, let me go next week; no, let me wait for a while!'"

The tabernacle in Jerusalem was King David's place of worship, and he was far from being a chameleon worshiper. Rather, he rejoiced with those who said, "Let us go to the house of the Lord" (Psalm 122:1). The same was true for believers in the early church. "They devoted themselves to the apostles' teaching and to fellowship, to the breaking of bread and to prayer. . . . Every day they continued to meet together in the temple courts" (Acts 2:42, 46).

What a joy it is to join with others in worship and fellowship! Praying and worshiping together, studying the Scriptures together, and caring for one another are essential for our spiritual growth and unity as believers.

Lawrence Darmani

Practice Gratitude Today

Spend time with another believer today praying, reading the Bible, worshiping, or listening to each other's concerns. Thank God for the fellowship of His people.

Rich toward God

1 TIMOTHY 6:6–11

Godliness with contentment is great gain.
1 Timothy 6:6

Growing up during the Great Depression, my parents knew deep hardship as children. As a result, they were thrifty adults—hard-working and grateful money stewards. At the same time, they were never greedy. They gave time, talent, and treasury to their church, charity groups, and the needy. Indeed, they handled their money wisely and gave cheerfully.

As believers in Jesus, my parents took to heart the apostle Paul's warning: "Those who want to get rich fall into temptation and a trap and into many foolish and harmful desires that plunge people into ruin and destruction" (1 Timothy 6:9).

Paul gave this advice to Timothy, the young pastor of the city of Ephesus, a wealthy city where riches tempted rich and poor alike. "The love of money is a root of all kinds of evil," Paul warned. "Some people, eager for money, have wandered from the faith and pierced themselves with many griefs" (v. 10).

What, then, is the antidote to greed? Being "rich toward God," said Jesus (Luke 12:21). By pursuing, appreciating, and loving our heavenly Father above all, He remains our chief delight. As the psalmist wrote, "Satisfy us in the morning with your unfailing love, that we may sing for joy and be glad all our days" (Psalm 90:14).

Rejoicing in Him daily relieves us of coveting, leaving us contented. May Jesus redeem our heart's desires, making us rich toward God!

Patricia Raybon

Practice Gratitude Today

Talk with God about the material possessions or financial resources you think you need to be happy. Ask God to help you be content. Then thank Him that He has already given you Himself.

The Joy of Remembering

PSALM 103:1–14

Praise the Lord, my soul, and forget not all his benefits.
Psalm 103:2

A longtime friend described the days surrounding his ninetieth birthday as "a time . . . to do a little reflecting, looking in the rearview mirror of my life, and spending many hours in what I call 'The Grace of Remembrance.' It's so easy to forget all the ways that the Lord has led! 'Forget not all his benefits'" (Psalm 103:2).

This was typical of the person I've known and admired for more than fifty years. Rather than reviewing disappointments, his letter was filled with thankfulness and praise to God.

First, he recalled the Lord's temporal mercies—his good health, the enjoyment of his wife and children, the joy and success of work, his enriching friendships, and the opportunities he'd had to serve God. He considered them all gifts—none deserved but all gratefully received.

Next, he reviewed God's spiritual mercies—the influence of Christian parents and the experience of God's forgiveness when he accepted Christ as a teenager. He concluded with the encouragement he'd received from churches, schools, and fellow Christians who cared and prayed for each other.

It's a model we should follow on a regular basis—the joy of remembering. "Praise the Lord, my soul; all my inmost being, praise his holy name" (v. 1). *David McCasland*

Practice Gratitude Today

Think back over your life so far. Where do you see God's mercies in your life circumstances, your family and friendships, and your relationship with God? Worship Him for His many gifts.

Another Chance

MICAH 7:1–3, 18–20

Once again you will have compassion on us.
You will trample our sins under your feet and
throw them into the depths of the ocean!
Micah 7:19 NLT

At the Second Chance Bike Shop, volunteers rebuild cast-off bicycles and donate them to needy kids. Shop founder Ernie Clark also donates bikes to needy adults, including the homeless, the disabled, and military veterans struggling to make it in civilian life. Not only do the bicycles get a second chance but sometimes the recipients do too. One veteran used his new bike to get to a job interview.

Second chances can transform a person's life, especially when the second chance comes from God. The prophet Micah extoled such grace during a time when the nation of Israel groveled in bribery, fraud, and other despicable sins. As Micah lamented, "The godly people have all disappeared; not one honest person is left on the earth" (Micah 7:2 NLT).

God would rightly punish evil, Micah knew. But being loving, He would give those who repented another chance. Humbled by such love, Micah asked, "Where is another God like you, who pardons the guilt of the remnant, overlooking the sins of his special people?" (v. 18 NLT).

We too can rejoice that God doesn't abandon us because of our sins if we ask for forgiveness. As Micah declared of God, "Once again you will have compassion on us. You will trample our sins under your feet and throw them into the depths of the ocean!" (v. 19 NLT).

God's love gives second chances to all who seek Him.

Patricia Raybon

Practice Gratitude Today

Where in your life do you need a second chance? Go to God in prayer, confessing any part of the brokenness that you're responsible for, and thank Him for His grace and loving restoration.

More than Conquerors

ROMANS 8:31–39

In all these things we are more than conquerors
through him who loved us.
Romans 8:37

When my husband coached our son's Little League baseball team, he rewarded the players with an end-of-year party and acknowledged their improvement over the season. One of our youngest players, Dustin, approached me during the event. "Didn't we lose the game today?"

"Yes," I said. "But we're proud of you for doing your best."

"I know," he said. "But we lost. Right?"

I nodded.

"Then why do I feel like a winner?" Dustin asked.

Smiling, I said, "Because you are a winner."

Dustin had thought that losing a game meant he was a failure even when he'd done his best. As believers in Jesus, our battle is not confined to a sports field. Still, it's often tempting to view a tough season of life as a reflection of our worth.

The apostle Paul affirmed the connection between our present suffering and our future glory as God's children. Having given Himself for us, Jesus continues to work on our behalf during our ongoing battle with sin and transforms us into His likeness (Romans 8:31–32). Though we'll all experience hardship and persecution, God's unwavering love helps us persevere (vv. 33–34).

As His children, we may be tempted to allow struggles to define our worth. However, our ultimate victory is guaranteed. We may stumble along the way, but we'll always be "more than conquerors" (v. 37).

Xochitl Dixon

Practice Gratitude Today

Where are you tempted to define your worth by your failures or wounds? Thank God that, in Christ, you are defined by His love.

The Joy of a Generous God

PSALM 36:5–12

They feast on the abundance of your house; you give them drink from your river of delights.
Psalm 36:8

Recently I walked into a hotel lobby that featured the largest arrangement of fresh flowers I have ever seen. It was bursting with color, perfectly arranged, and its fragrance was amazing. It stopped me in my tracks, and I lingered for a moment to admire its beauty. It made me think that there is something about abundance that captures our hearts. Think of the inviting beauty of a bowl overflowing with colorful fruit, or a countertop covered with three or four pies ready for enjoyment after a bountiful holiday meal.

The joy of abundance reminds me of the generosity of God. He makes our cup overflow (Psalm 23:5). He "is able to do immeasurably more than all we ask or imagine" (Ephesians 3:20). His grace is sufficient for any difficulty that life brings our way (2 Corinthians 12:9). And it is He who kills the fattened calf and calls for the best robe when the lost son returns (see Luke 15:20–24).

No wonder the psalmist rejoices: "How priceless is your unfailing love, O God! People take refuge in the shadow of your wings. They feast on the abundance of your house" (Psalm 36:7–8). Our God is abundantly good. Let's overflow with praise for His many blessings.

Joe Stowell

Practice Gratitude Today

Where do you see God's abundance in your life today? Make time to slow down and savor the bounty and beauty of God's provision.

Make a Joyful Noise

PSALM 98

Shout for joy to the LORD, all the earth,
burst into jubilant song with music.
Psalm 98:4

Back when I was searching for a church to attend regularly, a friend invited me to a service at her church. The worship leaders led the congregation in a song I particularly loved. So I sang with gusto, remembering my college choir director's advice to "project!"

After the song, my friend's husband turned to me and said, "You really sang loud." This was not a compliment! After that, I self-consciously monitored my singing, making sure I sang softer than those around me and always wondering if others judged my singing.

But one Sunday, I noticed the singing of a woman in the pew beside me. She seemed to sing with adoration, without a trace of self-consciousness. Her worship reminded me of the enthusiastic, spontaneous worship that David demonstrated in his life (2 Samuel 6:12–22). In Psalm 98, the psalmist suggests that "all the earth" should "burst into jubilant song" in worship (v. 4).

Verse 1 of Psalm 98 tells us why we should worship joyfully, reminding us that God "has done marvelous things." Throughout the psalm, the poet recounts these marvelous things: God's faithfulness and justice to all nations, His mercy, and His salvation. Dwelling on who God is and what He's done can fill our hearts with praise.

What marvelous things has God done in your life? Today is the perfect time to recall His wondrous works and give Him thanks. Lift your voice and sing! *Linda Washington*

Practice Gratitude Today

Play a favorite worship song and sing along, even if you don't consider yourself a very good singer. Find a private place to be alone, if you prefer. Pray the lyrics as you worship God with thankfulness.

When You're Afraid

JUDGES 7:8–15

When the angel of the LORD appeared to Gideon, he said, "The Lord is with you, mighty warrior."
Judges 6:12

I had a medical checkup scheduled, and although I'd had no recent health concerns, I dreaded the visit. I was haunted by memories of an unexpected diagnosis long ago. While I knew God was with me and I should simply trust Him, I still felt afraid.

I was disappointed in my fear and lack of faith. If God was always with me, why was I feeling such anxiety? Then one morning I believe He led me to the story of Gideon.

Called a "mighty warrior" (Judges 6:12), Gideon was fearful over his assignment to attack the Midianites. Although God had promised him His presence and victory, Gideon still sought multiple reassurances (vv. 16–23, 36–40).

However, God didn't condemn Gideon for his fear. He understood him. On the night of the attack, He assured Gideon again of victory, even giving him a way to assuage his fears (7:10–11).

God understood my fear too. His reassurance gave me the courage to trust Him. I experienced His peace, knowing that He was with me regardless of the outcome. In the end, my checkup was uneventful.

We have a God who understands our fears and who reassures us through the Scriptures and the Spirit (Psalm 23:4; John 14:16–17). May we worship Him in thankfulness, just as Gideon did (Judges 7:15).

Karen Huang

Practice Gratitude Today

Where do you feel disappointed with yourself for not being more confident, courageous, or full of faith? Thank God for understanding your fears and being with you amid those fears.

Honoring God with Thanks

PSALM 50:8–15

Call on me in the day of trouble; I will deliver you, and you will honor me.
Psalm 50:15

The doctor wasn't frowning, despite talking to my husband about his recent cancer diagnosis. Smiling, she offered a suggestion: start each day by giving thanks. "For at least three things," the doctor said. Dan agreed, knowing that gratitude opens our hearts to find encouragement in God's goodness. Thus, Dan starts each day with words of praise. *Thank You, God, for a good night's sleep. For my clean bed. For sunshine. For breakfast on the table. For a smile on my lips.*

Each word is heartfelt. But could it sound trivial? Does our praise in life's small details matter to almighty God? In Psalm 50, David's chief musician, Asaph, offers a clear answer. God has "no need of a bull from your stall or of goats from your pens" (v. 9). Instead of these once-formal Israelite sacrifices of gratitude, God wants His people to give Him our hearts and lives in gratitude (vv. 14, 23).

As my husband experienced, wholehearted gratitude helps our spirits flourish. Then when we call on the Lord "in the day of trouble," He will "deliver" us (v. 15). Does this mean Dan will be healed, spiritually and physically, during his two-year treatment? Or not until after this lifetime? We don't know. But for now, Dan delights in showing God that he's grateful for His love and for who God is: Redeemer. Healer. Friend. And friends delight to hear these beautiful words: Thank you.

Patricia Raybon

Practice Gratitude Today

What are three things you are grateful for? Give thanks to God for providing them, even if you are in painful or difficult circumstances.

A New Community

ACTS 2:1–12, 42–47

All the believers were together and had everything in common.
Acts 2:44

My friend Carrie's five-year-old daughter, Maija, has an interesting approach to playtime. She loves mixing together dolls from different play sets to come up with a new community. In the world of her imagination, everything belongs together. These are her people. She believes they are happiest when they're together, despite being different sizes and shapes.

Her creativity reminds me of God's purpose for the church. On the day of Pentecost, Luke tells us, "there were staying in Jerusalem God-fearing Jews from every nation under heaven" (Acts 2:5). Though these people were from different cultures and spoke different languages, the Holy Spirit's arrival made them a new community: the church. From then on, they were considered one body, unified by the death and resurrection of Jesus.

The leaders of this new body were a group of people Jesus brought together during His time on earth—His disciples. If Jesus hadn't united them, more than likely they would never have come together. And now more people—"about three thousand" (v. 41)—had become Christ followers. Thanks to the Holy Spirit, this once divided group "had everything in common" (v. 44). They were willing to share what they had with each other.

The Holy Spirit continues to bridge the gaps between people groups. We might not always get along, nor readily understand one another. But as believers in Christ, we belong together. *Linda Washington*

Practice Gratitude Today

Who in your church community doesn't look, talk, or think like you? Thank God that His body is made up of believers from every tribe, language, people, and nation (see Rev. 5:9).

Stories of Jesus

1 JOHN 1:1–4; JOHN 21:24–25

Jesus did many other things as well.
John 21:25

As a girl I loved to visit my small local library. One day, looking at the bookshelves holding the young adult section, I reasoned I could probably read every book. In my enthusiasm I forgot one important fact—new books were regularly added to the shelves. Although I gave it a valiant effort, there were simply too many books.

New books continue to fill more and more bookshelves. The apostle John likely would be amazed by the availability of books today since his five New Testament books—the gospel of John; 1, 2, and 3 John; and Revelation—were handwritten on parchment scrolls.

John wrote those books because he felt compelled by the Holy Spirit to give Christians an eyewitness account of Jesus's life and ministry (1 John 1:1–4). But John's writings contained only a small fraction of all that Jesus did and taught during His ministry. In fact, John said if everything Jesus did was written down, "the whole world would not have room for the books that would be written" (John 21:25).

John's claim remains true today. Despite all the books that have been written about Jesus, the libraries of the world still cannot contain every story of His love and grace. We can also celebrate that we have our own personal stories to share, and rejoice that we will be proclaiming them forever (Psalm 89:1)! *Lisa M. Samra*

Practice Gratitude Today

Share a story of Jesus's love and grace to you with someone today. Thank God that your story is just one of countless stories of His provision and care.

The Ups and Downs of Life

JOHN 16:31–33

I have told you these things, so that in me you may have peace.
John 16:33

A Facebook memory popped up, showing me a picture of my triumphant five-year-old when she'd won a fun and competitive game of Chutes and Ladders. I'd tagged my brother and sister in the post because we'd often played this board game when we were kids. Chutes and Ladders is based on a game that's been played for centuries, helping people learn to count and providing the thrill of being able to climb a ladder and win the game by getting to one hundred the fastest. But watch out! If you land on spot ninety-eight, you slide far down the chute, delaying—or even prohibiting—victory.

Isn't that just like life? Jesus lovingly prepared us for the ups and downs of our days. He said we'd experience "trouble" (John 16:33), but He also shared a message of peace. We don't have to be shaken by the trials we face. Why? Christ has overcome the world! Nothing is greater than His power, so we too can face whatever comes our way with "the mighty strength" He's made available to us (Ephesians 1:19).

Just like in Chutes and Ladders, life sometimes presents a ladder allowing us to happily ascend, and other times we tumble down a slippery slide. But we don't have to play the game of life without hope. We have the power of Jesus to help us overcome it all. *Katara Patton*

Practice Gratitude Today

Are you moving ahead in life, or do you feel like you're sliding backward? Whatever your current circumstance, praise God for His mighty power, and for overcoming the world.

The Wonder of Creation

GENESIS 1:9–13

Then God said, "Let the land produce vegetation: seed-bearing plants and trees on the land that bear fruit with seed in it."
Genesis 1:11

While Tim was hiking on Root Glacier in Alaska, he came across something he'd not seen before. Though Tim studies glaciers professionally, the vast number of small balls of moss were completely unfamiliar to him. After tracking the bright green balls for many years, Tim and his colleagues discovered that, unlike moss on trees, the "glacier mice" are unattached and—even more surprisingly—move in unison, like a herd or flock. At first, Tim and his colleagues suspected they were blown by the wind or were rolling downhill, but their research ruled out those guesses.

They haven't yet discovered exactly how the moss balls move. Such mysteries highlight God's creativity. In His work of creation, God appointed the land to "produce vegetation" in the form of plants and trees (Genesis 1:11). His design included glacier mice too, though most of us won't see them firsthand unless we visit a glacier that provides a suitable environment for them.

Glacier mice have been charming scientists with their fuzzy green presence since their discovery in the 1950s. When God observed the vegetation He'd created, He declared "that it was good" (v. 12). We're surrounded by God's botanical designs, each demonstrating His creative powers and inviting us to worship Him. We can delight in each of the trees and plants He's made—for they are good!

Kirsten Holmberg

Practice Gratitude Today

Spend a few minutes observing a plant: a tree, a flower, a houseplant. Consider the mysteries of how plants grow, feed themselves, and reproduce—and worship God for His creative power.

Unexpressed Gratitude

PSALM 107:31–43

Give thanks to the LORD, for he is good. . . . Let
the redeemed of the LORD tell their story.
Psalm 107:1–2

The whole reason for saying thanks is to let the giver of a gift know how much you appreciate something. Author G. B. Stern once said, "Silent gratitude isn't much use to anyone."

When our son was young, he sometimes needed to be reminded that avoiding eye contact, looking down at his feet, and mumbling some unintelligible words was not an acceptable thank-you. And after many years of marriage, my husband and I are still learning that it's important for us to continually express our gratitude to each other. When one of us feels appreciative, we try to verbalize it—even if we've said it many times before about the same thing. William Arthur Ward said, "Feeling gratitude and not expressing it is like wrapping a present and not giving it."

Showing our gratitude is obviously important in human relationships, but it's even more essential in our relationship with God. As we think about the many blessings we have received, do we express our thanks to Him throughout the day? And when we think of the amazing gift of His death and resurrection for forgiveness of our sins, do our hearts bubble over with awe and thanksgiving (Romans 6:23; 2 Corinthians 9:15)?

Take the reminder in Psalm 107:1 to heart each day: "Give thanks to the LORD, for he is good."

Cindy Hess Kasper

Practice Gratitude Today

As you notice God's gifts throughout your day, pause to express your gratitude to Him for His goodness to you.

Riding the Waves

PSALM 89:5–17

Who is like you, LORD God Almighty? You, LORD, are mighty, and your faithfulness surrounds you.
Psalm 89:8

As my husband strolled down the rocky beach taking photos of the Hawaiian horizon, I sat on a large rock fretting over another medical setback. Though my problems would be waiting for me when I returned home, I needed peace in that moment. I stared at the incoming waves crashing against the jagged black rocks. A dark shadow in the curve of the wave caught my eye. Using the zoom on my camera, I identified the shape as a sea turtle riding the waves peacefully. Its flippers spread wide and still. Turning my face into the salty breeze, I smiled.

The "heavens praise [God's] wonders" (Psalm 89:5). Our incomparable God rules "over the surging sea; when its waves mount up, you [God] still them" (v. 9). He "founded the world and all that is in it" (v. 11). He made it all, owns it all, manages it all, and purposes it all for His glory and our enjoyment.

Standing on the foundation of our faith—the love of our unchanging Father—we can "walk in the light of [His] presence" (v. 15). God remains mighty in power and merciful in His dealings with us. We can rejoice in His name all day long (v. 16). No matter what obstacles we face or how many setbacks we have to endure, God holds us as the waves rise and fall.

Xochitl Dixon

Practice Gratitude Today

Find a video or audio recording of ocean waves. Listen for a minute or two. Perhaps breathe along with the surf. Thank God that through the ups and downs of life, He is in control.

Singing with Violet

PHILIPPIANS 1:21–26

I desire to depart and be with Christ, which is better by far;
but it is more necessary for you that I remain in the body.
Philippians 1:23–24

An elderly woman named Violet sat on her bed in a Jamaican infirmary and smiled as some teenagers stopped to visit with her. The hot, sticky midday air came into her little group home unabated, but she didn't complain. Instead, she began racking her mind for a song to sing. Then a huge smile appeared and she sang, "I am running, skipping, jumping, praising the Lord!" As she sang, she swung her arms back and forth as if she were running. Tears came to those around her, for Violet had no legs. She was singing because, she said, "Jesus loves me—and in heaven I will have legs to run with."

Violet's joy and hopeful anticipation of heaven give new vibrancy to Paul's words in Philippians 1 when he referred to life-and-death issues. "If I am to go on living in the body, this will mean fruitful labor for me," he said. "I am torn between the two: I desire to depart and be with Christ, which is better by far" (vv. 22–23).

Each of us faces tough times that may cause us to long for the promise of heavenly relief. But as Violet showed joy despite her current circumstances, we too can keep "running, skipping, jumping, praising the Lord"—both for the abundant life He gives us here and for the ultimate joy that awaits us. *Dave Branon*

Practice Gratitude Today

What are you missing today that will be restored to you in the life to come? Praise God that He will wipe away every tear and make all things new.

A National Campout

LEVITICUS 23:33–43

Rejoice before the LORD your God for seven days.
Leviticus 23:40

We camped under the stars, with nothing between us and the infinite West African sky. No need for a tent in the dry season. But the fire was crucial. "Never let the fire go out," Dad said, prodding the logs with a stick. Fire kept wildlife at a distance. God's creatures are wonderful, but you never want a leopard or a snake meandering through your campsite.

Dad was a missionary to Ghana's Upper Region, and he had a knack for turning everything into a teaching moment. Camping was no exception.

God used campouts as a teaching point for His people too. Once a year, for an entire week, the Israelites were to live in shelters made of "branches from luxuriant trees—from palms, willows and other leafy trees" (Leviticus 23:40). The purpose was twofold. God told them, "All native-born Israelites are to live in such shelters so your descendants will know that I had the Israelites live in temporary shelters when I brought them out of Egypt" (vv. 42–43). But the event was also to be festive. "Rejoice before the LORD your God for seven days" (v. 40).

Camping may not be your idea of fun, but God instituted a one-week campout for the Israelites as a joyful way to recall His goodness. We easily forget the meaning at the heart of our holidays. Our festivals can be joyous reminders of the character of our loving God. He created fun too.

Tim Gustafson

Practice Gratitude Today

How can you disrupt your normal routine today to do something joyful and fun? Use this interruption to celebrate God's goodness and provision.

Broken Bones

PSALM 51:1–13

Let me hear joy and gladness; let the
bones you have crushed rejoice.
Psalm 51:8

Years ago, I played collegiate soccer as a goalkeeper. It was more fun than I can describe here, but all that fun came at a hefty price—one I continue to pay today. Being a goalie means that you are constantly throwing your body into harm's way to prevent the other team from scoring, often resulting in injuries. During the course of one season, I suffered a broken leg, several cracked ribs, a separated shoulder, and a concussion. Today, especially on cold days, I am visited by painful reminders of those broken bones.

David also had reminders of broken bones, but his injuries were spiritual, not physical. After David's moral collapse involving adultery with Bathsheba and the murder of her husband, God firmly disciplined him. But then David turned to God in repentance and prayed, "Let me hear joy and gladness; let the bones you have crushed rejoice" (Psalm 51:8).

God's chastening was so crushing that David felt like his bones were broken. Yet he trusted that the God of grace could both repair his brokenness and rekindle his joy. In our own failure and sin, it's a comfort to know that God loves us enough to pursue and restore us with His loving discipline.

Bill Crowder

Practice Gratitude Today

When have you experienced God's discipline or natural consequences for your sin? Thank God that He loves you enough to discipline you as His child (Hebrews 12:6).

Savor the Flavor

NEHEMIAH 8:1–12

All the people went away to eat and drink
. . . and to celebrate with great joy.
Nehemiah 8:12

In a fast-paced eat-and-run culture, few people make time to enjoy a leisurely meal in the company of friends. Someone has even remarked that the only way to enjoy a seven-course meal today is to get it all between two pieces of bread!

After many of the Israelite exiles in Babylon returned to Jerusalem to rebuild the temple and the walls of the city, they gathered to hear Ezra read from the Book of the Law given by God through Moses (Nehemiah 8:1). They listened to God's Word for hours, while teachers among them were "giving the meaning so that the people understood what was being read" (v.8).

When they wept because of their shortcomings, Ezra, along with Nehemiah the governor, told them this was not a time for sorrow but a time for rejoicing. The people were told to prepare a feast and share it with those who had nothing, "for the joy of the Lord is your strength" (v. 10). Then "all the people went away to eat and drink, to send portions of food and to celebrate with great joy, because they now understood the words that had been made known to them" (v. 12).

The spiritual banquet God has prepared for us in His Word is a cause for great joy. It is worth taking time to savor.

David McCasland

Practice Gratitude Today

Sit and listen to an audio recording of a favorite Bible passage without multitasking. If possible, invite someone else to listen with you. Thank God for the feast of wisdom that is His Word.

God's Great Love Cycle

ROMANS 13:8–10

Let no debt remain outstanding, except the
continuing debt to love one another.
Romans 13:8

As a new believer in Jesus at the age of thirty, I had lots of questions after committing my life to Him. When I started reading the Scriptures, I had even more questions. I reached out to a friend. "How can I possibly obey all God's commands? I just snapped at my husband this morning!"

"Just keep reading your Bible," she said, "and ask the Holy Spirit to help you love like Jesus loves you."

After more than twenty years of living as a child of God, that simple but profound truth still helps me embrace the three steps in His great love cycle. First, the apostle Paul affirmed that love is central in the life of a believer in Jesus. Second, by continuing to pay the "debt to love one another," followers of Christ will walk in obedience, "for whoever loves others has fulfilled the law" (Romans 13:8). Finally, we fulfill the law because "love does no harm to a neighbor" (v. 10).

When we experience the depth of God's love for us, demonstrated best through Christ's sacrifice on the cross, we can respond with gratitude. Our grateful devotion to Jesus leads to loving others with our words, actions, and attitudes. Genuine love flows from the one true God who is love (1 John 4:16, 19).

Loving God, help us get caught up in Your great love cycle!

Xochitl Dixon

Practice Gratitude Today

How have you experienced God's love recently? What would it look like today to love those around you in gratitude to God for the love He has for you?

A Joyful Heart

2 CHRONICLES 7:1–10

Shout for joy to the LORD, all the earth.
Psalm 100:1

My granddaughter's favorite tune is one of John Philip Sousa's marches. Sousa, known as "The March King," was an American composer in the late nineteenth century. Moriah isn't in a marching band; she's only twenty months old. She just loves the tune and can even hum a few notes. She associates it with joyful times. When our family gets together, we often hum this song along with claps and other boisterous noises, and the grandchildren dance or parade in circles to the beat. It always ends in dizzy children and lots of laughter.

Our joyful noise reminds me of the psalm that implores us to "worship the LORD with gladness" (Psalm 100:2). When King Solomon dedicated the temple in Jerusalem, the Israelites celebrated with praises (2 Chronicles 7:5–6). Psalm 100 may have been one of the songs they sang. The psalm declares: "Shout for joy to the LORD, all the earth. Worship the Lord with gladness; come before him with joyful songs. . . . Enter his gates with thanksgiving and his courts with praise; give thanks to him and praise his name" (vv. 1–2, 4). Why? "For the LORD is good and his love endures forever" (v. 5).

Our good God loves us! In grateful response, let's "shout for joy to the LORD" (Psalm 100:1). *Alyson Kieda*

Practice Gratitude Today

How can you "worship the LORD with gladness" or "shout for joy to the LORD" today? Whether with others or alone, take time to exuberantly worship God.

An Angry God?

EXODUS 33:18–19; 34:1–7

The LORD, the LORD, the compassionate and gracious God, slow to anger, abounding in love and faithfulness.
Exodus 34:6

When I studied Greek and Roman mythology in college, I was struck by how moody and easily angered the mythological gods were in the stories. The people on the receiving end of their anger found their lives destroyed, sometimes on a whim.

I was quick to scoff, wondering how anyone could believe in gods like that. But then I asked myself, *Is my view of the God who actually exists much different? Don't I view Him as easily angered whenever I doubt Him?* Sadly, yes.

That's why I appreciate Moses's request of God to "show me your glory" (Exodus 33:18). Having been chosen to lead a large group of people who often grumbled against him, Moses wanted to know that God would indeed help him with this great task. Moses's request was rewarded by a demonstration of God's glory. God announced to Moses His name and characteristics. He is "the compassionate and gracious God, slow to anger, abounding in love and faithfulness" (34:6).

This verse reminded me that God is not impulsive, suddenly striking out in anger. That's reassuring, especially when I consider the times I've lashed out at Him in anger or impatience. Also, He continually works to make me more like Himself.

We can see God and His glory in His patience with us, the encouraging word of a friend, a beautiful sunset, or—best of all—the whisper of the Holy Spirit inside of us. *Linda Washington*

Practice Gratitude Today

When have you felt that God was angry with you? Ask Him to remind you that He is compassionate and gracious. Thank Him that He is patient and abounding in love.

True Identity

1 JOHN 2:28–3:10

See what great love the Father has lavished on us,
that we should be called children of God!
1 John 3:1

As my friend reviewed the pictures I took of her, she pointed out the physical characteristics she saw as imperfections. I asked her to look closer. "I see a beautiful and beloved daughter of the almighty King of Kings," I said. "I see a compassionate lover of God and others, whose genuine kindness, generosity, and faithfulness have made a difference in so many lives." When I noticed the tears brimming her eyes, I said, "I think you need a tiara!" Later that afternoon, we picked out the perfect crown for my friend so she would never forget her true identity.

When we come to know Jesus personally, He crowns us with love and calls us His children (1 John 3:1). He gives us the power to persevere in faith so that "we may be confident and unashamed before him at his coming" (2:28). Though He accepts us as we are, His love purifies us and transforms us into His likeness (3:2–3). He helps us recognize our need for Him and repent as we rejoice in the power to turn away from sin (vv. 7–9). We can live in faithful obedience and love (v. 10), with His truth hidden in our hearts and His Spirit present in our lives.

My friend didn't really need a tiara or any other trinket that day. But we both needed the reminder of our worth as God's beloved children.

Xochitl Dixon

Practice Gratitude Today

Look at yourself in a mirror. What features do you tend to focus on and consider flaws? While still in front of the mirror, thank God that He sees you as His beautiful and beloved child.

Come Home

PSALM 91:1–2, 14–16

He is my refuge and my fortress, my God, in whom I trust.
Psalm 91:2

One early evening while I was jogging near a construction site in our neighborhood, a skinny, dirty kitten meowed at me plaintively and followed me home. Today, Mickey is a healthy, handsome adult cat, enjoying a comfortable life in our household and deeply loved by my family. Whenever I jog on the road where I found him, I often think, *Thank You, God. Mickey was spared from living on the streets. He has a home now.*

Psalm 91 speaks of "dwell[ing] in the shelter of the Most High" (v. 1), making our home with God. The Hebrew word for "dwell" here means "to remain," to stay permanently. As we remain in Him, He helps us to live according to His wisdom and to love Him above all (Psalm 91:14; John 15:10). God promises us the comfort of being with Him for eternity, as well as the security of His being with us through earthly hardship. Although trouble may come, we can rest in His sovereignty, wisdom, and love, and in His promises to protect and deliver us.

When we make God our refuge, we live "in the shadow of the Almighty" (Psalm 91:1). No trouble can touch us except that which His infinite wisdom and love allow. This is the safety of God as our home.

Karen Huang

Practice Gratitude Today

Where do you feel most secure and at home? If possible, go to that place to pray. Thank God that He is your refuge; you can rest in His sovereignty, wisdom, and love.

Singing Meadows

PSALM 65:8–13

The valleys are mantled with grain; they shout for joy and sing.
Psalm 65:13

I've often affectionately joked with my mother-in-law about her ability to talk to her dogs. She responds to their barks with loving understanding. Perhaps now she and dog owners everywhere will also listen for their canine pals to laugh. Scientists have discovered that many animals, including dogs, cows, foxes, seals, and parakeets, have "vocal play signals"—otherwise known as laughter. Identifying these accompanying sounds helps distinguish an animal's play behaviors from what might otherwise look like fighting to a human observer.

That animals express laughter and joy gives us a delightful glimmer of what it might look like for other parts of creation to praise God in their own way. As King David looked over his surroundings, it seemed to him that "the hills [were] clothed with gladness" and the meadows and valleys were "shout[ing] for joy" (Psalm 65:12–13). David recognized that God had cared for and enriched the land, providing both beauty and sustenance.

Even though our physical surroundings don't "sing" (v. 13) in a literal way, they bear witness to God's active work in His creation and, in turn, invite us to give praise to Him with our voices. May we—as part of the "whole earth"—be "filled with awe at [His] wonders" and respond to Him with "songs of joy" (v. 8). We can trust that He'll hear and understand them. *Kirsten Holmberg*

Practice Gratitude Today

In person or online, spend a few minutes watching God's joyful creation—a dog playing fetch, trees swaying in the wind, otters swimming. Thank God for the gladness and joy of His world.

Perfectly Imperfect in Christ

HEBREWS 4:12–16

We have a great high priest . . . who has been tempted in every way, just as we are—yet he did not sin.
Hebrews 4:14–15

The interior designer on the home improvement show raved about the handmade ceramic tiles selected for the home's new shower area. Different from commercially manufactured tiles, which are all identical, these handcrafted pieces were "imperfectly perfect." The imperfections gave each tile unique beauty, adding to the charm and style of an otherwise practical space.

I know little of style or charm, let alone how tiles might contribute positively or negatively to it. Yet while those tiles were imperfectly perfect, Jesus, in His coming to earth as a human being, was perfectly perfect. The writer of Hebrews affirmed, "We do not have a high priest who is unable to empathize with our weaknesses, but we have one who has been tempted in every way, just as we are—yet he did not sin" (4:15). At no time during His earthly journey did Jesus speak a sinful word or commit a sinful act. He is perfectly perfect.

The encouragement for us, as Hebrews says, is to "hold firmly to the faith we profess" in Jesus (v. 14) because He understands and empathizes with the struggles we endure. He has been there and done that—but perfectly. Our perfectly perfect Savior can help us with all things.

Bill Crowder

Practice Gratitude Today

What challenge or weakness are you facing today that you feel others don't understand? Thank Jesus that He lived a perfect life on your behalf and that He empathizes with your struggles.

Remembering to Praise

ISAIAH 63:7–9

I will tell of the kindnesses of the LORD.
Isaiah 63:7

When our congregation built our first church building, people wrote thankful reminders on the wall studs and concrete floors before the interior of the building was finished. Pull back the drywall from the studs and you'll find them there. Verse after verse from Scripture, written beside prayers of praise like "You are so good!" were left as a witness to future generations that regardless of our challenges, God had been kind and taken care of us.

We need to remember what God has done for us and tell others about it. Isaiah exemplified this when he wrote, "I will tell of the kindnesses of the LORD, the deeds for which he is to be praised, according to all the LORD has done for us" (Isaiah 63:7). Later, the prophet also recounted God's compassion for His people throughout history, even telling how "in all their distress he too was distressed" (v. 9). But if you keep reading the chapter, you'll notice Israel was again in a time of trouble, and the prophet longed for God's intervention.

Remembering God's past kindnesses helps when times are hard. Challenging seasons come and go, but His faithful character never changes. As we turn to Him with grateful hearts in remembrance of all He's done, we discover afresh that He's always worthy of our praise.

James Banks

Practice Gratitude Today

Place a reminder of God's past faithfulness to you somewhere in your home. Choose an object and location that will speak to you of God's goodness but will not be easily noticed by others.

The Debt Eraser

PSALM 103:1–12

As far as the east is from the west, so far has he removed our transgressions from us.
Psalm 103:12

I blinked back tears as I reviewed my medical bill. Considering my husband's severe cut in salary after a lengthy unemployment, even paying half of the balance would require years of small monthly installments. I prayed before calling the doctor's office to explain our situation and request a payment plan.

After leaving me on hold for a short time, the receptionist informed me the doctor had zeroed out our account.

I sobbed a thank-you. The generous gift overwhelmed me with gratitude. Hanging up the phone, I praised God. I considered saving the bill, not as a reminder of what I used to owe but as a reminder of what God had done.

My physician's choice to pardon my debt brought to mind God's choice to forgive the insurmountable debt of my sins. Scripture assures us God is "compassionate and gracious" and "abounding in love" (Psalm 103:8). He "does not treat us as our sins deserve" (v. 10). He removes our sins "as far as the east is from the west" (v. 12) when we repent and accept Christ as our Savior. His sacrifice erases the debt we once owed. Completely.

Once forgiven, we aren't defined by or limited by our past debt. In response to the Lord's extravagant gift, we can acknowledge all He's done. Offering our devoted worship and grateful affection, we can live for Him and share Him with others. *Xochitl Dixon*

Practice Gratitude Today

Who do you feel indebted to because of their generosity to you? Thank God that despite your great debt of sin, He joyfully forgave you because He is full of compassion, generosity, and love.

Blessed to Be a Blessing

2 KINGS 4:1–7

They brought the jars to her and she kept pouring.
2 Kings 4:5

During my years as a journalist, I enjoyed telling other people's stories, but I was trained to not share my own opinions. So years after I had felt God call me out of my journalism career, when I increasingly felt God directing me to write a blog and speak about Him, I was a little nervous about sharing my thoughts, especially about my faith. As I started blogging, I was afraid I'd run out of things to say. But week after week, I found encouraging words and insights to share. The more I wrote, the more ideas flowed. The same is still true now.

I have witnessed in my own life how God has filled me with more joy and inspiration when I've poured out my gifts and talents to serve others.

In 2 Kings, we read about a poor widow who went to the prophet Elisha for help. Her late husband's creditor wanted to seize her two sons. All she had at home was a small jar of olive oil. The prophet instructed her to collect empty jars from her neighbors and to keep pouring oil into the containers. "They brought the jars to her and she kept pouring" (4:5). She kept pouring until all the jars were miraculously filled. She could pay her family's debts with the extra oil.

God is faithful and always provides. He's blessed us with gifts and talents and resources to be a blessing to others. Let's not hide or dismiss our gifts but use them for His glory. *Nancy Gavilanes*

Practice Gratitude Today

What gift, talent, or resource has God given you today? How can you use it to bless someone? Thank God for faithfully providing enough to you that you can give to others.

God Is in Control

JOB 1:6–12, 20–22

The Lord gave and the Lord has taken away;
may the name of the Lord be praised.
Job 1:21

Carol couldn't understand why it was happening all at once. As if work wasn't bad enough, her daughter fractured her foot in school, and she herself came down with a severe infection. *What did I do to deserve this?* Carol wondered. All she could do was ask God for strength.

Job didn't know why calamity had hit him so hard either—pain and loss far greater than what Carol experienced. There's no indication he was aware of the cosmic battle for his soul. Satan wanted to test Job's faith, claiming he'd turn from God if he lost everything (Job 1:6–12). When disaster struck, Job's friends insisted he was being punished for his sins. That wasn't true, but he must have wondered, *Why me?*

Job's story offers a powerful lesson about suffering and about faith. We may try to discover the reason behind our pain, but perhaps there's a bigger story behind the scenes that we won't understand in our lifetime.

Like Job, we can hold on to what we do know: God is in full control. It's not an easy thing to say, but in the midst of his pain, Job kept looking to God and trusting in His sovereignty: "The Lord gave and the Lord has taken away; may the name of the Lord be praised" (v. 21). May we too keep trusting in God no matter what happens—and even when we don't understand.

Leslie Koh

Practice Gratitude Today

What is a loss in your life that has never made sense to you? Talk openly with God about it. End by thanking Him for His love and sovereignty.

Laughing Out Loud

GENESIS 21:1–7

God has brought me laughter, and everyone
who hears about this will laugh with me.
Genesis 21:6

Comedian John Branyan said, "We didn't think up laughter; that wasn't our idea. That was given to us by [God who] knew we were going to need it to get through life. He knew we were going to have hardship, He knew we were going to have struggles, He knew . . . stuff was going to happen. . . . Laughter is a gift."

A quick look at the creatures God made can bring laughter, whether because of their oddities (such as duck-billed platypuses) or antics (such as playful otters). God made mammals that live in the ocean and long-legged birds that can't fly. God clearly has a sense of humor, and because we're created in His image, we too have the joy of laughter.

We first see the word *laughter* in the Bible in the story of Abraham and Sarah. God promised this elderly couple a child: "A son who is your own flesh and blood will be your heir" (Genesis 15:4). And God told Abraham, "Look up at the sky and count the stars. . . . So shall your offspring be" (v. 5). When Sarah finally gave birth at ninety, Abraham named their son Isaac, which means "laughter." As Sarah exclaimed, "God has brought me laughter, and everyone who hears about this will laugh with me" (21:6). It amazed her that she could nurse a child at her age! God transformed her skeptical laughter when she'd heard she'd give birth (18:12) into laughter of sheer joy.

Thank God for the gift of laughter! *Alyson Kieda*

Practice Gratitude Today

Recall a favorite memory, video, joke, or photo that makes you laugh. Share it with someone and laugh together. Thank God for giving you laughter!

Catching Contentment

PSALM 131

I am like a weaned child with its mother;
like a weaned child I am content.
Psalm 131:2

In a psychiatrist's advice column, he responded to a reader named Brenda, who lamented that her ambitious pursuits had left her discontented. His words were blunt. Humans aren't designed to be happy, he said, "only to survive and reproduce." We're cursed to chase the "teasing and elusive butterfly" of contentment, he added, "not always to capture it."

I wonder how Brenda felt reading the psychiatrist's nihilistic words and how different she may have felt had she read Psalm 131 instead. In its words, David gives us a guided reflection on how to find contentment. He begins in a posture of humility, putting aside his kingly ambitions, and while wrestling with life's big questions is important, he puts those aside too (v. 1). Then he quiets his heart before God (v. 2), entrusting the future into His hands (v. 3). The result is beautiful: "Like a weaned child with its mother," he says, "I am content" (v. 2).

In a broken world like ours, contentment will at times feel elusive. In Philippians 4:11–13, the apostle Paul said contentment is something to be learned. But if we believe we're only designed to "survive and reproduce," contentment will surely be an uncatchable butterfly. David shows us another way: catching contentment through quietly resting in God's presence. *Sheridan Voysey*

Practice Gratitude Today

Where do you feel discontented with your life? Spend a few minutes silently before God, resting in His presence and the assurance that you are enough and you have enough in Christ.

Beyond the Stars

PSALM 8:1–9

You have set your glory in the heavens.
Psalm 8:1

After thirty years of service, the National Aeronautics and Space Administration retired the Space Shuttle Program. Five partially reuseable shuttles, across 135 missions, carried more than 355 people into space and helped construct the International Space Station. Since retiring the program, NASA has now shifted its focus to deep-space exploration.

The human race has invested massive amounts of time and money, with some astronauts even sacrificing their lives, to study the immensity of the universe. Yet the evidence of God's majesty stretches far beyond what we can measure.

When we consider the Sculptor and Sustainer of the universe who knows each star by name (Isaiah 40:26), we can understand why the psalmist David praised His greatness (Psalm 8:1). The Lord's fingerprints are on "the moon and the stars," which He "set in place" (v. 3). The Maker of the heavens and the earth reigns above all, yet He remains near all His beloved children, caring for each intimately and personally (v. 4). In love, God gives us great power, responsibility, and the privilege to care for and explore the world He's entrusted to us (vv. 5–8).

As we study our star-spattered night skies, our Creator invites us to seek Him with passion and persistence. He hears every prayer and song of praise flowing from our lips. *Xochitl Dixon*

Practice Gratitude Today

Step outside tonight to enjoy the night sky, or find a video or photo online showing the wonders of the universe. Thank God that He is infinitely more vast and majestic than His creation.

A Thankful Heart

COLOSSIANS 4:2–6

Devote yourselves to prayer, being watchful and thankful.
Colossians 4:2

Seneca, the great philosopher of ancient Rome, was once accused by Empress Messalina of adultery. After the senate sentenced Seneca to death, Emperor Claudius instead exiled him to Corsica, perhaps because he suspected the charge was false. This reprieve may have shaped Seneca's view of thankfulness when he wrote: "Homicides, tyrants, thieves, adulterers, robbers, sacrilegious men, and traitors there always will be, but worse than all these is the crime of ingratitude."

A contemporary of Seneca's, the apostle Paul, may have agreed. In Romans 1:21, he wrote that one of the triggers for the downward collapse of humankind was that they refused to give thanks to God. Writing to the church at Colossae, three times Paul challenged his fellow believers in Christ to gratitude. He said we should be "overflowing with thankfulness" (Colossians 2:7). As we let God's peace "rule in [our] hearts," we're to respond with thankfulness (3:15). In fact, gratitude ought to characterize our prayers (4:2).

God's great kindnesses to us remind us of one of life's great realities. He not only deserves our love and worship; He also deserves our thankful hearts. Everything that's good in life comes from Him (James 1:17).

With all we've been given in Christ, gratitude should be as natural as breathing. May we respond to God's gracious gifts by expressing our gratitude to Him. *Bill Crowder*

Practice Gratitude Today

As you go about your day, consider the relationships, opportunities, and material things you have to be thankful for. At the end of your day, write down as many of them as you can remember.

Redeeming the Season

PSALM 104:10–23

He made the moon to mark the seasons.
Psalm 104:19

Leisa wanted a way to redeem the season. So many of the autumn decorations she saw seemed to celebrate death, sometimes in gruesome and macabre ways.

Determined to counter the darkness in some small way, Leisa began to write things she was grateful for with a permanent marker on a large pumpkin. "Sunshine" was the first item. Soon visitors were adding to her list. Some entries were whimsical: "doodling," for instance. Others were practical: "a warm house," "a working car." Still others were poignant, like the name of a departed loved one. A chain of gratitude began to wind its way around the pumpkin.

Psalm 104 offers a litany of praise to God for things we easily overlook. "He makes springs pour water into the ravines," sang the poet (v. 10). "He makes grass grow for the cattle, and plants for people to cultivate" (v. 14). Even the night is seen as good and fitting. "You bring darkness, it becomes night, and all the beasts of the forest prowl" (v. 20). But then "the sun rises. . . . People go out to their work, to their labor until evening" (vv. 22–23). For all these things, the psalmist concluded, "I will sing praise to my God as long as I live" (v. 33).

In a world that doesn't know how to deal with death, even the smallest offering of praise to our Creator can become a shining contrast of hope.

Tim Gustafson

Practice Gratitude Today

Find someone or a group of people with whom to make a "chain of gratitude," either in person or by text. Take turns telling each other things you are grateful that God has given to you.

Cuddling In

PSALM 116:1–7

Return to your rest, my soul, for the LORD has been good to you.
Psalm 116:7

"Daddy, will you read to me?" my daughter asked. It's not an unusual question for a child to ask of a parent. But my daughter is eleven now. These days, such requests are fewer than they were when she was younger. "Yes," I said happily, and she curled up next to me on the couch.

As I read to her (from *The Fellowship of the Ring*), she practically melted into me. It was one of those glorious moments as a parent, when we feel perhaps just an inkling of the perfect love our Father has for us and His deep desire for us to "cuddle in" to His presence and love for us.

I realized in that moment that I'm a lot like my eleven-year-old. Much of the time, I'm focused on being independent. It's so easy to lose touch with God's love for us, a tender and protective love that Psalm 116 describes as "gracious and righteous . . . full of compassion" (v. 5). It's a love where, like my daughter, I can curl up in God's lap, at home in His delight for me.

Psalm 116:7 suggests that we might need to regularly remind ourselves of God's good love, and then crawl up into His waiting arms: "Return to your rest, my soul, for the LORD has been good to you." And indeed, He has.

Adam R. Holz

Practice Gratitude Today

How can you "cuddle in" with God today? Spend intentional time with Him, simply enjoying His tender love.

Getting a Grip on Gratitude

NUMBERS 11:1–11

Would they have enough if all the fish in
the sea were caught for them?
Numbers 11:22

The years of weariness caused by chronic pain and frustrations with my limited mobility had finally caught up with me. In my discontent, I became demanding and ungrateful. I began complaining about my husband's caregiving skills. I griped about the way he cleaned the house. Even though he's the best cook I know, I fussed about the lack of variety in our meals. When he finally shared that my grumbling hurt his feelings, I was resentful. He had no idea what I was going through. Eventually, God helped me see my wrongs, and I asked my husband and the Lord for forgiveness.

Longing for different circumstances can lead to complaining, and even a form of relationship-damaging self-centeredness. The Israelites were familiar with this dilemma. It seems they were never satisfied and always griping about God's provision (Exodus 17:1–3). Even though the Lord cared for His people in the wilderness by sending them "bread from heaven" (16:4), they began craving other food (Numbers 11:4). Instead of rejoicing over the daily miracles of God's faithful and loving care, the Israelites wanted something more, something better, something different, or even something they used to have (vv. 4–6). They took out their frustrations on Moses (vv. 10–14).

Trusting God's goodness and faithfulness can help us get a good grip on gratitude. Today we can thank Him for the countless ways He cares for us.

Xochitl Dixon

Practice Gratitude Today

What part of your life do you complain about the most? Talk with God about it, asking Him to remind you of things you have to be grateful for in that area.

Haystack Prayers

2 CORINTHIANS 1:8–11

You help us by your prayers.
2 Corinthians 1:11

Samuel Mills and four of his friends often gathered together to pray for God to send more people to share the good news of Jesus. One day in 1806, after returning from their prayer meeting, they got caught in a thunderstorm and took refuge in a haystack. Their weekly prayer gathering then became known as the Haystack Prayer Meeting, which resulted in a global mission movement. Today the Haystack Monument stands at Williams College in the United States as a reminder of what God can do through prayer.

Our heavenly Father is delighted when His children approach Him with a common request. It's like a family gathering where they're united in purpose, sharing a common burden.

The apostle Paul acknowledges how God helped him through the prayers of others during a time of severe suffering: "He will continue to deliver us, as you help us by your prayers" (2 Corinthians 1:10–11). God has chosen to use our prayers—especially our prayers together—to accomplish His work in the world. No wonder the verse continues: "Then many will give thanks . . . for the . . . answer to the prayers of many."

Let's pray together so we can also rejoice together in God's goodness. Our loving Father is waiting for us to come to Him so He can work through us in ways that reach far beyond anything we could ever imagine.

Poh Fang Chia

Practice Gratitude Today

Ask someone to join you in praying for something you've been asking God about. As you pray today, thank Him that He works through the prayers of His children.

Nowhere to Hide

GENESIS 3:6–13, 22–24

To him who loves us and has freed us
from our sins by his blood . . .
Revelation 1:5

I smelled something burning, so I hurried to the kitchen. Nothing was on the stove or in the oven. I followed my nose through the house. From room to room I went, eventually ending up downstairs. My nose led me to my office and then to my desk. I peeked beneath it and there, peering back at me with big eyes pleading for help, was Maggie, our dog—our very fragrant dog. What smelled like something burning when I was upstairs now had the distinct odor of skunk. Maggie had gone to the farthest corner of our house to escape the foul smell, but she couldn't get away from herself.

Maggie's dilemma brought to mind the many times I have tried to run away from unpleasant circumstances only to discover that the problem was not the situation I was in but me. Since Adam and Eve hid after sinning (Genesis 3:8), we've all followed their example. We run away from situations thinking we can escape the unpleasantness—only to discover that the unpleasantness is us.

The only way to escape ourselves is to stop hiding, acknowledge our waywardness, and let Jesus wash us clean (Revelation 1:5). I am grateful that when we do sin, Jesus is willing to give us a brand-new start.

Julie Ackerman Link

Practice Gratitude Today

What sin have you not been able to deal with on your own that you need to confess to God? Bring it to Him in prayer, confessing, repenting, and thanking Him that He is faithful to forgive your sins.

Impromptu Praise

ACTS 16:16–26

About midnight Paul and Silas were praying
and singing hymns to God.
Acts 16:25

During a short-term mission trip to Ethiopia, our team accompanied another team from a local ministry on an outreach to a group of young men who'd hit hard times and were living in shacks in a literal junkyard. They were such a delight to meet! We shared testimonies, encouraging words, and prayers together. One of my favorite moments that evening was when a local team member played his guitar and we got to worship with our new friends under the radiant moon. What a sacred moment! Despite their desperate situation, these men had hope and joy that can only be found in Jesus.

Acts 16 records another impromptu praise time. This one broke out in a jail in the city of Philippi. Paul and Silas had been arrested, beaten, flogged, and imprisoned while serving Jesus. Instead of giving in to despair, they worshiped God by "praying and singing" in their jail cell (v. 25). "Suddenly there was such a violent earthquake that the foundations of the prison were shaken. At once all the prison doors flew open, and everyone's chains came loose" (v. 26).

The jailer's first thought was to end his life, but when he realized the prisoners hadn't escaped, he was in awe of God, and salvation came to his family (vv. 27–34).

God delights in hearing us praise Him. Let's worship Him during both the highs and lows of life. *Nancy Gavilanes*

Practice Gratitude Today

Turn on music that you find worshipful. Choose a current high or low in your life to focus on as you worship God for the hope you have in Jesus.

Giving Credit

JEREMIAH 9:23–26

Let the one who boasts boast in the Lord.
1 Corinthians 1:31

In the early 1960s, some unusual paintings featuring a person or animal with huge, sad eyes became popular. Some considered the work kitschy or tacky, but others delighted in it. As the artist's husband began to promote his wife's creations, the couple grew quite prosperous. But the artist's signature—Margaret Keane—didn't appear on her work. Instead, Margaret's husband presented his wife's work as his own. Margaret fearfully remained silent about the fraud for twenty years until the couple's marriage ended. It took a courtroom "paint-off" between them to prove the true artist's identity.

The man's deception was clearly wrong, but even as followers of Jesus we may find it easy to take credit for talents we possess, leadership skills we display, or kind deeds to others. But those qualities are possible only because of God's grace. In Jeremiah 9, we find the prophet lamenting the lack of humility and the unrepentant hearts of the Israelite people. He wrote that the Lord says we shouldn't boast of our wisdom, our strength, or our riches but only of our understanding and knowledge that He is the Lord "who exercises kindness, justice and righteousness on earth" (v. 24).

Our hearts fill with gratitude as we realize the identity of the true Artist. "Every good and perfect gift is . . . from the Father" (James 1:17). All of the credit and all of the praise belong to the Giver of good gifts. *Cindy Hess Kasper*

Practice Gratitude Today

Make a list of things people have complimented you on—talents, accomplishments, character traits, perspectives. Praise God for giving you these abilities and achievements.

The Joy of Giving

1 THESSALONIANS 5:12–24

Encourage the disheartened, help the weak, be patient with everyone.
1 Thessalonians 5:14

It was a dreary week. I had been feeling lethargic and listless, although I couldn't figure out why. Near the end of the week, I found out that an aunt had kidney failure. I knew I had to visit her—but to be honest, I felt like postponing the visit. Still, I made my way to her place, where we had dinner, chatted, and prayed together. An hour later, I left her home feeling upbeat for the first time in days. Focusing on someone else rather than myself had somehow improved my mood.

Psychologists have found that the act of giving can produce satisfaction, which comes when the giver sees the recipient's gratitude. Some experts even believe that humans are wired to be generous!

Perhaps that's why Paul, when encouraging the church in Thessalonica to build up their faith community, urged them to "help the weak" (1 Thessalonians 5:14). Earlier, he had also cited Jesus's words, "It is more blessed to give than to receive" (Acts 20:35). While this was said in the context of giving financially, it applies as well to the giving of time and effort.

When we give, we get an insight into how God feels. We understand why He's so delighted to give us His love, and we share in His joy and the satisfaction of blessing others. I think I'll be visiting my aunt again soon.

Leslie Koh

Practice Gratitude Today

How can you give of your time, skill, or money to someone today? As you give, thank God that He delights in giving to you.

Extreme Kindness

JEREMIAH 52:31–34

When the kindness and love of God our
Savior appeared, he saved us.
Titus 3:4–5

Fast-food restaurant worker Kevin Ford hadn't missed a shift in twenty-seven years. After a video surfaced showing his humble gratitude for a modest gift he received to commemorate his decades of service, thousands of people rallied together to show kindness to him. "It's like a dream, a dream come true, that nobody can even think of this," he said when a fundraising effort brought in $250,000 in just over a week.

Jehoiachin, the exiled king of Judah, was also the recipient of extreme kindness. He'd been incarcerated for thirty-seven years before the benevolence of the Babylonian king resulted in his release. The king "freed him from prison. He spoke kindly to him and gave him a seat of honor higher than those of the other kings who were with him in Babylon" (Jeremiah 52:31–32). Jehoiachin was given a new position, new clothes, and a new residence. His new life was fully funded by the king.

This story pictures what happens spiritually when, unable to help ourselves, believers in Jesus's death and resurrection are rescued from their estrangement from God. They're brought from darkness and death into light and life; they're brought into the family of God because of the extreme kindness of God. *Arthur Jackson*

Practice Gratitude Today

What is one benefit of being in relationship with God and part of His family that you are grateful for today? Praise God for rescuing you from sin and death, because of His great kindness.

Creation's Song

PSALM 19:1–6

The heavens declare the glory of God; the skies proclaim the work of his hands.
Psalm 19:1

Using acoustic astronomy, scientists can observe and listen to the sounds and pulses of space. They've found that stars don't orbit in silence in the mysterious night sky but rather generate music. Like humpback whale sounds, the resonance of stars exists at wavelengths or frequencies that may not be heard by the human ear. Yet, the music of stars and whales and other creatures combine to create a symphony that proclaims the greatness of God.

Psalm 19:1–4 says, "The heavens declare the glory of God; the skies proclaim the work of his hands. Day after day they pour forth speech; night after night they reveal knowledge. They have no speech, they use no words; no sound is heard from them. Yet their voice goes out into all the earth, their words to the ends of the world."

In the New Testament, the apostle Paul reveals that in Jesus "all things were created: things in heaven and on earth, visible and invisible; . . . all things have been created through him and for him" (Colossians 1:16). In response, the natural world's heights and depths sing to their Maker. May we join creation and sing out the greatness of the One who "with the breadth of his hand marked off the heavens" (Isaiah 40:12).

Remi Oyedele

Practice Gratitude Today

Find a video online of whale song. Thank God for the parts of creation that you cannot see, hear, or sense for yourself.

Joy in Hard Places

HABAKKUK 3:16–19

Yet I will rejoice in the Lord, I will be joyful in God my Savior.
Habakkuk 3:18

Whenever she was unable to take my phone call, my friend's voicemail recording invited me to leave her a message. The recording cheerfully concluded, "Make it a great day!" As I reflected on her words, I realized that it's not within our power to make every day "great"—some circumstances truly are devastating. But a closer look might reveal something redeeming and beautiful in my day, whether things are going well or poorly.

Habakkuk wasn't experiencing easy circumstances. God had shown the prophet coming days when none of the crops or livestock—on which God's people depended—would be fruitful (3:17). It would take more than mere optimism to endure the coming hardships. As a people group, Israel would be in extreme poverty. Habakkuk experienced heart-pounding, lip-quivering, leg-trembling fear (v. 16).

Yet despite that, Habakkuk said he would "rejoice in the Lord" and "be joyful" (v. 18). He proclaimed his hope in the God who provides the strength to walk in difficult places (v. 19).

Sometimes we go through seasons of deep pain and hardship. But no matter what we've lost—or wanted but never had—we can, like Habakkuk, rejoice in our relationship with a loving God. Even when it feels like we have nothing else, He will never fail or abandon us (Hebrews 13:5). He, the One who "provide[s] for those who grieve," is our ultimate reason for joy (Isaiah 61:3). *Kirsten Holmberg*

Practice Gratitude Today

What is one thing redeeming or beautiful about today? Thank God that no matter your circumstances, He will never fail or abandon you.

A Gratitude Visit

ROMANS 16:1–16

I commend to you our sister Phoebe, . . . for she has been the benefactor of many people, including me.
Romans 16:1–2

Counting your blessings promotes good physical health, according to a study by some American doctors. Volunteers who kept weekly gratitude journals reported fewer aches and pains than those who recorded daily hassles or neutral events.

A "gratitude visit" was developed by Dr. Martin E. P. Seligman to promote strong emotional health. He tells people to think of someone who has made an important difference in their lives. He asks them to write the story of how that person has helped them and then to visit that person and read the story aloud. Tests show that a year later the people who had done so were happier and reported fewer episodes of depression. Even more important, think of what it must have done for those who were thanked!

The apostle Paul had a long list of people who had helped him and for whom he was grateful (Romans 16:1–16). He wrote that Phoebe had been a "benefactor of many," Priscilla and Aquila had "risked their lives" for his life, and Mary had "worked very hard" for the believers in Rome. And Paul took time to write his thanks in a letter to the church at Rome.

Who has helped to shape your life? Could you make a gratitude visit—for their sake and for yours? *Anne Cetas*

Practice Gratitude Today

Plan a time when you can write your story of how someone helped you and when you can deliver the story to that person. If possible, visit in person; a video call would be another option.

Grandmother Research

ZEPHANIAH 3:17–20

He will take great delight in you.
Zephaniah 3:17

Researchers at Emory University used MRI scans to study the brains of grandmothers. They measured empathetic responses to images that included their own grandchild, their own adult child, and one anonymous child. The study showed that grandmothers have a higher empathy toward their own grandchild than even their own adult child. This is attributed to what they call the "cute factor"—their own grandchild being more adorable than the adult.

Before we say "Well, duh!" we might consider the words of James Rilling, who conducted the study: "If their grandchild is smiling, [the grandmother is] feeling the child's joy. And if their grandchild is crying, they're feeling the child's pain and distress."

One prophet gives an "MRI" of God's feelings as He looks upon His people: "He will take great delight in you; in his love he will . . . rejoice over you with singing" (Zephaniah 3:17). Some translate this to say, "You will make His heart full of joy, and He will sing loudly." Like an empathetic grandmother, God feels our pain: "In all their distress he too was distressed" (Isaiah 63:9). And He feels our joy: "The Lord takes delight in his people" (Psalm 149:4).

When we feel discouraged, it's good to remember that God has real feelings for us. He's not a cold, faraway God, but one who loves and delights in us. It's time to draw close to Him, feel His smile, and listen to His singing. *Kenneth Petersen*

Practice Gratitude Today

What are you feeling today? Joy? Pain? Contentment? Anger? Gratitude? Fear? Thank God that He knows and feels what you're feeling.

Ask the Man Who Owns One

PSALM 66:1, 8–20

Let me tell you what [God] has done for me.
Psalm 66:16

In the early 1900s, the Packard Motor Car Company generated a slogan to entice buyers. "Ask the man who owns one" became a powerful tagline, one that contributed to the company's reputation for manufacturing the dominant luxury vehicle in that era. What Packard seemed to understand is that personal testimony is compelling to the hearer: a friend's satisfaction with a product is a powerful endorsement.

Sharing with others our personal experiences of God's goodness to us also makes an impact. God invites us to declare our gratitude and joy not only to Him but also to those around us (Psalm 66:1). The psalmist eagerly shared in his song the forgiveness God granted him when he turned from his sins (vv. 18–20).

God has done amazing works in the course of history, such as parting the waters of the Red Sea (v. 6). He also does amazing work in each of our personal lives: giving us hope in the midst of suffering, giving us the Holy Spirit to understand His Word, and providing for our daily needs. When we share with others our personal experiences of God's work in our lives, we're giving something of much greater value than an endorsement of a particular purchase—we're acknowledging God's goodness and encouraging one another along the journey of life.

Kirsten Holmberg

Practice Gratitude Today

Make time today to tell someone, whether in person or online, about God's provision and presence in your life.

More Than Skin-Deep

PSALM 32

Blessed is the one . . . whose sins are covered.
Psalm 32:1

José, a young believer in Jesus, was visiting his brother's church. As he entered the sanctuary prior to the service, his brother's face fell when he saw him. José's tattoos, covering both arms, were visible since he was wearing a T-shirt. His brother told him to go home and put on a long-sleeved shirt, for many of José's tattoos reflected the ways of his past. José suddenly felt dirty. But another man overheard the brothers' interaction and brought José to the pastor, telling him what had happened. The pastor smiled and unbuttoned his shirt, revealing a large tattoo on his chest—something from his own past. He assured José that because God had made him pure from the inside out, he didn't need to cover his arms.

David experienced the joy of being made pure by God. After confessing his sin to God, the king wrote, "Oh, what joy for those whose disobedience is forgiven, whose sin is put out of sight!" (Psalm 32:1 NLT). He could now "shout for joy" with others "whose hearts are pure!" (v. 11 NLT). The apostle Paul later quoted Psalm 32:1–2 in Romans 4:7–8, a passage declaring that faith in Jesus leads to salvation and a pure standing before Him (see Romans 4:23–25).

Our purity in Jesus is much more than skin-deep, for He knows and purifies our hearts (1 Samuel 16:7; 1 John 1:9). May we rejoice in His purifying work today.

Tom Felten

Practice Gratitude Today

How do you feel blemished or disqualified because of past sin either that you committed or that was committed against you? Praise God that He has cleansed you completely in Christ.

Worthy of All Praise

PSALM 18:1–6

I love you, LORD, my strength.
Psalm 18:1

Many consider Ferrante and Teicher to be the greatest piano duet team of all time. Their collaborative presentations were so precise that their style was described as four hands but only one mind. Hearing their music, one can begin to grasp the amount of effort required to perfect their craft.

But there's more. They loved what they did. In fact, even after they retired in 1989, Ferrante and Teicher would occasionally show up at a local piano store just to play an impromptu concert. They simply loved making music.

David also loved making music, but he teamed up with God to give his song a higher purpose. His psalms affirm his struggle-filled life and his desire to live in deep dependence upon God. In the midst of his personal failures and imperfections, his praise expressed a kind of spiritual "perfect pitch," acknowledging the greatness and goodness of God even in the darkest of times. The heart behind David's praise is simply stated in Psalm 18:1: "I love you, LORD, my strength."

David continued, "I called to the LORD, who is worthy of praise. . . . In my distress I called to the LORD" (vv. 3, 6). Regardless of our situation, may we likewise lift our hearts to praise and worship our God. He's worthy of all praise! *Bill Crowder*

Practice Gratitude Today

What do you love to do to the glory of God? Set aside time today to worship God by exercising your skills, abilities, and gifts.

The Remedy for Jealousy

1 SAMUEL 18:5–15

From that time on Saul kept a jealous eye on David.
1 Samuel 18:9 NLT

I gladly agreed to babysit my grandkids while their parents went out for the evening. After hugs, I asked the boys what they did over the weekend. Both had separate adventures. Bridger, age three, recounted breathlessly how he got to stay overnight with his aunt and uncle—and he had ice cream and rode a carousel and watched a movie! Next it was five-year-old Samuel's turn. When asked what he did, he said, "Camping." "Did you have fun?" I asked. "Not so much," he answered forlornly.

Samuel experienced the age-old feeling of jealousy. He forgot how much fun he had camping with his dad when he heard his brother excitedly tell about his weekend.

All of us can fall prey to jealousy. King Saul gave in to the green-eyed monster of jealousy when the praise David received exceeded his: "Saul has slain his thousands, and David his tens of thousands" (1 Samuel 18:7). Saul was outraged and "from that time on . . . kept a jealous eye on David" (v. 9 NLT). He was so incensed he tried to kill David!

The comparison game is foolish and self-destructive. Someone will always have something we don't or enjoy experiences different from ours. But God has already given us many blessings, including both life on this earth and the promise of eternal life to all who believe. Depending on His help and focusing on Him in thankfulness can help us to overcome jealousy. *Alyson Kieda*

Practice Gratitude Today

Whose life are you envious of? Consider what you feel is missing from your own life. Talk honestly with God about it; end by thanking Him for specific things He has given you.

Uncertain Times

PHILIPPIANS 4:6–9

The peace of God, which transcends all understanding,
will guard your hearts and your minds in Christ Jesus.
Philippians 4:7

During a major economic downturn several years ago, many people lost their jobs. Sadly, my brother-in-law was one of them. Writing to me about their situation, my sister shared that although there were uncertainties, they had peace because they knew that God would care for them.

Believers in Jesus can have peace in the midst of uncertainties because we have the assurance that our heavenly Father loves His children and cares for our needs (Matthew 6:25–34). We can bring all our concerns to Him with an attitude of thankfulness, trusting Him to meet our needs and give us peace (Philippians 4:6–7).

"The peace of God, which transcends all understanding," writes the apostle Paul, "will guard your hearts and your minds through Christ Jesus" (v. 7). To say the peace of God transcends all understanding reveals that we can't explain it, but we can experience it as He guards our hearts and minds.

Our peace comes from the confidence that the Lord loves us and He is in control. He alone provides the comfort that settles our nerves, fills our minds with hope, and allows us to relax even in the midst of changes and challenges. *Poh Fang Chia*

Practice Gratitude Today

What uncertainty or challenge seems to exclude peace from your life today? Thank God that His peace doesn't depend on your circumstances but on His constant presence with you.

All of Me

MATTHEW 27:45–54

Offer your bodies as a living sacrifice, holy and pleasing to God—this is your true and proper worship.
Romans 12:1

Young Isaac Watts found the music in his church sadly lacking, and his father challenged him to create something better. Isaac did. His hymn "When I Survey the Wondrous Cross" has been called the greatest in the English language and has been translated into many other languages.

Watts's worshipful third verse ushers us into the presence of Christ at the crucifixion: "See from His head, His Hands, His feet, / sorrow and love flow mingled down. / Did e'er such love and sorrow meet / or thorns compose so rich a crown?"

The crucifixion Watts describes so elegantly stands as history's most awful moment. We do well to pause and stand with those around the cross. The Son of God strains for breath, held by crude spikes driven through His flesh. After tortured hours, a supernatural darkness descends. Finally, mercifully, the Lord of the universe dismisses His anguished spirit. An earthquake rattles the landscape. Back in the city, the thick temple curtain rips in half. Graves open, and dead bodies resurrect, walking about the city (Matthew 27:51–53). These events compel the Roman centurion who crucified Jesus to say, "Surely he was the Son of God!" (v. 54).

"The Cross reorders all values and cancels all vanities," says the Poetry Foundation in commenting on Watts's poem. The song could only conclude: "Love so amazing, so divine demands my soul, my life, my all."

Tim Gustafson

Practice Gratitude Today

Read the lyrics of Isaac Watts's "When I Survey the Wondrous Cross" or listen to a recording of the hymn. Pray the words, thanking Jesus for the mercy and power of His crucifixion.

Unlimited

ISAIAH 40:21–28

The LORD is the everlasting God, the Creator of the ends of the earth. He will not grow tired or weary.
Isaiah 40:28

There I am, sitting in the shopping mall food court, my body tense and my stomach knotted over looming work deadlines. As I unwrap my burger and take a bite, people rush around me, fretting over their own tasks. *How limited we all are*, I think to myself, *limited in time, energy, and capacity*.

I consider writing a new to-do list and prioritizing the urgent tasks, but as I pull out a pen, another thought enters my mind: a thought of One who is infinite and unlimited, who effortlessly accomplishes all that He desires.

This God, Isaiah says, can measure the oceans in the hollow of His hand and collect the dust of the earth in a basket (Isaiah 40:12). He names the stars of the heavens and directs their path (v. 26), knows the rulers of the world and oversees their careers (v. 23), considers islands mere specks of dust and the nations like drops in the sea (v. 15). "To whom will you compare me?" He asks (v. 25). "The LORD is the everlasting God," Isaiah replies. "He will not grow tired or weary" (v. 28).

Stress and strain aren't good for us, but on this day they deliver a powerful lesson. The unlimited God is not like me. He accomplishes everything He wishes. I finish my burger, and then pause once more. And silently worship. *Sheridan Voysey*

Practice Gratitude Today

Make a list of the tasks, deadlines, and unknowns that feel stressful today. Take your list to God in prayer, thanking Him that He is sovereign and unlimited in power and love.

Consider the Source

JAMES 1:12–18

Every good and perfect gift is from above, coming
down from the Father of the heavenly lights.
James 1:17

I love cinnamon. I love cinnamon rolls, cinnamon graham crackers, cinnamon candies, cinnamon toast, cinnamon apples, and cinnamon pretzels. Cinnamon is one of those spices that makes other things taste better. However, it never crossed my mind to think about where cinnamon comes from. Then, on a recent trip to Sri Lanka, I learned that 90 percent of all the cinnamon in the world comes from that island nation located in the Indian Ocean. For all of the cinnamon I've enjoyed over the years, I never stopped to consider its source.

Sadly, my walk with Christ is sometimes like that. God has blessed me with a wonderful wife, five children, and grandchildren who are more fun than a barrel of monkeys. In the midst of my enjoyment of them, however, I sometimes fail to consider the source of those blessings—what the hymn writer called the "fount of every blessing." James put it like this: "Every good and perfect gift is from above, coming down from the Father of the heavenly lights, who does not change like shifting shadows" (1:17).

How ungrateful we would be to enjoy the rich blessings of life without thanking the Father who is the source of all creation.

Bill Crowder

Practice Gratitude Today

What good things do you tend to take for granted because they are such a familiar part of your life? Pause to thank God for providing you with the good things you have.

God's Gift of Grace

EPHESIANS 4:4–8

To each one of us grace has been given as Christ apportioned it.
Ephesians 4:7

As I was grading another stack of papers for a college writing class I teach, I was impressed with one particular paper. It was so well written! Soon, though, I realized it was too well written. Sure enough, a little research revealed that the paper had been plagiarized from an online source.

I sent the student an email to let her know that her ruse had been discovered. She was getting a zero on this paper, but she could write a new paper for partial credit. Her response: "I am humiliated and very sorry. I appreciate the grace you are showing me. I don't deserve it." I responded by telling her that we all receive Jesus's grace every day, so how could I deny showing her grace?

There are many ways God's grace enhances our lives and redeems us from our errors. Peter says it gives us salvation: "We believe it is through the grace of our Lord Jesus that we are saved" (Acts 15:11). Paul says it helps us not to be overtaken by sin: "Sin shall no longer be your master, because you are not under the law, but under grace" (Romans 6:14). Elsewhere, Peter says grace allows us to serve: "Use whatever gift you have received to serve others, as faithful stewards of God's grace" (1 Peter 4:10).

Grace. So freely given by God (Ephesians 4:7). May we use this gift to love and encourage others. *Dave Branon*

Practice Gratitude Today

Where do you see God's grace at work in your life? Thank Him for the grace He's freely given to you, and ask Him how you can share His grace with someone today.

Just a Whisper

JOB 26:7–14

How faint the whisper we hear of him!
Job 26:14

The whispering wall in New York City's Grand Central Station is an acoustic oasis from the clamor of the area. This unique spot allows people to communicate quiet messages from a distance of thirty feet. When one person stands at the base of a granite archway and speaks softly into the wall, sound waves travel up and over the curved stone to the listener on the other side.

Job heard the whisper of a message when his life was filled with noise and the tragedy of losing nearly everything (Job 1:13–19; 2:7). His friends blabbered their opinions, his own thoughts tumbled endlessly, and trouble had invaded every aspect of his existence. Still, the majesty of nature spoke softly to him about God's divine power.

The splendor of the skies, the mystery of the earth suspended in space, and the stability of the horizon reminded Job that the world was in the palm of God's hand (26:7–11). Even a churning sea and a rumbling atmosphere led him to say, "These are but the outer fringe of his works; how faint the whisper we hear of him!" (v. 14).

If the world's wonders represent just a fragment of God's capabilities, it's clear that His power exceeds our ability to understand it. In times of brokenness, this gives us hope. God can do anything, including what He did for Job as He sustained him during suffering.

Jennifer Benson Schuldt

Practice Gratitude Today

Spend a few minutes outside observing nature—the clouds in the sky, a bird on a tree limb, a cool breeze on your face. Thank God for these whispers of His divine power and sovereignty.

Back from the Dead

EPHESIANS 2:1–10

[God] made us alive with Christ even when
we were dead in transgressions.
Ephesians 2:5

Can a man be officially alive after being declared legally dead? That question became international news when a man from Ohio showed up in good health after being reported missing more than twenty-five years earlier. At the time of his disappearance, he had been unemployed, addicted, and hopelessly behind in child support payments. So he decided to go into hiding. On his return, however, he discovered how hard it is to come back from the dead. When the man went to court to reverse the ruling that had declared him legally dead, the judge turned down his request, citing a three-year time limit for changing a death ruling.

That unusual request of a human court turns out to be a common experience for God. Paul's letter to the Ephesians tells us that though we were spiritually dead, God "made us alive with Christ" (2:5). Yet declaring and making us spiritually alive was a deeply painful matter for God. Our sin and its consequent spiritual death required the suffering, death, and resurrection of God's Son (vv. 4–7).

It's one thing to show evidence of physical life. Our challenge is to show evidence of spiritual life. Having been declared alive in Christ, we are called to live in gratitude for the immeasurable mercy and life given to us.

Mart DeHaan

Practice Gratitude Today

Where do you see evidence of spiritual life in yourself? Thank God for rescuing you from death, filling you with His Spirit, and making you into the image of His Son, Jesus.

Lavish Expressions of Love

2 CORINTHIANS 9:6–15

You will be enriched in every way so that you can be generous on every occasion.
2 Corinthians 9:11

On our wedding anniversary, my husband, Alan, gives me a large bouquet of fresh flowers. When he lost his job during a corporate restructure, I didn't expect this extravagant display of devotion to continue. But on our nineteenth anniversary, the color-splashed blossoms greeted me from their spot on our dining room table. Because he valued continuing this annual tradition, Alan saved some money each month to ensure he'd have enough for this show of affection.

My husband's careful planning exhibited exuberant generosity, similar to what Paul encouraged when he addressed the Corinthian believers. The apostle complimented the church for their intentional and enthusiastic offerings (2 Corinthians 9:2, 5), reminding them that God delights in generous and cheerful givers (vv. 6–7). After all, no one gives more than our loving Provider, who's always ready to supply all we need (vv. 8–10).

We can be generous in all kinds of giving, caring for one another because the Lord meets all of our material, emotional, and spiritual needs (v. 11). As we give, we can express our gratitude for all God has given us. We can even motivate others to praise the Lord and give from all God has given them (vv. 12–13). Openhanded giving, a lavish expression of love and gratitude, can demonstrate our confidence in God's provision for all His people. *Xochitl Dixon*

Practice Gratitude Today

How can you give to someone today to help meet a material, emotional, or spiritual need? Thank God that no one is more generous or giving than God Himself.

Great Things!

PSALM 126

What, then, shall we say in response to these things?
If God is for us, who can be against us?
Romans 8:31

On November 9, 1989, the world was astonished by the news of the fall of the Berlin Wall. The wall that had divided Berlin, Germany, was coming down, and the city that had been divided for twenty-eight years would be united again. Though the epicenter of joy was Germany, an onlooking world shared in the excitement. Something great had taken place!

When Israel returned to her homeland in 538 BC after being exiled for almost seventy years, it was also momentous. Psalm 126 begins with an over-the-shoulder look at that joy-filled time in the history of Israel. The experience was marked by laughter, joyful singing, and international recognition that God had done great things for His people (v. 2). And what was the response of the recipients of His rescuing mercy? Great things from God prompted great gladness (v. 3). Furthermore, His works in the past became the basis for fresh prayers for the present and bright hope for the future (vv. 4–6).

You and I need not look far in our own experiences for examples of great things from God, especially if we believe in God through His Son, Jesus. Nineteenth-century hymn writer Fanny Crosby captured this sentiment when she wrote, "Great things He hath taught us, great things He hath done, and great our rejoicing through Jesus the Son." Yes, to God be the glory, great things He has done! *Arthur Jackson*

Practice Gratitude Today

Think back over your life. What are some of the great things God has done for you? Praise Him for those things.

A Thanksgiving Blessing

LUKE 14:12–14

When you give a banquet, invite the poor, the crippled,
the lame, the blind, and you will be blessed.
Luke 14:13–14

Wanda Dench sent a text inviting her grandson to Thanksgiving dinner, not knowing he'd recently changed his phone number. The text instead went to a stranger, Jamal. Jamal didn't have plans, and so, after clarifying who he was, asked if he could still come to dinner. Wanda said, "Of course you can." Jamal joined the family dinner in what has since become a yearly tradition for him. A mistaken invitation became an annual blessing.

Wanda's kindness in inviting a stranger to dinner reminds me of Jesus's encouragement in Luke's gospel. During a dinner party at a "prominent" Pharisee's house (Luke 14:1), Jesus noticed who was invited and how the guests jostled for the best seats (v. 7). Jesus told His host that inviting people based on what they could do for him in return (v. 12) meant the blessing would be limited. Instead, Jesus told the host that extending hospitality to people without the resources to repay him would bring even greater blessing (v. 14).

For Wanda, inviting Jamal to join her family for Thanksgiving dinner resulted in the unexpected blessing of a lasting friendship that was a great encouragement to her after her husband's death. When we reach out to others, not because of what we might receive but because of God's love flowing through us, we receive far greater blessing and encouragement.

Lisa M. Samra

Practice Gratitude Today

Do you know someone who may be alone for Thanksgiving? Invite that person to join you sometime this holiday weekend. Thank God that He invited you into His family when you had nothing to give.

Game of Thanks

COLOSSIANS 3:12–17

Whatever you do, . . . do it all in the name of the Lord Jesus, giving thanks to God the Father through him.
Colossians 3:17

Every autumn we throw a scrumptious Thanksgiving feast on the campus of the university where I work. Our students love it! Last year a group of students played a game at their table. They challenged each other to name something they were thankful for in three seconds or less, without repeating what someone else had said. Anyone who hesitated was out of the game.

There are all kinds of things that students gripe about—tests, deadlines, rules, and a host of other college-type complaints. But these students had chosen to be thankful. And my guess is that they all felt a lot better after the game than they would have if they had chosen to complain.

While there will always be things to complain about, if we look carefully there are always blessings to be thankful for. When Paul describes our newness in Christ, thankfulness is the only characteristic mentioned more than once. In fact, it is mentioned three times. "Be thankful," he says in Colossians 3:15. Sing to God "with gratitude in your hearts" (v. 16). And whatever you do, make sure you are "giving thanks to God the Father" (v. 17). Paul's instruction to be thankful is astonishing when we consider that he wrote this letter from prison!

Today, let's make the choice to have an attitude of thankfulness.

Joe Stowell

Practice Gratitude Today

Set a timer for three minutes. During that time, list as many things that you are thankful for as you can.

Giving Thanks Always

ISAIAH 12:1–6

Give praise to the LORD, proclaim his name; make known among the nations what he has done.
Isaiah 12:4

In the seventeenth century, Martin Rinkart served as a clergyman in Saxony, Germany, for more than thirty years during times of war and plague. One year he conducted more than four thousand funerals, including his wife's, and at times food was so scarce that his family went hungry. Although he could have despaired, his faith in God remained strong and he gave thanks continually. In fact, he poured his gratitude into a song, "Nun danket alle Gott," which became the well-loved English hymn "Now Thank We All Our God."

Rinkart followed the example of the prophet Isaiah, who instructed God's people to give thanks at all times, including when they'd disappointed God (Isaiah 12:1) or when enemies oppressed them. Even then they were to exalt God's name, making "known among the nations what he has done" (v. 4).

We might give thanks easily during harvest celebrations such as Thanksgiving, when we're enjoying an abundant feast with friends and family. But can we express our gratitude to God in difficult times, such as when we're missing someone from our table or when we're struggling with our finances or when we're locked in conflict with someone close to us?

Let's echo Pastor Rinkart, joining hearts and voices as we give praise and thanks to "the eternal God, whom earth and heaven adore." We can "sing to the LORD, for he has done glorious things" (v. 5).

Amy Boucher Pye

Practice Gratitude Today

What difficulty, loss, or struggle are you experiencing today? Bring it to God in prayer. Then thank Him for the things He has provided for you.

Loved Well

EPHESIANS 3:14–21

I pray that you . . . grasp how wide and long and high and deep is the love of Christ.
Ephesians 3:17–18

We were gathered with family for Thanksgiving dinner when someone asked if each person would share what he or she was thankful for. One by one we talked. Three-year-old Joshua was thankful for music, and Nathan, aged four, for horses. We were all silenced, though, when Stephen (who was soon to turn five) answered, "I'm thankful that Jesus loves me so well." In his simple faith, he understood and was grateful for the love of Jesus for him personally. He told us that Jesus showed His love by dying on a cross.

The apostle Paul wanted the believers in the church at Ephesus to understand how well God loved them, and that was his prayer: that they would "have power, together with all the Lord's holy people, to grasp how wide and long and high and deep is the love of Christ" (Ephesians 3:18). He prayed that they would be rooted and grounded in that love.

To ground ourselves in God's love, it's helpful to review these verses frequently or even memorize them. We can also take a few minutes each day to thank the Lord for the specific ways He shows His love to us. This will help us to grow in our belief and be thankful—as Stephen is—that Jesus loves us so well. *Anne Cetas*

Practice Gratitude Today

Write out Ephesians 3:17–19 on a note card and put it where you will see it often. Memorize it over the next few days. Thank God for His love, which is too wonderful to fully comprehend.

The Perfect Prayer Partner

ROMANS 8:31–34

[Jesus] is at the right hand of God and is also interceding for us.
Romans 8:34

Few sounds are as beautiful as hearing someone who loves you praying for you. When you hear a friend pray for you with compassion and God-given insight, it's a little like heaven touching earth.

How good it is to know that because of God's kindness to us our prayers can also touch heaven. Sometimes when we pray, we may struggle with words and feelings of inadequacy, but Jesus taught His followers that we "should always pray and not give up" (Luke 18:1). God's Word shows us that one of the reasons we can do this is that Jesus Himself "is at the right hand of God and is also interceding for us" (Romans 8:34).

We never pray alone, because Jesus is praying for us. He hears us as we pray and speaks to the Father on our behalf. We don't have to worry about the eloquence of our words, because no one understands us like Jesus. He helps us in every way, presenting our needs before God the Father. He also knows when the answers we ask for would not be good for us, handling every request or concern with perfect wisdom and love.

Jesus is the perfect prayer partner—the friend who intercedes for us with immeasurable kindness. His prayers for us are beautiful beyond words and should encourage us to always pray with thankfulness.

James Banks

Practice Gratitude Today

Sit in silence before the Father, confident that Jesus is interceding on your behalf. After a few minutes, thank Jesus for knowing your every need and always being with you through His Spirit.

Hallelujah!

REVELATION 11:15–18

He will reign for ever and ever.
Revelation 11:15

Astonishingly, it took George Frideric Handel only twenty-four days to write the orchestral music for the *Messiah* oratorio—today perhaps the world's most famous musical composition, one performed thousands of times every year around the world. The magnificent work reaches its climax nearly two hours after it begins with the most famous part of the oratorio, the "Hallelujah" chorus.

As the trumpets and timpani announce the beginning of the chorus, voices layer on top of each other as the choir sings the words of Revelation 11:15: "And he shall reign for ever and ever." It's a triumphant declaration of the hope of eternity in heaven with Jesus.

Many of the words in *Messiah* come from the book of Revelation, the apostle John's account of a vision he had near the end of his life describing events culminating with the return of Christ. In Revelation, John returned again and again to the theme of the return of the resurrected Jesus to earth—when there would be great rejoicing with the sound of choirs (19:1–8). The world will rejoice because Jesus will have defeated the powers of darkness and death and established His kingdom of peace.

One day, all the people of heaven will sing together in a magnificent choir proclaiming the majesty of Jesus and the blessing of His forever reign (7:9). Until then, we live, work, pray, and wait in hope.

Lisa M. Samra

Practice Gratitude Today

Listen to a recording of the "Hallelujah" chorus. Praise God that, through Jesus, He has defeated darkness and death and invited you into a new, eternal life of love and peace.

Honoring God

JOHN 15:1–5

If you remain in me and I in you, you will bear much fruit.
John 15:5

The church service was still in progress, and we had some visitors there that morning. The speaker was only halfway through his sermon when I noticed one of our visitors walking out. I was curious and concerned, so I walked out to talk with her.

"You're leaving so soon," I said, approaching her. "Is there a problem I can help with?" She was frank and forthright. "Yes," she said, "my problem is that sermon. I don't accept what the preacher is saying." He had said that no matter what we accomplish in life, the credit and praise belong to God. "At least," the woman moaned, "I deserve some credit for my achievements!"

I explained to her what the pastor meant. People do deserve recognition and appreciation for what they do. Yet even our gifts and talents are from God, so He gets the glory. Even Jesus, the Son of God, said, "The Son can do nothing by himself; he can do only what he sees his Father doing" (John 5:19). He told His followers, "Apart from me you can do nothing" (15:5).

We acknowledge the Lord as the one who helps us to accomplish everything. *Lawrence Darmani*

Practice Gratitude Today

What accomplishments, skills, or successes are you most proud of? Pause to thank God for giving you the gifts, talents, and abilities you have.

The Other 80 Percent

PSALM 69:29–36

Let heaven and earth praise him, the seas
and all that move in them.
Psalm 69:34

Recently I saw a billboard stating that 80 percent of all life on Earth is found in the seas. That staggering number is difficult to process, largely because most of that life is out of sight.

As I considered this, it reminded me of how much greater God's creation is than we typically appreciate. While we can easily have our breath taken away by a majestic mountain range or a panoramic sunset, we sometimes fail to see His extraordinary work in the details that require more careful study and examination. Not only is much of God's creation hidden by the oceans, but other parts are also too small for our eyes to observe. From the microscopically small to the unsearched reaches of the universe, it is all the work of our Creator. In those magnificent structures—seen and unseen—God's creative glory is revealed (Romans 1:20).

As we grow to understand the wonder of creation, it must always point us to the Creator Himself—and call us to worship Him. As the psalmist said, "Let heaven and earth praise him, the seas and all that move in them" (Psalm 69:34). If creation itself gives praise to the Creator, we can and should certainly join the chorus. What a mighty God we serve!

Bill Crowder

Practice Gratitude Today

Find an article or video about life in the ocean or another part of Earth that is hard to observe. Praise God for the wonders of His creation—and how He is more wondrous still.

Tears of Praise

PSALM 30

Sing the praises of the Lord, you his faithful people; praise his holy name.
Psalm 30:4

Years ago, I cared for my mom as she was in hospice. I thanked God for the four months He allowed me to serve as her caregiver and asked Him to help me through the grieving process. I often struggled to praise God as I wrestled with my mixed emotions. But as my mom breathed her last breath and I wept uncontrollably, I whispered, "Hallelujah." I felt guilty for praising God in that devastating moment until, years later, I took a closer look at Psalm 30.

In David's song "for the dedication of the temple," he worshiped God for His faithfulness and mercy (vv. 1–3). He encouraged others to "praise his holy name" (v. 4). Then David explored how intimately God entwines hardship and hope (v. 5). He acknowledged times of grief and rejoicing, times of feeling secure and being dismayed (vv. 6–7). His cries for help remained laced with confidence in God (vv. 7–10). The echo of his praise wove through David's moments of wailing and dancing, grief and joy (v. 11). Acknowledging the mystery and complexity of enduring affliction and anticipating God's faithfulness, David proclaimed his endless devotion to God (v. 12).

Like David, we can sing, "Lord my God, I will praise you forever" (v. 12). Whether we're happy or hurting, God can help us declare our trust in Him and lead us to worship Him with joyful shouts and tears of praise.

Xochitl Dixon

Practice Gratitude Today

In what current circumstance do you feel both grief and joy? Thank God for entwining hope with hardship and peace with anguish.

Shout for Joy

PSALM 100

Shout for joy to the Lord, all the earth.
Psalm 100:1

Duke University's basketball fans are known as Cameron Crazies. When Duke plays archrival North Carolina, the Crazies are given these instructions: "This is the game you've been waiting for. No excuses. Give everything you've got. Cameron [Stadium] should never be less than painfully loud tonight." Clearly, Duke fans take allegiance seriously.

The songwriter of Psalm 100 took his allegiance to the Lord seriously and wanted others to do the same. "Shout for joy to the Lord," he exclaimed (v. 1). His people were to freely express their praise to God because He was the covenant God of Israel, the God over all other so-called gods. They were called to focus all their energies on Him and His goodness.

God's goodness and grace should motivate us to freely express our love and allegiance to Him with shouts of joy. This may mean that those who are more reserved must push back the boundaries of restraint and learn what it means to be expressive in their praise to God. Those who are so expressive that they miss the beauty of silence may need to learn from those whose style is more reflective.

Worship is a time to focus on our Creator, Redeemer, and Shepherd, and celebrate what He has done. *Marvin Williams*

Practice Gratitude Today

Joyfully and freely express your praise to God today. Celebrate Him and thank Him for His love and goodness.

Celestial Communion

1 CORINTHIANS 11:23–26

Whenever you eat this bread and drink this cup,
you proclaim the Lord's death until he comes.
1 Corinthians 11:26

When Apollo 11's Eagle lunar module landed on the moon's Sea of Tranquility on July 20, 1969, the space travelers took time to recover from their flight before stepping onto the moon's surface. Astronaut Buzz Aldrin had received permission to bring bread and wine so he could take Communion. After reading Scripture, he tasted the first foods ever consumed on the moon. Later, he wrote: "I poured the wine into the chalice our church had given me. In the one-sixth gravity of the moon the wine curled slowly and gracefully up the side of the cup." As Aldrin enjoyed this celestial Communion, his actions proclaimed his belief in Christ's sacrifice on the cross and the guarantee of His second coming.

The apostle Paul encourages us to remember how Jesus sat with His disciples "on the night he was betrayed" (1 Corinthians 11:23). Christ compared His soon-to-be sacrificed body to the bread (v. 24). He declared the wine as a symbol of "the new covenant" that secured our forgiveness and salvation through His blood shed on the cross (v. 25). Whenever and wherever we take Communion, we're proclaiming our trust in the reality of Jesus's sacrifice and our hope in His promised second coming (v. 26).

No matter where we are, we can celebrate our faith in the one and only risen and returning Savior—Jesus Christ—with confidence.

Xochitl Dixon

Practice Gratitude Today

When will you find yourself outside of your normal rhythms and routines today or in the coming week? In that unusual place, pause to thank God for His sacrificial love.

God's Rescue

PSALM 40:1–4

He lifted me out of the slimy pit, out of the mud and mire;
he set my feet on a rock and gave me a firm place to stand.
Psalm 40:2

A compassionate volunteer was called a "guardian angel" for his heroic efforts. Jake Manna was installing solar panels at a jobsite when he joined an urgent search to find a missing five-year-old girl. While neighbors searched their garages and yards, Manna took a path that led him into a nearby wooded area where he spotted the girl waist-deep in a marsh. He waded carefully into the sticky mud to pull her out of her predicament and return her, damp but unharmed, to her grateful mother.

Like that little girl, David also experienced deliverance. The singer "waited patiently" for God to respond to his heartfelt cries for mercy (Psalm 40:1). And He did. God leaned in, paid close attention to his cry for help, and responded by rescuing him from the "mud and mire" of his circumstances (v. 2)—providing sure footing for David's life. The past rescues from the muddy marsh of life reinforced his desire to sing songs of praise, to make God his trust in future circumstances, and to share his story with others (vv. 3–4).

When we find ourselves in life challenges such as financial difficulties, marital turmoil, and feelings of inadequacy, let's cry out to God and patiently wait for Him to respond. He's there, ready to help us in our time of need and give us a firm place to stand. *Marvin Williams*

Practice Gratitude Today

Openly share your difficulties with God in prayer. Ask Him to deliver you, and thank Him that you can wait in patient hope, knowing that He is good.

Reflecting God's Glory

EXODUS 31:1–11

The heavens declare the glory of God; the skies proclaim the work of his hands.
Psalm 19:1

The twelfth-century Chinese artist Li Tang painted landscapes animated with people, birds, and water buffalo. Because of his genius with fine line sketches on silk, Li Tang is considered a master of Chinese landscape art. For centuries, artists from around the world have depicted what they see in God's art gallery of creation: "The heavens declare the glory of God; the skies proclaim the work of his hands" (Psalm 19:1). The Bible tells us that our creativity as human beings comes from being made in the image of the Master Creator (Genesis 1:27).

God chose artists who worked with wood, gold, silver, bronze, and gems to create the furnishings, utensils, altars, and garments that were used when the ancient Israelites worshiped Him in the tabernacle (Exodus 31:1–11). These artistic renderings of spiritual realities prompted and guided the priests and the people in their worship of the Lord who had called them to be His people.

Through many types of artistic expression, we reflect the beauty of creation and honor the Creator and Redeemer of this marvelous world.

Dennis Fisher

Practice Gratitude Today

Look up online a favorite painting, song, sculpture, or art piece, and spend a few minutes considering it. Thank God for how we can reflect His infinite artistry in our own creativity.

The Christmas Gift of Speech

LUKE 1:62–75

[Zechariah's] mouth was opened and his tongue set free, and he began to speak, praising God.
Luke 1:64

A postsurgical stroke had robbed Tom of his ability to speak, and he faced a long rehab journey. Weeks later, we were pleasantly surprised when he showed up at our church's Thanksgiving service. We were even more surprised when he stood up to speak. Searching for what to say, he jumbled his words, repeated himself, and confused days and time. But one thing was clear: he was praising God! It's possible to have your heart break and be blessed at the same moment. This was that kind of moment.

In the "pre-Christmas story" in Luke's gospel, we meet a man who lost the gift of speech. Gabriel the angel appeared to Zechariah the priest and told him he would be the father of a great prophet (1:11–17). Zechariah and his wife were elderly, so he doubted it. That's when Gabriel told him he would not speak "until the day this happens" (v. 20).

The day did happen. And at the ceremony to name the miracle baby, Zechariah spoke. With his first words he praised God (v. 64). Then he said, "Praise be to the Lord, the God of Israel, because he has come to his people and redeemed them" (v. 68).

Like Zechariah, as soon as he was able, Tom's response was to praise God. Their hearts were inclined toward the One who made their tongues and their minds. Regardless of what faces us this season, we can respond the same way. *Tim Gustafson*

Practice Gratitude Today

Whether in private or with others, pray out loud, listening to the sounds of your words. Thank God for your voice, with which you can praise Him and communicate with others.

Renewed Vision

1 SAMUEL 1:10–18; 2:1–2

My heart rejoices in the LORD; in the LORD my horn is lifted high.
1 Samuel 2:1

After a painful minor surgery on my left eye, my doctor recommended a vision test. With confidence, I covered my right eye and read each line on the chart with ease. Covering my left eye, I gasped. How could I not realize I'd been so blind?

While adjusting to new glasses and renewed vision, I thought of how daily trials often caused me to be spiritually nearsighted. Focusing only on what I could see up close—my pain and ever-changing circumstances—I became blind to the faithfulness of my eternal and unchanging God. With such a limited perspective, hope became an unattainable blur.

First Samuel 1 tells the story of another woman who failed to recognize God's trustworthiness while focusing on her current anguish, uncertainty, and loss. For years, Hannah had endured childlessness and endless torment from Peninnah, the other wife of her husband, Elkanah. Hannah's husband adored her, but contentment evaded her. One day, she prayed with bitter honesty. When Eli the priest questioned her, she explained her situation. As she left, he prayed that God would grant her request (1:17). Though Hannah's situation didn't change immediately, she walked away with confident hope (v. 18).

Her prayer in 1 Samuel 2:1–2 reveals a shift in Hannah's focus. Even before her circumstances improved, Hannah's renewed vision changed her perspective and her attitude. She rejoiced in the ongoing presence of God—her Rock and everlasting hope. *Xochitl Dixon*

Practice Gratitude Today

What difficulty, loss, or struggle is stealing your focus today? Talk with God about it. End by thanking Him for being your unchanging Rock and everlasting hope.

Don't Forget the Giver

DEUTERONOMY 6:4–12

Be careful that you do not forget the Lord.
Deuteronomy 6:12

It was just before Christmas, and her kids were having a difficult time with gratitude. She knew how easy it was to slip into that kind of thinking, but she also knew she wanted something better for the hearts of her children. So she went through the house and placed red bows on light switches, the pantry and refrigerator doors, the washing machine and dryer, and the water faucets. With each bow there was a handwritten note: "Some of the gifts God gives us are easy to overlook, so I've put a bow on them. He is so good to our family. Let's not forget where the gifts come from."

In Deuteronomy 6, we see that the future of the nation of Israel involved the conquest of existing places. So they would move into large flourishing cities they did not build (v. 10), occupy houses filled with good things they didn't provide, and benefit from wells and vineyards and olive groves they didn't dig or plant (v. 11). All these blessings could be easily traced back to a single source—"the Lord your God" (v. 10). And while God lovingly provided these things and more, Moses wanted to make sure the people were careful not to forget (v. 12).

During certain seasons of life, it's easy to forget. But let's not lose sight of God's goodness, the source of all our blessings. *John Blase*

Practice Gratitude Today

Walk around your home, reminding yourself that everything you own is a gift from God. Praise Him for His loving provision.

Mell's Smiley Face

ROMANS 5:1–5

We also glory in our sufferings, because we know
that suffering produces perseverance.
Romans 5:3

Some people think you shouldn't draw in your Bible, but I'm glad my daughter Melissa drew in hers. In the margin next to Romans 5, she used a green ink pen to draw a small, simple smiley face, and circled verse 3.

How could she have known that her family and friends would need this passage when she left us so suddenly in a car accident at age seventeen? How could she know that these verses would tell her story, while guiding our lives and the lives of others over the following years?

Romans 5 begins by explaining our justification through faith, which gives us peace with God through Jesus (v. 1). Melissa had that peace. And right now she is enjoying the fruits of her faith, as verse 2 describes: we "boast in the hope of the glory of God." Imagine the smiley face she could draw now!

And then there's the rest of us—all of us left behind when loved ones precede us in death. Somehow, we "glory in our sufferings." Why? Our suffering brings perseverance, which brings character, which brings us hope (vv. 3–4).

We feel helpless in times of tragedy, but we are never hopeless. God pours His love into our hearts—and with it the great hope of His glory. It's all part of God's mysterious yet marvelous plan. *Dave Branon*

Practice Gratitude Today

Write out Romans 5:3 on a note card and put it where you will it see often, or place it as the wallpaper on your phone. Thank God that He uses your suffering to produce something of value.

In Living Color

REVELATION 4:1–6

The one who sat there had the appearance of jasper and ruby. A rainbow that shone like an emerald encircled the throne.
Revelation 4:3

When Xavier McCoury put on the glasses Aunt Celena sent for his tenth birthday, he burst into tears. Born color-blind, Xavier had only ever seen the world in shades of gray, white, and black. With his new EnChroma glasses, however, Xavier saw color for the first time. His euphoria at witnessing the beauty around him made his family feel like they'd beheld a miracle.

Witnessing God's colorfully radiant brilliance also evoked a powerful reaction in the apostle John (Revelation 1:17). After encountering the full glory of the resurrected Christ, John glimpsed "a throne in heaven with someone sitting on it. And the one who sat there had the appearance of jasper and ruby. A rainbow that shone like an emerald encircled the throne. . . . From the throne came flashes of lightning" (4:2–3, 5).

In a different time, Ezekiel had a similar vision, seeing "what looked like a throne of lapis lazuli," with a figure above the throne who "looked like glowing metal, as if full of fire" (Ezekiel 1:26–27). This magnificent figure was surrounded with rainbowlike radiance (v. 28).

One day we will meet the resurrected Christ face-to-face. These visions give us just a tiny hint of the magnificence that awaits us then. As we celebrate the beauty of God's creation here and now, may we live in anticipation of the glory yet to be revealed. *Remi Oyedele*

Practice Gratitude Today

What part of creation or natural wonder fills you with awe? Thank God for the beauty of His creation—and that it only hints at the glory and magnificence of God Himself.

A Remote Location

MARK 8:1–13

My God will meet all your needs according to
the riches of his glory in Christ Jesus.
Philippians 4:19

Tristan da Cunha Island is famous for its isolation. It is the most remote inhabited island in the world, thanks to the 288 people who call it home. The island is located in the South Atlantic Ocean, 1,750 miles from South Africa—the nearest mainland. Anyone who might want to drop by for a visit has to travel by boat for six days because the island has no airstrip.

Jesus and His followers were in a somewhat remote area when He produced a miraculous meal for thousands of hungry people. Before His miracle, Jesus said to His disciples, "[These people] have already been with me three days and have nothing to eat. If I send them home hungry, they will collapse on the way" (Mark 8:2–3). Because they were in the countryside where food was not readily available, they had to depend fully on Jesus. They had nowhere else to turn.

Sometimes God allows us to end up in desolate places where He is our only source of help. His ability to provide for us is not necessarily linked with our circumstances. If He created the entire world out of nothing, God can certainly meet our needs—whatever our circumstances—out of the riches of His glory in Christ Jesus (Philippians 4:19).

Jennifer Benson Schuldt

Practice Gratitude Today

In what part of your life do you feel far away from help, satisfaction, or solutions? In prayer, thank God that His ability to provide does not depend on you or your circumstances.

Mosaic of Beauty

LUKE 1:46–55

My soul glorifies the Lord and my spirit
rejoices in God my Savior.
Luke 1:46–47

Sitting in the courtyard of the Church of the Visitation in Ein Karem, Israel, I was overwhelmed with the beautiful display of sixty-seven mosaics containing the words of Luke 1:46–55 in as many languages. Traditionally known as the Magnificat from the Latin word meaning "to magnify," these verses are Mary's joyous response to the announcement that she will be the mother of the Messiah.

Each plaque contains Mary's words, including: "My soul glorifies the Lord and my spirit rejoices in God my Savior. . . . The Mighty One has done great things for me" (vv. 46, 49). The biblical hymn etched in the tiles is a song of praise as Mary recounts the faithfulness of God to her and the nation of Israel.

A grateful recipient of God's grace, Mary rejoices in her salvation (v. 47). She acknowledges that God's mercy has extended to the Israelites for generations (v. 50). Looking back over God's care for the Israelites, Mary praises God for His powerful acts on behalf of His people (v. 51). She also thanks God, recognizing that her daily provision comes from His hand (v. 53).

Mary shows us that recounting the great things God has done for us is a way to express praise and can lead us to rejoice. This Christmas season, consider God's goodness as you reflect on the year. In doing so, you may create a mosaic of great beauty with your words of praise.

Lisa M. Samra

Practice Gratitude Today

Think back over your past year. How has God shown His goodness to you? Praise Him for His faithfulness, mercy, provision, and power.

Stress to Peace

PHILIPPIANS 4:4–8

Do not be anxious about anything, but in every situation, by prayer and petition, with thanksgiving, present your requests to God.
Philippians 4:6

Moving ranks as one of the biggest stressors in life. We moved to our current home after I'd lived in my previous one for nearly twenty years. I'd lived alone in that first home for eight years before I got married. Then my husband moved in, along with all his things. Later, we added a child, and that meant even more stuff.

Our moving day to the new house wasn't without incident. Five minutes before the movers arrived, I was still finishing up a book manuscript. And the new home had several sets of stairs, so it took double the time and twice as many movers as planned.

But I wasn't feeling stressed out by the events of that day. Then it hit me: I'd spent many hours finishing writing a book—one chock-full with Scripture and biblical concepts. By God's grace, I'd been poring over the Bible, praying, and writing to meet my deadline. So I believe the key was my immersion in Scripture and in prayer.

Paul wrote, "Do not be anxious about anything, but in every situation, by prayer and petition, with thanksgiving, present your requests to God" (Philippians 4:6). When we pray—and "rejoice in" God (v. 4)—we refocus our mind from the problem to our Provider. We may be asking God to help us deal with a stressor, but we're also connecting with Him, which can provide a peace "which transcends all understanding" (v. 7). *Katara Patton*

Practice Gratitude Today

What stressor is preoccupying you today? Tell God about one thing you can rejoice in amid the stress.

The Cost

JOHN 19:25–30

When he had received the drink, Jesus said, "It is finished." With that, he bowed his head and gave up his spirit.
John 19:30

Michelangelo's works explored many facets of the life of Jesus, yet one of the most poignant was also one of the most simple. In the 1540s he sketched a pietà (a picture of Jesus's mother holding the body of the dead Christ) for his friend Vittoria Colonna. Done in chalk, the drawing depicts Mary looking to the heavens as she cradles her son's still form. Rising behind Mary, the upright beam of the cross carries these words from Dante's *Paradise*, "There they don't think of how much blood it costs." Michelangelo's point was profound: when we contemplate the death of Jesus, we must consider the price He paid.

The price paid by Christ is captured in His dying declaration, "It is finished" (John 19:30). The word for "it is finished" (*tetelestai*) was used in several ways—to show a bill had been paid, a task finished, a sacrifice offered, a masterpiece completed. Each of them applies to what Jesus did on our behalf on the cross. Perhaps that's why the apostle Paul wrote, "May I never boast except in the cross of our Lord Jesus Christ, through which the world has been crucified to me, and I to the world" (Galatians 6:14).

Jesus's willingness to take our place is the eternal evidence of how much God loves us. As we contemplate the price He paid, may we also celebrate His love and give thanks for the cross. *Bill Crowder*

Practice Gratitude Today

Search online for a picture of *Pietà for Vittoria Colonna* or another artistic depiction of Jesus's crucifixion. Spend a few minutes looking at the picture, thanking Jesus for His sacrifice.

Praising through Problems

JOB 1:13–22

Shall we accept good from God, and not trouble?
Job 2:10

"It's cancer." I wanted to be strong when Mom said those words to me. But I burst into tears. You never want to hear those words even one time. But this was Mom's third bout with cancer. After a routine mammogram and biopsy, Mom learned that she had a malignant tumor under her arm.

Though Mom was the one with bad news, she had to comfort me. Her response was eye-opening for me: "I know God is always good to me. He's always faithful." Even as she faced a difficult surgery, followed up by radiation treatments, Mom was assured of God's presence and faithfulness.

How like Job. Job lost his children, his wealth, and his health. But after hearing the news, Job 1:20 tells us "he fell to the ground in worship." When advised to curse God, he said, "Shall we accept good from God, and not trouble?" (2:10). What a radical initial response. Though Job later complained, ultimately he accepted that God had never changed. Job knew that God was still with him and that He still cared.

For most of us, praise is not our first response to difficulties. Sometimes the pain of our circumstances is so overwhelming that we lash out in fear or anger. But watching Mom's response reminded me that God is still present, still good. He will help us through hard times.

Linda Washington

Practice Gratitude Today

What feels difficult, painful, or overwhelming right now? Pause to thank God that even in that circumstance, He is present and He is good.

For Love or Money

LUKE 19:1–10

Watch out! Be on your guard against all kinds of greed;
life does not consist in an abundance of possessions.
Luke 12:15

Irish poet Oscar Wilde said, "When I was young I thought that money was the most important thing in life; now that I am old I know that it is." His comment was made tongue in cheek; he lived only to age forty-six, so he never truly was old. Wilde fully understood that life is not about money.

Money is temporary; it comes and it goes. So life must be about more than money and what it can buy. Jesus challenged the people of His generation—rich and poor alike—to a recalibrated value system. In Luke 12:15, Jesus said, "Watch out! Be on your guard against all kinds of greed; life does not consist in an abundance of possessions." In our culture, where there's an abiding focus on more and newer and better, there's something to be said both for contentment and for perspective about how we view money and possessions.

Upon meeting Jesus, a rich young ruler went away sad because he had many possessions he didn't want to give up (Luke 18:18–25), but Zacchaeus the tax collector gave away much of what he'd spent his life acquiring (19:8). The difference is embracing the heart of Christ. In His grace, we can find a healthy perspective on the things we possess—so they don't become the things that have us. *Bill Crowder*

Practice Gratitude Today

Which of your possessions feel like they possess you? How can you be generous with what you have today, remembering and thanking God that His heart toward you is generous?

The Light of Hope

PSALM 42

Put your hope in God, for I will yet praise
him, my Savior and my God.
Psalm 42:11

My mother's shiny red cross should have been hanging next to her bed at the cancer care center. And I should have been preparing for holiday visits between her scheduled treatments. All I wanted for Christmas was another day with my mom. Instead, I was home . . . hanging her cross on a fake tree.

When my son Xavier plugged in the lights, I whispered, "Thank You." He said, "You're welcome." My son didn't know I was thanking God for using the flickering bulbs to turn my eyes toward the ever-enduring Light of hope—Jesus.

The writer of Psalm 42 expressed his raw emotions to God (vv. 1–4). He acknowledged his "downcast" and "disturbed" soul before encouraging readers: "Put your hope in God, for I will yet praise him, my Savior and my God" (v. 5). Though he was overcome with waves of sorrow and suffering, the psalmist's hope shone through the remembrance of God's past faithfulness (vv. 6–10). He ended by questioning his doubts and affirming the resilience of his refined faith: "Why, my soul, are you downcast? Why so disturbed within me? Put your hope in God, for I will yet praise him, my Savior and my God" (v. 11).

For many of us, the Christmas season stirs up both joy and sorrow. Thankfully, even these mixed emotions can be reconciled and redeemed through the promises of the true Light of hope—Jesus.

Xochitl Dixon

Practice Gratitude Today

How are both grief and joy present for you this Christmas season? Honestly share your sorrows with God. Then thank Him for being the Light of the World, who came to redeem and reconcile.

December 21

Dancing before the Lord

MARK 14:1–9

Some of those present were saying indignantly to
one another, "Why this waste of perfume?"
Mark 14:4

A number of years ago, Carolyn and I visited a small church where during the worship service a woman began to dance in the aisle. She was soon joined by others. Carolyn and I looked at each other, and an unspoken agreement passed between us: "Not me!" We come from church traditions that favor a serious liturgy, and this other form of worship was well beyond our comfort zone.

But if Mark's story of the woman's "waste" in anointing Jesus means anything at all, it suggests that our love for Jesus may express itself in ways that others find uncomfortable (Mark 14:1–9). A year's wages were involved in the woman's anointing. It was a seemingly unwise act that invited the disciples' scorn. The word Mark uses to describe their reaction means "to snort" and suggests disdain and mockery. The woman may have cringed, fearing Jesus's response. But He commended her for her act of devotion and defended her from His own disciples, for Jesus saw the love that prompted her action despite others considering it impractical. He said, "Why are you bothering her? She has done a beautiful thing to me" (v. 6).

Different forms of worship—informal, formal, quiet, exuberant—represent a sincere outpouring of love for Jesus. He's worthy of all worship that comes from a heart of love. *David H. Roper*

Practice Gratitude Today

How can you worship God today in a way that feels extravagant, impractical, or out of your comfort zone? Let your gratitude to God pour out in sincere, loving worship.

Sweet Company

JOHN 14:15–26

The Spirit of truth . . . lives with you and will be in you.
John 14:17

The elderly woman in the nursing home didn't speak to anyone or request anything. It seemed she merely existed, rocking in her creaky old chair. She didn't have many visitors, so one young nurse would often go into her room on her breaks. Without asking the woman questions to try to get her to talk, she simply pulled up another chair and rocked with her. After several months, the elderly woman said to her, "Thank you for rocking with me." She was grateful for the companionship.

Before He went back to heaven, Jesus promised to send a constant companion to His disciples. He told them He would not leave them alone but would send the Holy Spirit to be in them (John 14:17). That promise is still true for believers in Jesus today. Jesus said that the triune God makes His "home" with us (v. 23).

The Lord is our close and faithful companion throughout our entire life. Let us enjoy His sweet company today. *Anne Cetas*

Practice Gratitude Today

Spend a few minutes simply being in the presence of the Holy Spirit, enjoying His company in silence. Thank God that He is a friend who is with you always.

God's Most Comforting Commitment

JOSHUA 1:1–9

The Lord your God will be with you wherever you go.
Joshua 1:9

Years ago, our family visited Four Corners, the only place in the United States where four states meet at one location. My husband stood in the section marked Arizona. Our oldest son, AJ, hopped into Utah. Our youngest son, Xavier, held my hand as we stepped into Colorado. When I scooted into New Mexico, Xavier said, "Mom, I can't believe you left me in Colorado!" We were together and apart as our laughter was heard in four different states. Now that our grown sons have left home, I have a deeper appreciation of God's promise to be near all His people wherever they go.

After Moses died, God called Joshua into leadership and guaranteed His presence as He expanded the Israelites' territory (Joshua 1:1–4). God said, "As I was with Moses, so I will be with you; I will never leave you nor forsake you" (v. 5). Knowing His people would struggle with doubt and fear, God built a foundation of hope on these words: "Have I not commanded you? Be strong and courageous. Do not be afraid; do not be discouraged, for the LORD your God will be with you wherever you go" (v. 9).

No matter where God leads us or our loved ones, even through difficult times, His most comforting commitment assures us that He's always present.

Xochitl Dixon

Practice Gratitude Today

Where in your life does it feel like God isn't with you? In prayer, thank God that His loving presence doesn't depend on your feelings or circumstances.

Extreme Measures

LUKE 19:1–10

The Son of Man came to seek and to save the lost.
Luke 19:10

A few years ago, a friend of mine lost track of her young son while walking through a swarm of people at Union Station in Chicago. Needless to say, it was a terrifying experience. Frantically she yelled his name and ran back up the escalator, retracing her steps in an effort to find her little boy. The minutes of separation seemed like hours, until suddenly—thankfully—her son emerged from the crowd and ran to the safety of her arms.

Thinking of my friend who would have done anything to find her child fills me with a renewed sense of gratitude for the amazing work God did to save us. From the time God's first image bearers—Adam and Eve—wandered off in sin, He lamented the loss of fellowship with His people. He went to great lengths to restore the relationship by sending His one and only Son "to seek and to save the lost" (Luke 19:10). Without the birth of Jesus, and without His willingness to die to pay the price for our sin and to bring us to God, we would have nothing to celebrate at Christmastime.

So this Christmas, let's be thankful that God took extreme measures by sending Jesus to reclaim our fellowship with Him. Although we once were lost, because of Jesus we have been found! *Joe Stowell*

Practice Gratitude Today

When have you lost someone or something precious to you, even if only for a short time? In prayer, reflect on how God was willing to do anything to get you back.

The Yard-Sale Christmas

1 TIMOTHY 6:6–10, 17–19

Godliness with contentment is great gain.
1 Timothy 6:6

A mom felt she'd been overspending on family Christmas gifts, so one year she decided to try something different. For a few months before the holiday, she scrounged through yard sales for inexpensive, used items. She bought more than usual but for far less money. On Christmas Eve, her children excitedly opened gift after gift after gift. The next day there were more! Mom had felt guilty about not getting new gifts, so she had additional gifts for Christmas morning. The kids began opening them but quickly complained, "We're too tired to open any more. You've given us so much!" That's not a typical response from children on a Christmas morning!

God has blessed us with so much, but it seems we're always looking for more: a bigger house, a better car, a larger bank account. Paul encouraged Timothy to remind people in his congregation that "we brought nothing into the world, and we can take nothing out of it. But if we have food and clothing, we will be content with that" (1 Timothy 6:7–8).

God has given us our very breath and life—besides providing for our needs. How refreshing it might be to enjoy and be content with His gifts and to say, "You've given us so much! We don't need more." As Paul wrote, "Godliness with contentment is great gain" (v. 6).

Anne Cetas

Practice Gratitude Today

Make a list of as many gifts from God as you can. Thank Him for your life and breath—and everything else He's given you.

Living Testament

2 TIMOTHY 2:1–10

Remember Jesus Christ, raised from the dead,
descended from David. This is my gospel.
2 Timothy 2:8

Watchman Nee was arrested for his faith in Christ in 1952, and he spent the rest of his life in prison. He died in his jail cell on May 30, 1972. When his niece came to collect his few possessions, she was given a scrap of paper that a guard had found by his bed. On it was written his life's testimony:

"Christ is the Son of God who died for the redemption of sinners and was resurrected after three days. This is the greatest truth in the universe. I die because of my belief in Christ—Watchman Nee."

Tradition says that the apostle Paul also was martyred for his faith in Christ. In a letter written shortly before his death, Paul exhorted his readers: "Remember Jesus Christ, raised from the dead, descended from David. This is my gospel, for which I am suffering. . . . But God's Word is not chained" (2 Timothy 2:8–9).

We may not be called to be martyred as witnesses to the reality of Christ—as millions of His followers through the centuries have been—but we are all called to be a living testament of Jesus's work on our behalf. No matter the outcome, from a heart of gratitude for God's gracious gift we can tell others what Jesus has done for us.

Dennis Fisher

Practice Gratitude Today

Who can you tell today about something Jesus has done for you? Let your gratitude for Jesus's work in your life overflow in your words.

Carried by Love

ISAIAH 46:1–10

I have made you and I will carry you.
Isaiah 46:4

My four-year-old grandson sat on my lap and patted my bald head, studying it intently. "Papa," he asked, "what happened to your hair?" "Oh," I laughed, "I lost it over the years." His face turned thoughtful. "That's too bad," he responded. "I'll have to give you some of mine."

I smiled at his compassion and pulled him close for a hug. Reflecting later on his love for me in that cherished moment also caused me to ponder God's selfless, generous love.

G. K. Chesterton wrote: "We have sinned and grown old, and our Father is younger than we." By this he meant that the "Ancient of Days" (Daniel 7:9) is untainted by sin's decay—God is ageless and loves us exuberantly with a love that never falters or fades. He's fully willing and able to fulfill the promise He made to His people in Isaiah 46: "Even to your old age and gray hairs I am he, I am he who will sustain you. I have made you and I will carry you" (v. 4).

Five verses later He explains, "I am God, and there is none like me" (v. 9). The great "I AM" (Exodus 3:14) loves us so deeply that He went to the extreme of dying on the cross to bear the full weight of our sin, so that we might turn to Him and be free of our burden and gratefully worship Him forever!

James Banks

Practice Gratitude Today

Where has your body, mind, or heart been affected by sin's decay? Take that hurt to God, and thank Him that through Christ He has defeated the curse of sin and death.

The Wonder of Nature

JOB 36:26–33

My ears had heard of you but now my eyes have seen you.
Job 42:5

Growing up around the woods and waters of Midwest America, I've been fascinated with natural wildlife native to our region. But on a recent trip to the California coast, I found myself staring in breathtaking wonder at snorting elephant seals, barking sea lions, and a forest of silent redwoods. I watched pelicans soar in formation, and I saw migrating whales spouting in the distance. Together they are just a sampling of the millions of species that make up the intricate and delicate balance of nature.

According to the Bible, the variety of the natural world is designed to do far more than inspire childlike wonder. The mysteries of nature can help us come to terms with a God who allows inexpressible, unexplainable pain and suffering.

We see this in the epic story of Job. While he was suffering, Job didn't know that God had such a high regard for him that he allowed Satan to test his faith with a series of losses.

What emerges is this eventual, unavoidable conclusion: a Creator who has the wisdom and power to design the wonders of nature is great enough to be trusted with pain and suffering that are beyond our ability to understand. In awe, Job proclaimed, "I know that you can do all things" (42:2). We can trust that kind of God—no matter what.

Mart De Haan

Practice Gratitude Today

What aspect of creation, large or small, fills you with wonder? Thank God that He has the wisdom and power to understand and order all of creation—including your life.

Carried through the Storm

PSALM 107:1–3, 23–32

He stilled the storm to a whisper; the
waves of the sea were hushed.
Psalm 107:29

During Scottish missionary Alexander Duff's first voyage to India in 1830, he was shipwrecked in a storm off the coast of South Africa. He and his fellow passengers made it to a small, desolate island; a short time later, one of the crew found a Bible belonging to Duff washed ashore on the beach. When the book dried, Duff read Psalm 107 to his fellow survivors, and they took courage. Finally, after a rescue and yet another shipwreck, Duff arrived in India.

Psalm 107 lists some of the ways God delivered the Israelites. Duff and his shipmates no doubt identified with and took comfort in the words: "He stilled the storm to a whisper; the waves of the sea were hushed. They were glad when it grew calm, and he guided them to their desired haven" (vv. 29–30). And, like the Israelites, they too gave "thanks to the Lord for his unfailing love and his wonderful deeds for mankind" (v. 31).

We see a parallel to Psalm 107:28–30 in the New Testament (Matthew 8:23–27; Mark 4:35–41). Jesus and His disciples were in a boat at sea when a violent storm began. His disciples cried out in fear, and Jesus—God in flesh—calmed the sea. We too can take courage! Our powerful God and Savior hears and responds to our cries and comforts us in the midst of our storms.

Alyson Kieda

Practice Gratitude Today

What storm are you experiencing today? Recall a time in your past that God delivered you from a difficulty or struggle. Thank Him for His love, faithfulness, and power.

A New Day

PSALM 118:19–29

This is the day the LORD has made. We will rejoice and be glad in it.
Psalm 118:24 NLT

In a morning meeting I recently attended, the person who opened the gathering began by praying, "Lord, thanks for today. It is the beginning of a new day we have never seen before." Although the idea seemed obvious, that prayer got me thinking about a couple of different things. First, because each day is a new opportunity, it will be filled with things we cannot anticipate or even prepare for. Therefore, it's important that we recognize our limitations and lean heavily on God—intentionally choosing to live in His grace and strength rather than relying on our own resources.

The second thing that occurred to me is that the newness of each day is a gift worth celebrating. Perhaps this reality was what prompted the psalmist to declare, "This is the day the LORD has made. We will rejoice and be glad in it" (Psalm 118:24 NLT).

Of course, we face many unknowns today—and some could be difficult. But the treasure of each brand-new day is so special that Moses was led to write, "Teach us to number our days, that we may gain a heart of wisdom" (90:12). Every new day is a precious gift. May we thankfully embrace each one with confident trust and humble celebration.

Bill Crowder

Practice Gratitude Today

How will you celebrate the gift that is today? Your celebration could be simple or elaborate, just between you and God or something you invite others into. However it looks, thank God for today.

Breath of Life

GENESIS 2:4–8

Then the LORD God . . . breathed into
his nostrils the breath of life.
Genesis 2:7

On a cold and frosty morning, as my daughter and I walked to school, we enjoyed seeing our breath turn to vapor. We giggled at the various steamy clouds we could each produce. I received the moment as a gift, reveling in being with her and being alive.

Our breath, which is usually invisible, was seen in the cold air, and it made me think about the Source of our breath and life—the Lord our Creator. For He who formed Adam out of the dust of the ground, giving him the breath of life (Genesis 2:7), also gives life to us and to every living creature. All things come from Him—even our very breath, which we inhale without thinking about it.

We may be tempted, living with today's conveniences and technology, to forget our beginnings and that God is the one who gives us life. But when we pause to remember that God is our Creator, we can build an attitude of thankfulness into our daily routines. We can ask Him for help and acknowledge the gift of life with humble, thankful hearts. May our gratitude spill out and touch others, so that they also may give thanks to the Lord for His goodness and faithfulness.

Amy Boucher Pye

Practice Gratitude Today

While breathing in and out deeply, consider everything your body does without you thinking about it: blood pumps; neurons fire; organs function; hormones regulate. Thank God for His love, care, and provision.

The Writers

James Banks Pastor, Peace Church, Durham, North Carolina. Author: *Prayers for Prodigals*, *Praying the Prayers of the Bible*, and *Peace through Prayer*.

John Blase Poet, adjunct seminary professor, literary agent, and part-time UPS employee living in Hot Springs, Arkansas. Author: *The Jubilee*, *Know When to Hold 'Em*, *Touching Wonder*, and *All Is Grace*.

Amy Boucher Pye London-based writer, speaker, retreat leader, and spiritual director. Author: *Transforming Love: How Friendship with Jesus Changes Us* and *7 Ways to Pray*.

Dave Branon Former senior editor, Our Daily Bread Publishing. Author: *Beyond the Valley* and *Lands of the Bible Then and Now: Experience the Book of Acts in Scripture and Photos*.

Anne Cetas Former managing editor, *Our Daily Bread*. Author: *Finding Jesus in Everyday Moments*.

Poh Fang Chia Country director, Our Daily Bread Ministries, Singapore.

Winn Collier Pastor, All Souls Church, Charlottesville, Virginia. Author: *Restless Faith* and *Let God*.

Bill Crowder Former vice president of ministry content, Our Daily Bread Ministries. Author: *Windows on Christmas*, *God of Surprise*, *Gospel on the Mountains*, *Wisdom for Our Worries*, *King Solomon*, and *Joseph*.

Lawrence Darmani Novelist and publisher in Accra, Ghana. Author: *Grief Child*.

Dennis DeHaan (1932–2014) Former editor, *Our Daily Bread*.

Mart DeHaan Former president, Our Daily Bread Ministries. Author: *A Matter of Faith: Understanding True Religion.*

Xochitl Dixon Blogs at xedixon.com. Author: *Sacred Strides, Waiting for God*, and *Different Like Me.*

Estera Pirosca Escobar Romanian by birth but living in the United States, she is national field director for International Friendships, Inc. Through that outreach she has seen many international students trust Jesus as Savior.

Tom Felten Executive editor, *Our Daily Bread.* He has a leadership role at Forest Hills Bible Chapel in Grand Rapids and serves at Michigan's Upper Peninsula Bible Camp in the summers.

Dennis Fisher Former senior research editor, Our Daily Bread Ministries. Former chairperson, C. S. Lewis Studies Consultation for the Evangelical Theological Society.

Nancy Gavilanes Author, speaker, podcaster, Bible school instructor, and life coach. Author: *Abounding Faith, Crossing Your Jordan River, Waiting on God Well, God-Given Dreams*, and *Feisty Faith.*

Tim Gustafson Senior content editor and content developer, *Our Daily Bread.* Author: *Brother to Brother.*

C. P. Hia Special assistant to the president, Our Daily Bread Ministries. Based in Singapore.

Kirsten Holmberg Speaker and author, residing in Idaho. Author: *Advent with the Word: Approaching Christmas through the Inspired Language of God.*

Adam R. Holz Director, Focus on the Family's website Plugged In. Author: *Beating Busyness.*

Karen Huang Book editor in Singapore. Author: *Letters to a Single Woman.*

Arthur Jackson Midwest region urban director, PastorServe. Former pastor.

Cindy Hess Kasper Former senior content editor, Our Daily Bread Ministries; has written for *Our Daily Bread* since 2006.

Alyson Kieda Former editor, Our Daily Bread Ministries.

Randy Kilgore Writer and workplace chaplain. Founder of Desired Haven Ministries in Massachusetts. Author: *Made to Matter: Devotions for Working Christians.*

Leslie Koh Editor, Our Daily Bread Ministries, Singapore. Former journalist for *The Strait Times* newspaper in Singapore.

Karen Kwek Former book editor based in Singapore.

Monica La Rose Editor, Our Daily Bread Ministries. Holds a master's in theology from Calvin Seminary, Grand Rapids, Michigan.

Albert Lee Former assistant to the president, Our Daily Bread Ministries, Singapore.

Julie Ackerman Link Began writing for *Our Daily Bread* in 2000. Author: *Above All, Love* and *Hope for All Seasons.*

Matt Lucas President and CEO of Our Daily Bread Ministries.

David McCasland Longtime writer for *Our Daily Bread*, beginning in the late 1990s. Author: *Oswald Chambers: Abandoned to God* and *Eric Liddell: Pure Gold.*

Elisa Morgan Cohost of *Discover the Word* and *God Hears Her*, productions of Our Daily Bread Ministries. President emerita, Mothers of Preschoolers (MOPS) International. Author: *You Are Not Alone, Christmas Changes Everything*, and *Fruitful Living.*

Harold Myra Award-winning editor, author, and publishing executive. Former CEO of Christianity Today International.

Remi Oyedele Finance professional and freelance writer. Blogs at www.wordzpread.com.

Glenn Packiam Lead pastor, New Life Downtown, Colorado Springs. Author: *Blessed Broken Given: How Your Story Becomes Sacred in the Hands of Jesus, Discover the Mystery of Faith*, and *Secondhand Jesus.*

Katara Patton Executive editor, VOICES at Our Daily Bread Ministries. Author: *Successful Mothers of the Bible* and *Navigating the Blues.*

Kenneth Petersen Former publisher, Our Daily Bread Publishing. Author: *Farm Sweet Farm: 75 Devotions*, *A Bushel of Reasons to Love Country Living*, and *Oh Happy Day: Soul- Stirring Inspirations with a Gospel Music Twist.*

Karen Pimpo Project manager in marketing communications. Contributing writer for *Our Daily Bread.* Sings in the Grand Rapids Symphony Chorus.

Patricia Raybon Writer, journalist, supporter of Bible translation projects. Author: *I Told the Mountain to Move* and *My First White Friend.*

David Roper Former pastor and founder of Idaho Mountain Ministries. Author: *A Man to Match the Mountain* and *Teach Us to Number Our Days.*

Lisa M. Samra Writer, facilitator of mentoring relationships with women, developer of focus groups focusing on spiritual formation.

Jennifer Benson Schuldt Technical writer living in the Chicago area. Has written for *Our Daily Bread* since 2015.

Julie Schwab Editor and professor with a BA in creative writing and an MA in theological studies.

Joe Stowell Former president of both Moody Bible Institute and Cornerstone University. Author of more than twenty books.

Sheridan Voysey Writer, speaker, and broadcaster in Oxford, England. Author: *Resurrection Year* and *Resilient.*

Linda Washington Writer of fiction and nonfiction books for kids, teens, and adults. Author: *God and Me* and *The Soul of C. S. Lewis.*

Marvin Williams Pastor, Trinity Church, Lansing, Michigan. Author: *Loving God, Loving Others.*

Mike Wittmer Professor of Bible, Cornerstone Theological Seminary; pastor, Cedar Springs Baptist Church. Author: *Heaven Is a Place on Earth*, *The Last Enemy*, and *Despite Doubt.*

Karen Wolfe Native of Jamaica who now lives in the United States. Holds a biblical studies degree from New Orleans Baptist Theological Seminary.

Spread the Word by Doing One Thing.

- Give a copy of this book as a gift.
- Share the QR code link via your social media.
- Write a review of this book on your blog, favorite bookseller's website, or at ourdailybreadpublishing.org.
- Recommend this book to your church, small group, or book club.

Our Daily Bread.

Connect with us.

Our Daily Bread Publishing
PO Box 3566, Grand Rapids, MI 49501, USA
Email: books@odbm.org